Genuine Happiness

Genuine Happiness

Meditation as the
Path to Fulfillment

B. Alan Wallace

Foreword by His Holiness the Dalai Lama

WILEY

John Wiley & Sons, Inc.

Published by John Wiley & Sons, Inc., Hoboken, New Jersey
Published simultaneously in Canada

For general information about our other products and services, please contact our Customer Care Department within the United States at (800) 762–2974, outside the United States at (317) 572–3993 or fax (317) 572–4002.

Wiley also publishes its books in a variety of electronic formats. Some content that appears in print may not be available in electronic books. For more information about Wiley products, visit our web site at www.wiley.com.

Library of Congress Cataloging-in-Publication Data:

Wallace, B. Alan.
   Genuine happiness : meditation as the path to fulfillment / B. Alan Wallace ; foreword by H.H. the Dalai Lama.
      p. cm.
   Includes bibliographical references and index.
   ISBN 0-471-46984-X (cloth)
   1. åAnåapåanasmôrti. 2. Meditation—Buddhism. I. Title.
   BQ5630.A6W35 2005
   294.3'4435—dc22
      ISBN 978-1-68442-585-3 (paperback)

2004027098

Printed in the United States of America

Contents

PART THREE
Cultivating a Good Heart

PART FOUR
Exploring the Nature of Consciousness

Foreword by His Holiness the Dalai Lama

MEDITATION IS AN INSTRUMENT or technique to shape or transform the mind. According to my own meager experience of meditation as a simple Buddhist monk, as I get older, even though many of the problems I face become more serious and my responsibilities become more challenging, my mind is becoming calmer. The result of a calmer mind is that I am happier. When faced with problems, my peace of mind is largely undisturbed. This is certainly the result of meditation.

Meditation is important as a tool for transforming the mind. We do not have to think of it as something religious. Like compassion and the spirit of forgiveness, I would include it among our basic good human qualities. When we are born we are quite free from ideology, but we are not free from the need for human affection. Compassion, love and forgiveness, the spirit of harmony, and a sense of brotherhood and sisterhood are all taught by our religious traditions. And yet this does not mean that if you accept the value of compassion or forgiveness then you must take up religion as a whole. Meditation is the same; we can use it as a means of strengthening our basic good human qualities.

Generally speaking, our awareness is normally attracted toward physical sensory experiences and mental concepts. With meditation we learn to withdraw our mind inward; we don't let it chase after sensory objects. However, we don't withdraw it so much that it becomes dull. We have to maintain a very full state of alertness and mindfulness so that an awareness of our natural state of mind emerges. This is a state of mind in which awareness is not afflicted by memories and thoughts of the past, nor is it afflicted by thoughts of the future, anticipations, fears, and hopes. Rather, our mind remains in a natural and neutral state.

When we withdraw our mind from external objects, it's almost as if we can't recognize it as our mind. There is a kind of absence, a kind of vacuity. However, as we slowly progress and get used to it, we begin to notice an underlying clarity, a luminosity. And that's when we begin to realize and appreciate the natural state of the mind.

Now, the Buddhist tradition of meditation includes many different techniques and practices. But it is very important to be skillful in how we apply them. We need a balanced approach, combining studying and learning with the practices of contemplation and meditation. Otherwise, there is a danger that too much intellectualization will kill the more contemplative practices. But then, too much emphasis on practical implementation without study can kill the understanding.

In this book, Alan Wallace describes a range of meditation techniques from the simplest mindfulness of breathing up to the exalted methods of Dzogchen. From a perspective of long experience of study and practice, he has tried to present these techniques with reference to the universal qualities of the human mind, free from the cultural embellishments that may have become associated with them as they were developed in India, Tibet, and elsewhere. This is, I believe, entirely appropriate. When the Buddha and other great teachers of the past first gave these instructions, they did not do so in order that only Indians, Tibetans, or Asians should benefit, but in order that all sentient beings should find peace and happiness. It is my prayer, too, that whoever puts these instructions and words of advice into effect may find the tranquility and insight that is their fruit.

September 29, 2003

Acknowledgments

THIS BOOK IS BASED on a series of lectures I gave in Santa Barbara from the autumn of 2000 through the spring of 2001. These lectures were recorded and then transcribed by many volunteers among my students, to whom I am deeply grateful. These raw transcripts were then edited into book form by Brian Hodel, after which I made various changes, which he polished once again. It has been a pleasure working with Brian, and I thank him for his unflagging enthusiasm and skillful editing. The manuscript was then sent to my agent, Patricia van der Leun, who coached me with enormous patience in writing a book proposal and polishing my writing style. It was thanks to her that the manuscript was submitted to John Wiley & Sons, and due to the kind interest on the part of Thomas Miller, executive editor, general interest books, that it was accepted for publication. I have very much enjoyed working with Teryn Johnson, the editor at John Wiley & Sons who line-edited the manuscript and made other helpful suggestions. I am grateful to all those who have contributed to this book, especially my many teachers, including His Holiness the Dalai Lama, Geshe Rabten, and Gyatrul Rinpoche, without whom my life in Dharma and this book that has resulted from it would have been impossible. Finally, I wish to express my thanks for the loving support of my wife, Vesna A. Wallace, and stepdaughter, Sarah, who have brought so much joy to my life.

Introduction

OVER THE PAST THIRTY-FOUR years that I have studied and practiced Buddhism, I have trained under the guidance of sixty teachers from the East and West. Most of my spiritual mentors have been Tibetan, but I have also learned from meditation masters trained in the Theravada traditions of Burma, Thailand, and Sri Lanka. Among the wide range of meditation practices to which I have been exposed, I have found none more beneficial than the following five Buddhist meditations:

- Meditative quiescence
- The Four Applications of Mindfulness (of the body, feelings, mind, and mental objects)
- The Four Immeasurables (compassion, loving-kindness, empathetic joy, and equanimity)
- Dream yoga
- Dzogchen, the Great Perfection

As far as I'm concerned, these are the greatest hits of the Buddhist meditative tradition because they present a direct path leading to the realization of our deepest nature and the potentials of consciousness. These meditations are the essential Buddhist practices for refining the attention, cultivating mindfulness, opening the heart, investigating the nature of the waking state and its relation to dreaming, and finally probing the nature of awareness itself. Each takes you a step further on the path to enlightenment, yet you don't have to believe in any specific creed to engage in them, and you can swiftly see for yourself how they alleviate the afflictions of the mind and bring you a greater sense of well-being and fulfillment.

I have not watered these meditations down for popular consumption; nor have I mixed them with cultural additives from the traditional Asian civilizations in which they have long been preserved. While I admire those cultures, I was born and raised in the West, and it is important to recognize that these practices are as powerful for us in the modern world as they were for Asians centuries ago. Although they originated in India and Tibet, these practices are universal in their application. The issues they address are fundamental to human existence throughout the world and throughout human history, and never have they been more relevant than today.

I have titled this book *Genuine Happiness* because the meditations herein present a path to inner fulfillment and human flourishing. This is a happiness gained not through the outer conquest of nature or the acquisition of wealth and fame, but through the conquest of our inner obscurations and the realization of the natural resources inherent in our hearts and minds.

As you introduce yourself to these ways of exploring and training the mind, you will delve into deeper and deeper states of awareness to open up the inner resources of consciousness. In the midst of active daily life it is easy for our minds to become scattered, and our attention becomes dysfunctional by oscillating between dullness and compulsive agitation. The first three chapters present techniques for overcoming these states by cultivating meditative quiescence or tranquility called, in Sanskrit, *shamatha*. The practices are designed to collect and focus the mind through the cultivation of inner stillness, stability, and clarity. This process of fine-tuning our attention moves us toward a state called, in Sanskrit, *sukha*, meaning *genuine happiness*: a state that arises only from a healthy, balanced mind.

To aid you in this process, I have begun each chapter with a guided meditation. Each practice lasts twenty-four minutes, a period called, in Sanskrit, a *ghatika*, which is often said to be the ideal duration for a meditation session when one first begins to practice. Along with introductory material and commentary, a few words at the beginning of each meditation will set our motivation, and we will always end with a short dedication of merit. I suggest that you follow the chapters in order, devoting a week or two to each practice before moving on to the next step of meditative development.

As you sharpen your mind through meditation, you might wonder how you can use this new tool—a stable, serviceable mind—in ways that bring greater richness and clarity, greater wisdom and understanding into your life. You could begin with what the Buddha himself described as a fast track to liberation, the fundamental insight teaching of the whole Buddhist Dharma: the Four Applications of Mindfulness. Their meaning boils down to a recommendation familiar to both East and West: "know thyself." Socrates expressed this universal theme when he commented, "I am still unable . . . to know myself; and it really seems to me ridiculous to look into other things before I have understood that."

In the Buddhist practice of the Four Applications of Mindfulness, we begin by attending closely to the nature of the body. Next we shift our focus to physical and mental feelings: pleasure, pain, and indifference. Observing closely, like a scientist who has never encountered a feeling before, we examine the nature of the phenomena "feelings," rather than identifying with them. How do feelings arise and vanish; what is their nature; and how are they influenced by observation? Then we focus on other mental processes and consciousness itself, and finally on the diverse phenomena that appear to the mind's eye. To what extent can this array of mental events—imagery, dreams, and thoughts—be observed? What is their nature? The Four Applications of Mindfulness were the first forms of Buddhist meditation I encountered, and I am still awed by their profundity and effectiveness.

Following the Four Applications of Mindfulness we will delve into an array of practices that provide a strong foundation for empathy: the Four Immeasurables of loving-kindness, compassion, empathetic joy, and equanimity. These "skillful means" are a perfect complement to the wisdom practices of the Four Applications of Mindfulness. You will find that mindfulness and loving-kindness enhance each other. From there we will explore daytime and nighttime dream yoga before arriving finally at the pinnacle of the Buddhist teachings, Dzogchen, usually translated as the "Great Perfection." Here we move beyond any "ism," a domain of realization that can be compared with contemplative practices found in the Christian, Jewish, Sufi, Taoist, and Vedanta traditions. Despite their differences in doctrine, ritual, and practice, I am convinced that there is an intimate connection among contemplative traditions at the deepest levels of realization, a common ground beneath all the differences. And this common ground is the happiness we are all seeking in our heart of hearts.

I believe that all human beings are yearning for genuine happiness, a quality of well-being deeper than transient pleasure, entertainment, or intellectual stimulation. In Buddhism, the source of this deep yearning, what the great fourteenth-century Tibetan master Tsongkhapa called our *eternal longing*, is at the deepest level of our own being, *buddha-nature*, or primordial consciousness. This quest for genuine happiness sharply contrasts with our attraction to fleeting pleasures. There is nothing wrong with savoring the pleasures of life: pleasures that we experience from being with dear friends and loved ones, delicious food, and wonderful weather are aroused by stimuli coming in through the five physical senses. We also experience pleasures that require no sensory input, for instance when we think of a pleasant memory. But when the stimulus is withdrawn, the pleasure vanishes. Genuine happiness, on the other hand, is not stimulus-driven. Aristotle called such happiness *eudaimonia*, and he equated it with the human good, with the mind working in accordance with virtue, especially the best and most complete virtue. Augustine, the great fifth-century Christian philosopher and theologian, called genuine happiness a *truth-given joy*, a sense of well-being that arises from the nature of truth itself. In the Buddhist understanding this is not a truth that we *learn*, nor is it a truth outside of us. It is the truth that we *are*, in our innermost nature.

In modern societies, there is a widespread fixation on what Buddhists call the Eight Mundane Concerns: (1) seeking the acquisition of material goods and (2) trying not to lose those you have; (3) striving for stimulus-driven pleasures and (4) doing your best to avoid pain and discomfort; (5) seeking praise and (6) avoiding abuse; (7) yearning for a good reputation and (8) fearing disgrace.

We strive for the mundane, good things of life not only because they bring pleasure, but because these are symbols of what we really want. There is nothing intrinsically wrong with these pleasurable stimuli, but we can have all of that and still feel unfulfilled. So what is it that we truly yearn for? The Buddha suggested that our deepest desire for genuine happiness is based not on successfully adjusting outer circumstances, but on something that arises from within, free of the effects of good fortune and adversity. Therefore in Buddhist practice, in our quest for genuine happiness, we cultivate what is sometimes called *renunciation*, though the term I prefer is a *spirit of emergence*, which is my translation from the Tibetan words *nge jung*. Part of the experience of this spirit of emergence is the recognition that genuine happiness is not to be found in mere pleasurable stimuli but from dispelling the inner causes of suffering and discontent. With this motivation one seeks to definitively emerge, once and for all, from the true causes of suffering and realize the innate bliss of consciousness untainted by the afflictions of the mind.

Today in the West, there are two main psychological trends. The older, and until recently the dominant one, is negative psychology. It is based on attacking a mental problem, as in the case of a neurosis or psychosis that has come to your attention. You wouldn't go to the psychologist unless you were aware of the problem; then the therapist would seek a solution. This traditional approach is now being complemented with positive psychology, which asks: What wholesome qualities might we cultivate to achieve above-normal mental health? How can we accentuate the positive?

Buddhism uses both approaches. Pinpointing the nature of frustration, dissatisfaction, anxiety, irritation, and the like pertains to the first of the Four Noble Truths: the reality of suffering. Here the Buddha said, "This is the reality of suffering. Recognize it!" Don't remain in denial; move toward understanding. The Buddha began to "turn the wheel of Dharma" with his teachings on the Four Noble Truths. Since then, traditional Buddhist teachers often begin explaining the Buddhadharma with a discussion of the reality of suffering and the ocean of *samsara*—the cycle of existence, in which we compulsively take rebirth after rebirth under the influence of our mental afflictions, especially that of delusion. Once we have begun to fathom the reality of suffering, we turn to the other noble truths: the origin of suffering, the possibility of its cessation, and the path that leads to the end of suffering. This is the Buddha's earliest teaching.

Many wonder, however, whether it is harmful to attend closely to the reality of suffering. After all, if you attend closely to the reality of suffering within yourself and in the world around you, before long this may appear overwhelming. You begin to observe yourself, and you begin to see how dissatisfaction, or *duhkha*, pervades your life. Even when everything is temporarily going well, it's hard to avoid the fact that this won't last, and this recognition brings anxiety in its wake: "What will become of me?" From the start, Buddhism encourages us to look suffering in the eye, and there is a lot to be said for this. But there is a danger of fixating too much on the problems of existence. Do you want run the risk of leading a life where suffering fills your world because you attend to it so closely? Is there anything else that is authentically Buddhist that might complement this approach?

There is. The reality of suffering is balanced by the Great Perfection, Dzogchen. The basic premise of the Great Perfection is that our fundamental nature has always been that of primordial perfection, a purity and innate bliss that is there just waiting to be discovered. Here is the simplest (but by no means the easiest!) of Buddhist paths: seek out a qualified spiritual mentor and have him or her point out the nature of your own pristine awareness, known in Tibetan as *rigpa*. Fathom and identify the very essence of awareness itself in its natural state before it becomes conceptually structured, distorted, and obscured. Then linger right there. Maintain that awareness while walking, talking, eating, or driving—always and everywhere. By sustaining the recognition of pristine awareness that is never distorted or afflicted in any way, you find that it is primordially pure. This awareness is not something to be developed or attained. It is present right now. So simply pick up the thread of utter purity of your own awareness and maintain it continuously. By so doing, it will become clearer and clearer and the path will open for you of its own accord. The first four types of meditation explained in this book are preparations for the culminating stage.

To sum up, part I of this book explains three methods for developing meditative quiescence: mindfulness of breathing, settling the mind in its natural state, and cultivating awareness of simply being aware. Part II addresses the Four Applications of Mindfulness—of the body, feelings, the mind, and phenomena at large. These are the fundamental Buddhist teachings on the cultivation of contemplative insight. Part III discusses the Four Immeasurables—loving-kindness, compassion, empathetic joy, and equanimity—which are the heart's path to genuine happiness. Part IV begins with an explanation of the spirit of awakening—the altruistic yearning to achieve enlightenment for the benefit of the world—then proceeds to the daytime and nighttime practices of dream yoga, and finally Dzogchen.

By training the attention in the cultivation of meditative quiescence and exploring the Four Applications of Mindfulness, the Four Immeasurables, dream yoga, and Dzogchen, we have the opportunity to release and rest in the utterly pure awareness of the immediate present. This is the Buddhist version of "follow your bliss." This doesn't mean "follow pleasurable stimuli." Rather, it refers to something that is prior to pleasurable stimuli, something that carries through both the pleasant and the unpleasant, something deeper. We have all had glimpses of it, so we shouldn't think this is something mysterious and difficult to realize. I suspect there is no one who has not experienced the following: a moment when your heart felt full, you were utterly relaxed, a smile came to your face, and you were pervaded by a sense of well-being—and you hadn't a clue why. Nothing especially good had happened just beforehand. You were not thinking about anything nice, not tasting anything good, no pleasurable stimuli were coming in. Yet there it was: your heart, your very being, was offering you its own joy. This is the first hint of a sense of genuine happiness that comes from the nature of awareness itself. So this is what this book is all about: following the scent of genuine happiness to its source by probing into the nature of consciousness and tapping your inner, natural resources to the full.

PART I

Refining the Attention

Mindfulness of Breathing

METHODS FOR REFINING THE attention were already developed to a very sophisticated degree in India 2,500 years ago, during the time of Gautama the Buddha. These advanced states of *samadhi*, or meditative concentration, were found to yield profound states of serenity and bliss, and many contemplatives cultivated these states as ends in themselves. Gautama's great innovation was to further develop these methods of *samadhi*, then apply this refined, focused attention to the direct, experiential investigation of the mind and its relation to the rest of the world. In this way, the cultivation of *shamatha*, or meditative quiescence, is analogous to the development of the telescope for the sustained, precise observation of celestial phenomena. The only instrument we have for directly observing mental phenomena is mental awareness, and this is honed into a fine tool by the development of *shamatha*.

The Buddha taught dozens of techniques to refine, stabilize, and clarify the attention. One in particular is especially appropriate for highly discursive, conceptual, imaginative, mentally talkative people: mindfulness of breathing. From the earliest records we have of the Buddha's own pursuit of liberation, on the night of his enlightenment, he first stabilized his mind with the practice of *shamatha*, then applied it to *vipashyana*, the cultivation of contemplative insight into the nature of reality.

Mindfulness of breathing was the first Buddhist meditation I began practicing, and I often recommend it to my students as the first step on the meditative path. I began learning it from books in

1970, especially the writings of the Thai monk Buddhadasa. I was leading the life of a reclusive college student at the time, spending a lot of time reading about the contemplative traditions of the world, and beginning to study the Tibetan language. A few years later, when I was living as a monk in the mountains above Dharamsala, India, I received personal instruction in the technique from two Theravada Buddhist meditation teachers who had trained in Burma and Thailand, Goenka and Kitti Subho. In 1980, I traveled to Sri Lanka, solely to meditate, and I then had the opportunity to train for months in this practice under the renowned scholar and contemplative Balangoda Anandamaitreya. Over the years, I have also been taught variations of this practice by a number of Tibetan lamas, but I have relied primarily on my Theravada teachers for this kind of meditation.

Practice

In our practices for refining and balancing the attention, we will begin with the Buddhist strategy of moving from the coarse to the subtle, from the easy to the more difficult. This approach begins with mindfulness of breathing, proceeds to settling the mind in its natural state, and concludes with the practice of simply being aware of being aware. In each of these practices, we start the session by establishing a suitable bodily posture, and cultivating three qualities as we "settle the body in its natural state": relaxation, stillness, and vigilance.

Relaxation

There are two postures I would recommend for this practice: sitting or lying down. Generally, the optimal and most widely recommended posture is sitting cross-legged on a cushion. If this is too uncomfortable, you may sit in a chair, with both feet resting on the ground. But another, less commonly used posture is lying down on the back, with your arms outstretched to your sides, palms up, and your head resting on a pillow. This is especially useful if you have a back problem or if you are physically tired or ill.

Whatever posture you adopt, let your body rest at ease, with your spine straight but not rigid. Relax your shoulders, with your arms loosely dropping to your sides. Allow gravity to take over. Now bring your awareness to your face. It's best if your eyes are hooded, not completely shut. Soften the muscles of your face, specifically the jaw, temples, and forehead. Soften your eyes. Let your face be as relaxed as that of a sleeping baby. Then complete this initial relaxation process by taking three slow, deep, gentle breaths through the nostrils. As you inhale, breathe smoothly and deeply down to the bottom of your abdomen. Like filling a pot with water, feel your abdomen slowly fill and expand, then breathe into your diaphragm, and finally into the upper chest. Then release the breath fully, without forcing it out. Do this three times, keeping your awareness present in the body, especially noting the sensations of the in- and out-breaths. Following these deep breaths, return to normal, unregulated respiration. Let this quality of bodily relaxation be an outer expression of your mind: let your awareness be at ease, releasing all your cares; simply be present in the here and now.

As you breathe in and out, direct your attention to the tactile sensations of the passage of the breath at the apertures of your nostrils or above your upper lip. Take a moment to locate the sensation. Rest your attention right where you feel the incoming and outgoing breaths. Once in a while, check to see that you are still breathing down into the abdomen. This will happen naturally if your body is settled, with your back straight and your belly relaxed and soft.

Stillness

Throughout each meditation session, let your body be as still as possible, with a minimum of fidgeting; remain motionless as a mountain. This helps to bring about the same quality in the mind: one of stillness, where your attention is focused and continuous.

Vigilance

Even if you are lying down, let your posture reflect a sense of vigilance, not just collapsing into drowsiness. If you are sitting up, either on a cushion or in a chair, slightly raise your sternum, while keeping the belly soft and relaxed. In this way, you will naturally breathe into your abdomen first, and when the respiration deepens you may feel your diaphragm and chest expanding as well. Sit at attention, without slouching forward or tilting to either side. This physical posture also reinforces this same quality of vigilance mentally.

Mindfulness of Breathing

Maintaining focused attention is vital for virtually everything we do throughout the day, including working, driving, relating to others, enjoying times of recreation and entertainment, and engaging in spiritual practice. Therefore, the theme for this session is learning to focus the attention. Whatever your normal level of attention—whether you are usually scattered or composed—the quality of your attention can be improved, and this brings with it extraordinary benefits. In this practice, we shift from a compulsively conceptual, fragmented mode of awareness to one of deeper simplicity, moving into a witnessing or observing mode. In addition to honing the attention, this meditation will enhance your health, tune your nervous system, allow you to sleep better, and improve your emotional balance. This is a different way of applying our minds, and it improves with practice. The specific method we will follow is the cultivation of mindfulness of breathing.

Due to habit, thoughts are bound to intrude. When they come, just release them as you exhale, without identifying with them, without emotionally responding to them. Watch the thought emerge, pass before you, and then fade away. Then rest your attention in the sense of repose, not dull and sluggish, but at ease. For the time being, if all you can accomplish in one *ghatika*, or twenty-four minutes, is to bring forth a sense of mental relaxation, that's great. Maintain your attention right where you feel the sensations of the in- and out-breaths.

Maintain mindfulness of your breathing as continuously as you can. The term *mindfulness* in this context refers to the faculty of focusing continuously upon a familiar, chosen object without distraction. In Tibetan and Sanskrit, the word translated as *mindful-ness* also means *remembering*. So the cultivation of mindfulness means maintaining an unbroken flow of remembering, remembering, remembering. It doesn't involve any internal commentary. You are simply remembering to attend to the stream of tactile sensations of the in- and out-breaths. The quality of awareness you are cultivating here is a kind of bare attention, a simple witnessing, with no mental analysis or conceptual elaboration. In addition to sustaining mindfulness, it's crucial to apply introspection intermittently throughout the session. This does not mean thinking about yourself. Rather, it is the internal monitoring of your mental state. By means of introspection, looking within, you can determine whether your attention has disengaged from the breath and has wandered off to sounds, other sensations in your body, or vagrant thoughts, memories, or anticipations of the future. Introspection entails quality control, monitoring the processes of both the mind and the body. From time to time, see if any tension has built up around your eyes or forehead. If so, release it. Let your face soften and relax. Then spend a few minutes seeing if you can divide your attention while remaining at ease. Be mindful of your breath, but also be aware of how your mind is operating.

Let me emphasize that this is not a concentration technique in the Western sense. We are not bearing down with tight, focused effort. It is essential to maintain a physical and mental sense of relaxation, and on that basis we gradually enhance the stability and then the vividness of attention. This entails a spacious quality of awareness, and within that spaciousness, a sense of openness and ease; mindfulness comes to rest on the breath, like a hand laid gently on a child's head. As the vividness of attention increases, you will notice sensations even between breaths. As the turbulence of the mind subsides, you will find that you can simply attend to the tactile sensations of the breath, rather than your thoughts about it.

I'll now introduce a technique you may find useful on occasion, a simple device of counting that, done with precision, may bring greater stability and continuity to your attention. Once again, with a luxurious sense of being at ease and giving your overworked and overwrought conceptual mind a rest, place your attention on the tactile sensations of the breath. After exhaling, just as the next in-breath begins, mentally count "one." Maintaining an erect posture, with the chest raised so the breath flows back in effortlessly, breathe in and follow the tactile sensations of the breath, letting your conceptual mind rest. Then experience the wonderful sense of refreshment as the breath is released, all the way out, until reaching the next turnaround point. Cultivate a "Teflon mind"—a mind to which nothing sticks, that doesn't cling to thoughts about the present, past, or future. In this manner, count from one to ten. You may then repeat counting to ten, or continue counting up from ten to higher numbers. This is a practice of simplifying rather than suppressing your discursive mind. You are reducing mental activity to just counting, taking a holiday from compulsive thinking throughout the entire cycle of the breath. Practice for several minutes before ending this session.

To bring any worthy endeavor to a close in a meaningful fashion, Buddhists dedicate merit. Something has been drawn together in our hearts and minds by applying ourselves to this wholesome activity. After completing a meditation session, you may want to dwell for a minute or so to dedicate the merit of your practice, that it may lead to the fulfillment of whatever you find to be most meaningful for yourself and for others. With intention and attention, that goodness can be directed wherever we wish.

For Further Contemplation

The Buddha praised the practice of mindfulness of breathing as an exceptionally effective way to balance and purify the mind:

> Just as in the last month of the hot season, when a mass of dust and dirt has swirled up, a great rain cloud out of season disperses it and quells it on the spot, so too concentration by mindfulness of breathing, when developed and cultivated, is peaceful and sublime, an ambrosial dwelling, and it disperses and quells on the spot unwholesome states whenever they arise.

In the practice of *shamatha* we consciously rest our awareness upon our breathing. The breath is like a steed and awareness is its rider. Attending to the breath is unlikely to arouse craving or aversion. Shifting into neutral, we neither aggravate nor distort the mind. Therefore, you might expect this practice to be rather boring. The object of attention doesn't seem very interesting, just the same old breath. And yet once you have developed some continuity, there are surprises in store. You will find a sense of well-being and balance that arises in a quiet, serene way, as if you are listening to waves rolling into shore. You can rest in that serenity and settle deeper and deeper. Your mind is like a stream, and you are simply not polluting it with distractions. Those who have studied the natural environment know that if you stop contaminating a polluted river, its self-purifying ability will come to the fore. The same is true for the natural healing properties of the mind.

We all know something about the earth's natural resources and the importance of conserving them, but don't we also have *internal* natural resources? Might not the mind, in a very practical, everyday sense, become its own source of well-being? Whenever I see His Holiness the Dalai Lama, I feel I am meeting a man whose heart, mind, and spirit are overflowing with uncontrived goodwill, compassion, and cheer. He must have done some extraordinary exploration of his inner resources to open up such a wellspring. Since we all have an eternal longing to find real satisfaction that fills the heart, a longing that looks for more than a continuous stream of pleasurable stimuli, for something deeper, something more fulfilling, how can we tap into that resource? *Shamatha* is like a drilling platform from which to begin fathoming our inner natural resources.

If you are drawn to the practice of breath awareness, do it for at least one session a day, though two would be best—one in the morning and one in the evening. Twenty-four minutes is a duration that Indian and Chinese yogis settled on independently. In ancient Chinese theory, it is said that twenty-four minutes is the duration required for the *qi*, or vital energies in your body, to go through one complete cycle. For the Indians the same time period was considered optimal for one's meditation sessions when one first begins to practice. Later you may wish to extend this longer. Keep in mind that twenty-four minutes is only a small fraction of the approximately sixteen hours a day that you are awake. If that is the only spiritual practice you do, if there is no carryover to everything else, then no matter what happens in that twenty-four minutes, it will not have a very transformative effect on your life as a whole. There is just too much competition from the activities of the other fifteen and a half hours.

Mindfulness in Daily Life

Here are some guidelines drawn from the teachings of Asanga, a great fifth-century Indian Buddhist adept, that may help you extend your practice into daily life:

Restrain your six senses (mental awareness as well as the five physical senses) from objects that arouse craving or hostility. This doesn't mean that you should never be thinking about anything pleasant or unpleasant. Simply avoid dwelling on them in ways that upset the equilibrium of your mind. If you want to attend to them, do so, but don't feed the mental afflictions of attachment and aversion. That would be like polluting a mountain stream. Similarly, if you focus on things that are disappointing in yourself or in others, they will become your reality. So avoid dwelling on those things that arouse hostility, irritation, negativity, craving, anxiety, and grasping.

Furthermore, don't become attached to the input from your senses. When a monk walks down the road, he is to cast his gaze downward so that he doesn't focus on things that may catalyze craving or hostility. The point is this: don't go to places where you are bound to succumb to obsessive desires. Sensual craving is one of the five hindrances that the Buddha taught as obstructing the process of refining the attention. Another is malice. When you are troubled by someone's negative behavior toward you, attend to that person with compassion. Being dominated by angry, hateful thoughts simply poisons the mind. Protect your mind from malice as you would shelter a child from injury.

During ordinary activities, when you are walking, eating, or cleaning, bring greater mindfulness to your movements. Be mindful of your diet. Consume food that is not difficult to digest, and in quantities that are not too large or too small. If you want to turn eating into a Dharma event, partake of your food so that you can nourish your body and use it to be of service to the world. And get enough sleep. Even with the best of intentions, your practice will be impaired if you're not getting enough sleep. Try to fall asleep with wholesome thoughts. Provide yourself with an interval between sleep and your daily activities, with all of their concerns and responsibilities. It is optimal to meditate just before retiring.

It is often said that spiritual practice will not be fruitful over the long term unless you take satisfaction in it. Of course you will not enjoy every moment because sometimes the path gets rugged—not because Dharma is thorny, but because our habit-driven minds are. On the whole, it is important to find and follow a path that makes the heart sing. When breath awareness starts to go well, it becomes enjoyable. In simplicity you find that the scent of spiritual progress is strong and pure. But you can also develop an attachment to simplicity. You may start yearning for solitude and want to disengage from the world, thinking, "This feels so good—all I need is the breath." That may alienate you, keeping you from engaging with others, making you less inclined to offer what you can to those around you. It's important not to devalue engagement with others or the reality of our interconnectedness with them. We have something to offer others and there is something to be received from them. That is a key element in the meaning of life, and you don't want to shut that out because you enjoy mindfulness of breathing so much.

Buddhism is not just meditation; nor, for that matter, is any contemplative path merely a set of techniques, a cookbook for the soul. Meditation becomes woven into the whole fabric of life. And, generally speaking, spiritual practice brings with it a mood of focusing critically on how we live. Why do we engage in the kinds of things we do from day to day? Among the many desires that come to mind and the many that we may pursue, are there some that are not worth investing a life into, things that we do merely out of habit? Some desires, such as the wish to be a good father, mother, brother, or sister, are worthy aspirations. In your work, you want to do your job well and in a way that gives you satisfaction. Assuming the work is wholesome, there is value to that. But aren't there some desires that are more important than others, calling on us to prioritize and make sacrifices? The issue in spiritual practice in general is the simplification and prioritization of desires. What do we want most? Could some desires merely represent something else we really want? Notice how many people, especially well-known people who have made it to the top of their professions, fall into alcoholism and drug abuse? I was impressed when I recently heard the actress Gwenyth Paltrow comment in an interview that when it comes to being a celebrity with adoring fans and great wealth, "If that is all you have, you don't have much." May not some of us be striving diligently in the wrong directions, not being quite in touch with our true aspirations?

In my case, when I was twenty, I sensed that having a girlfriend, a car, a good education, and fine prospects for a successful career just wasn't enough. I discovered that fixation on the mundane, and the transient didn't ultimately deliver on the initial promises. So while we are immersed in the ongoing flux of the happiness and pain of life, the spirit of emergence can guide us in seeking out a path of increasing sanity. Keeping our feet on the ground, becoming psychologically more healthy and less neurotic—that alone will bring a greater sense of well-being. And there is a smooth curve flowing from mental health to spiritual maturation. That implies that even taking the first baby steps toward mental health is part of spiritual practice.

Going beyond desires for things that are merely symbols of true happiness leads to deeper understanding. We begin to see that we are interrelated with our fellow human beings, other sentient beings, the entire environment. We are now, and have always been, inextricably interconnected with those around us. In Buddhism the notion of an isolated, independent individual, an autonomous ego, is not based on reality. Such an ego has never existed; it's nothing more than a habitual mental construct, and a deluded one at that. This assertion is more than merely a belief; it is a working hypothesis that we will carefully examine as we proceed through these practices, not merely accepting anything as dogma. If we are interrelated from our core, and we return to the question *What do we seek?* our search is not for ourselves alone but for ourselves in relation to all others. The questions become, "What do I seek in relationship to you?" "How can we venture together?" As soon as possible, cultivate an altruistic motivation for your practice of mindfulness of breathing and for whatever other practice you do. Aspire to bring forth the full capacity of your own buddha-nature. Manifest it completely, whatever that might entail. As a result, you will experience a capacity for compassion, for wisdom, and for energy, or power of the spirit itself, power to heal, and power to create.

How can this be unveiled? By simplifying and focusing our desires in the same manner as we cultivate attention. Eventually a point is reached where all our other desires become derivatives of the one wish: "May I realize perfect spiritual awakening for the benefit of all beings." That is the simple, single desire of *bodhichitta*, the spirit of awakening. Then, when that is the only desire that lingers, for a moment release it. Let it go and just be present. Similarly, when you focus the attention, when the mind settles, becomes more centered on the breath, release that. Release and be present in the sheer state of being aware. That will reveal to you the very nature of awareness itself.

2

Settling the Mind
in Its Natural State

WE MOVE NOW FROM the practice of mindfulness of breathing to the more subtle meditation of settling the mind in its natural state. After spending four years in India, studying with many Tibetan and Theravada Buddhist teachers, I was encouraged by His Holiness the Dalai Lama, who had ordained me as a monk, to join my teacher Geshe Rabten in establishing a Tibetan Buddhist monastery for Westerners in Switzerland. This was something of a homecoming for me, for I had lived for years in Switzerland when I was growing up. Shortly after I moved there, Geshe Rabten taught his monastic and lay students the practice of Mahamudra, designed to fathom the nature of consciousness. This consists of two parts: *shamatha* and *vipashyana*. The *shamatha* technique he taught is identical to the one presented here. Since then, I have received similar teachings from the late Tibetan contemplative Khenpo Jigmé Phuntsok, perhaps the most renowned yogi in all of Tibet, and from Gyatrul Rinpoche, whose guidance and example has been a profound source of inspiration.

Practice

Rest your body in its natural state, as described in the previous chapter. For this practice, it is important to leave your eyes open, with your gaze resting vacantly in the space in front of you. Blink whenever you feel like it, and let your eyes remain relaxed. Although leaving your eyes open may seem a bit awkward if you've never done this before in meditation, try to get used to it. Don't let your eyes become strained in any way, any more than they are when daydreaming. In this practice your head may be slightly inclined. The tongue is pressed gently against the palate. Throughout the twenty-four minutes of this session, your body should be at ease and still, apart from the natural movements of breathing. Bring to mind the three qualities of the posture: relaxation, stability, and vigilance.

Before venturing into the main practice, spend a few moments in discursive meditation, bringing to mind your motivation for this session. In the broader context of your spiritual practice, or of your life in general, what do you most deeply and meaningfully yearn for? How could you find greater meaning, fulfillment, satisfaction, and happiness in your life? This aspiration may pertain not only to your individual well-being but may include all those with whom you come in contact, the world at large. I encourage you to bring to mind your most meaningful motivation. It will enrich your practice.

Let's begin to stabilize this marvelous instrument, the mind, to refine its focus and attention by counting twenty-one breaths. In a purely observational mode, place your attention once again upon the tactile sensations created when the air enters and exits your nostrils. Also direct your introspective awareness to the state of your mind, seeing whether it is agitated, calm, drowsy, or alert. Let your mindfulness of the breathing and your introspective vigilance upon the mind be coupled with a sense of being profoundly at ease, relaxed from your core. With this simple technique, at the beginning of your next inhalation, mentally count "one," then simply observe the tactile sensations of the in-breath and out-breath. At the very beginning of the next in-breath, count "two." In this way, go from one to twenty-one, without losing count. Though thoughts are bound to intrude, just let them go, release them with each out-breath, and direct your awareness back to your breathing.

Now we'll highlight a second aspect of this practice: increasing vividness by settling the mind in its natural state. We have six doors of perception, including the five physical senses of sight, sound, smell, taste, and touch. But we have another avenue, a direct perception into another realm of reality—the sixth domain of mental experience. So take an interest now in the domain of the mind, this field of experience in which thoughts, images, feelings, emotions, memories, desires, fears, and at night, dreams, all occur. For the time being, we will also maintain a peripheral mindfulness of the breathing. Metaphorically, let's keep one hand of the attention on the buoy of the breath. To expand the metaphor, imagine you are out in the ocean in a gentle swell rising and falling, with one hand on a buoy to give you some stability, a point of reference. Now, wearing a facemask, you sink your head beneath the surface of the waves, aware with your body of the rise and fall of the incoming swells but attending to whatever lies in the ocean depths, in the transparent, luminous water.

In this state of awareness, observe whatever comes up in the mind with no preference as to whether thoughts are arising or not, no preference for nice thoughts as opposed harsh thoughts. Do this without intervention or manipulation, without control. Let the thought rise up, pass before you, then fade away. Meanwhile, let your awareness rest, abiding in its own stillness, even while the mind is active. In this way, the mind gradually settles in its *natural* state, which is quite distinct from its *habitual* state. Habitually, the mind oscillates between excitation and laxity. But with this practice the mind gradually comes to rest in its ground state, calm and clear.

Finally, in the same fashion, without control or identification, simply rest in a mode of observation, sometimes called "naked awareness." Perceive as nakedly as you can whatever arises in this space, whether it wells up from inside like an emotion or feeling, or appears more as an object of the mind—for example, mental chitchat or memories. See if your awareness can be so deeply relaxed that you can observe these mental events without intervention. Can you watch each mental event so passively that it plays out its own life—it arises, it lingers, it passes—as if it were uninfluenced by your awareness of it? Watch carefully, but remain relaxed.

It is very important to this practice that there be no preference for having a calm and quiet mind as opposed to an active and discursive mind. It *is* appropriate to have a preference for not being carried away by the events of the mind and not grasping onto them. Discover whether it is possible for you to be calm even when the thoughts passing through your mind are disturbed.

Continue breathing normally into the abdomen. If you become disoriented, return to the breath, stabilize a bit, and then hover in the space of the mind once again. Try to maintain this meditative state for the full twenty-four minutes.

To bring this session to a close, dedicate whatever benefit, whatever has been meaningful in this practice, to the fulfillment of your aspirations for your own well-being and happiness and for that of those around you. May the greatest possible good be derived from this practice.

For Further Contemplation

In order to make the attention malleable, or, serviceable, we have begun with two practices that train the attention with *shamatha*, or meditative quiescence. Such attention has two qualities: stability and vividness, both achieved by cultivating mindfulness and introspection. The first chapter centered on attention to the breath; here we focus on the mind. In the early Pali literature, the Buddha referred to this practice as the cultivation of "unfastened mindfulness." Parallels can easily be drawn between this *shamatha* technique and the "sitting" practice of Soto Zen, as well as the contemporary Vipassana tradition. In the Tibetan Buddhist tradition it is variously called "settling the mind in its natural state," "quiescence focused on conceptualization," and "taking the mind and appearances as the path." While such practice certainly yields many insights into the nature of the mind, it is properly classified as a *shamatha* practice, not as *vipashyana*, for it doesn't entail any investigation into the nature of phenomena. This method of settling the mind has the special advantage of leading to insight into the relative nature of consciousness.

Practicing breath awareness provides a clear measure of attentional stability. You are either on the breath or not. If you choose to be on the breath, but then five seconds later you have become distracted, you know your stability needs improvement. Keep returning to the breath, cultivating continuity and stability, maintaining the breath as a point of reference. Furthermore, pay attention to the vividness and clarity of your apprehension of the tactile sensations of the in-breaths and out-breaths. Can you pick up sensations even between breaths, or do they fade? Even if sensations of the breath grow faint or disappear, maintain your attention on the region where they last appeared. As vividness increases, you will find that what you are sensing has greater richness. The technique is straightforward: you maintain mindfulness of the breathing, in which you seek continuity, all the while monitoring the mind with introspective vigilance for the occurrence of laxity or excitation.

The first step toward developing attentional stability and vividness is by using a clear object of the mind, such as the breath. But in this technique of observing the mind, you move on to something subtler, where attentional stability and vividness are not locked onto a specific object. Here you bring awareness into the domain of your mind, stabilize there—vividly, clearly—and whatever comes up rises and passes unobstructed. In the cacophony of the mind, the awareness itself remains stable. Using a metaphor cited by Sogyal Rinpoche, your awareness is like a gracious host in the midst of unruly guests. The guests come and go, they may have food fights at times, but the host is calm and serene.

Even when you are observing whatever arises in the space of your mind, there are still objects of awareness. The subject/object dichotomy has shifted from subjective attention to the objective breath to a subjective awareness of the objective phenomena arising in the domain of the mind. Therefore, you are observing thoughts and memories within the domain of the mind as objects of awareness. Just as with mindfulness of breathing, you can cultivate attentional stability and vividness, but you are not controlling your mind, as you *were* doing with mindfulness of the breath.

Here you are not trying to modify, identify with, or judge the contents of the mind. Stability and vividness are still present, but these are qualities of subjective awareness, not the objective contents of the mind, which come and go, sometimes chaotically. As your awareness becomes more stable, you grow familiar with this subjective stability, even in the midst of mental agitation. When you are not identifying with the objects, not judging, intervening, suppressing, or empowering mental activities, simply observe how the mind settles.

Upon observing the rising and passing of mental phenomena, you have probably found little that is stable. The mind is filled with fleeting thoughts, images, memories, and so forth. You may wonder how you are to attain stability when the mind is so turbulent. Keep in mind that the stability to be cultivated here is not to be found within the objective contents of the mind but in your subjective awareness of them. By this I mean that you settle in the stillness of the space of the mind, even when that space is filled with movement. So this requires a stability of *not* being carried away by thoughts and emotions. Furthermore, because your attention isn't focused on a fixed point, the stability of awareness has a free-flowing quality.

The nineteenth-century Tibetan contemplative Lerab Lingpa summarized the essence of this practice with the advice to settle the mind "without distraction and without grasping." On the one hand, don't let your attention be abducted by any of the contents of the mind, drifting off to the past or future or into conceptual elaborations about the present. On the other hand, whatever arises in the field of the mind, don't grasp onto it, identify with it, cling to it, or push it away. Don't even prefer to be free of thoughts. As Lerab Lingpa advised:

> Whatever kinds of mental imagery occur—be they gentle or violent, subtle or gross, of long or short duration, strong or weak, good or bad—observe their nature, and avoid any obsessive evaluation of them as being one thing and not another. Let the heart of your practice be consciousness in its natural state, limpid and vivid.

Have you ever seen a falcon hovering in midair as it scans the ground in search of a meal? There is nothing for this bird to hold onto, but with sensitive monitoring of its wings and the air currents, it can remain motionless relative to the ground, as it moves through the air. It hovers by not grasping, yet there is stability. You too can motionlessly hold your attention in "midair" in the space of your mind. If you would like to deepen your meditation—your contemplative inquiry into the nature of your own existence, your relation to the surrounding environment and other beings—the ability to sustain continuous, clear attention is crucial. Right now we are simply developing a tool, refining our attention so that it takes on a greater degree of stability and vividness. Another nineteenth-century Tibetan meditation master, Düdjom Lingpa, described the results of this practice as follows:

By applying yourself to this practice constantly at all times, both during and between meditation sessions, eventually all coarse and subtle thoughts will be calmed in the empty expanse of the essential nature of your mind. You will become still in an unfluctuating state, in which you will experience joy like the warmth of a fire, clarity like the dawn, and nonconceptuality like an ocean unmoved by waves.

The seventeenth-century contemplative Panchen Lozang Chökyi Gyaltsen, who was the tutor of the Fifth Dalai Lama, summarized the results:

In that way, the reality of the mind is insightfully perceived, and yet it is ungraspable and undemonstrable. "Whatever appears, loosely attend to it without grasping"—this is the quintessential advice that passes on the torch of the Buddha. . . . Moreover, whatever good and bad objects of the five senses arise, awareness clearly, luminously takes on any appearance, like the reflections in a limpid mirror. You have the sense that it cannot be recognized as being this and not being that.

Within the broad context of science and academic scholarship, we in the West are prone to a very restricted, prejudiced, and essentially unscientific view of the mind's potential for objective observation. The five outer senses, with their extensions through the instruments of technology, are thought to provide us with "objective" information, whereas the mind, directed inward, is considered too "subjective" to provide reliable data on whatever it may be observing. According to this view, empiricism—the exploration of reality through observation and experiment (as opposed to reliance on dogmatism or pure rationalism)—must be focused on the physical world and cannot be applied to the mind, which is only responsible for thinking and remembering. But the mind does so much more. As you watch your mind in meditation, you are not simply remembering something from the past, you are observing mental events in the present. Furthermore, you can tell from moment to moment if your mind is agitated or calm, whether you are interested or bored, happy, sad, or indifferent. You know this by means of direct observation, not indirectly with your five physical senses. But unfortunately in the modern Western tradition, such introspection has been marginalized, limiting scientific exploration.

Buddhism maintains that we have six modes of observation, and only one of them, mental perception, provides direct access to mental events. Brain scientists may get at them indirectly by finding neural correlations with mental states and processes, and behavioral psychologists can study them indirectly by observing mind-to-behavior relationships. But our only immediate access to mental events is by way of the mental perception. This is a crucial point but one that is generally ignored in our civilization—that mental perception, too, has empirical validity.

Of course, the ideal of objectivity is central to the humanities and the sciences. One who fails that test is considered to be a poor scientist and a poor scholar. But is objectivity possible in an area that *seems* to be an entirely subjective realm: the private, inner realm of your thoughts, memories, feelings, desires, mental imagery, and dreams? This, of course, depends on how one defines "objective." Let me offer two definitions of objectivity. One is objectivity as a way of engaging with reality, seeking understanding, that is as free as possible from individual bias. Here personal preferences must be set aside. An open-mindedness and a willingness to hear different, opposing, or unfamiliar voices, to consider ideas afresh and give them a fair shake, is one model of objectivity. I don't see any downside to that. In Buddhism there are said to be three criteria for a suitable student and one of them is objectivity: ascertaining what is being perceived, what is offered to you by reality, so to speak, without distorting it, overlaying it, or undercutting it by means of expectations, biases, or preferences. Such objectivity is just as crucial for contemplative inquiry as it is for scientific and scholarly inquiry.

Another type of objectivity is often stipulated as an ideal for science: the principle of attending to phenomena that are unrelated to any individual perceiver. When you look at the moon and then close your eyes, the moon is still out there. The moon is therefore said to be objectively real, and it is therefore a suitable object for scientific study. Science is not only trying to be free of prejudice and bias, but it is also looking at the objective world that is out there, independent of any observer. Notice, however, that if you start calling that matrix of objects that exist independently of any individual observer the "objective world," the "physical world," and then equate that with the "natural world," something is left out of nature: all of those real and natural phenomena that do not exist independently of the individual observer, like your thoughts, emotions, dreams, and the whole realm of your subjective life. Thoughts and the like are excluded because they have no existence independent of the observer. This falsely implies that thoughts are less real and not part of the natural world because they are not public. But this is nothing more than a bias, a subjectively prejudiced exclusion of mental phenomena from the natural world.

Yet from a pragmatic standpoint, aside from the fascination of exploring the nature of consciousness, mental events, and their relation to physical reality, of what value is this mode of contemplative inquiry to us personally? In that regard let me suggest that this practice is the very pursuit of genuine happiness mentioned earlier: "The truth shall make you free." Any Buddhist tradition that is true to the core of the Buddha's own teachings never veers far from this pragmatic ideal. Buddhism starts with the reality of suffering and goes right to the source of the suffering, of discontent, dissatisfaction, malaise, lack of meaning and fulfillment, grief, despair, and so on. Then it asks: does suffering have causes or does it arise randomly? If you opt for the latter, your inquiry hits a dead end. But if you adopt the working hypothesis that happiness and sorrow have causes, further inquiry is meaningful. Once we focus on the nature of our emotional states, our affective states of happiness and sorrow in all their gradations, then we can begin probing their causes.

Observe how the internal workings of the mind can prime you for dissatisfaction. For example, if someone belittles you, this may throw you into self-doubt and sadness. Must one opinion out of millions ruin your day? You descend down the slippery slope of negativity, worrying about your value as a person and so on, but your reaction needn't be automatic. There's no one-to-one correspondence between outer events and our inner emotional states.

In 1971, I began living with Tibetan refugees who had fled their country at the risk of their lives and had taken up residence in the Indian hill town of Dharamsala only a decade earlier. I found to my amazement that these were the happiest people I had ever met in my life. External factors that might prop up their happiness were few and far between. They were poor, they had lost their homeland, each one had gone through personal tragedy, and many were in bad health. By means of the intelligent and pragmatic quest to free ourselves from that which impedes us, we too may discover the source of genuine well-being.

Lifestyle Conducive to Practice

To advance our practice, we need a lifestyle that is conducive to greater balance and serenity, greater day-to-day well-being, one that allows our practice to flow into daily life, bringing us greater meaning and happiness. Let's be guided by this often-quoted statement by Atisha, the revered eleventh-century Indian master who played a pivotal role in revitalizing Buddhism in Tibet:

> As long as the conditions for meditative quiescence are incomplete, meditative concentration will not be accomplished even if you meditate diligently for a thousand years.

Atisha is saying that techniques need to be placed within the context of a supportive lifestyle. It's not enough to be skilled or earnest for twenty-four minutes. Skill and commitment will not work even in a thousand years if the context—a conducive lifestyle and a conducive environment—is not present. There's no point in applying ourselves to spiritual practice, then getting no benefit. Life is too short.

If you are intent on elevating your attention to exceptionally high degrees of stability and clarity so that your mind becomes optimally serviceable, the general counsel from the Buddhist tradition is to radically simplify your life. Withdraw into solitude where you can devote yourself to contemplative practice with as few distractions as possible. But most of us are unable to do this. I have modified the following recommendations of Asanga, which he designed specifically for those dedicated entirely to a life of contemplation, so that his counsel can be carried over to an active life. And though these recommendations are specifically for developing *shamatha*, they also apply more generally to the quest for deepening spiritual practice.

The six inner and outer requisites for training the attention begin with finding a suitable environment. Your environment is conducive to practice if it has five qualities:

1. Food, shelter, clothing, and other basics are easily obtained.

2. It is a pleasant location where you are not disturbed by people, carnivorous animals, and so forth. There must be a sense that your environment is relatively safe so you can be at ease.

3. The land is good. You might want to move away from an area where you can't breathe the air or drink the water, or where disease is prevalent. When you look at monasteries, in Tibet or Europe, you will notice that the monks generally have great aesthetic taste. They place monasteries in inspiring locations. If you can arrange to have a view that opens

your mind to a sense of spaciousness and relaxation, that's perfect.

4. Have good companions. The Buddha once said that the whole of spiritual practice is having spiritual friends. Practice goes much better if you have companions for mutual support. A sense of alienation from the people around you causes difficulties.

5. Finally, make sure people don't disrupt your mind during the daytime and that the nights are peaceful. Buddhist contemplatives have passed down the aphorism that for deep meditative practice "sound is a thorn." You can close your eyes but it is not so easy to close your ears. If you have a choice, choose well where you live.

The second recommendation is to have few desires. Free yourself from craving possessions of either high quality or in large quantity, as well as indulging in other mundane concerns.

Contentment is the third requisite. Look at what you have and see if it isn't already adequate. If it is, be content. How can someone who is materially well-off yet still unsatisfied be called "wealthy" in any meaningful sense? The person just has a lot of baggage. But whether you have many or a few possessions, if you are content, then true wealth is yours.

Fourth is simplicity of lifestyle. Once, when I was coordinating a *shamatha* retreat with about a dozen people devoting themselves solely to this practice for one year, the Tibetan contemplative Gen Lamrimpa, who was the primary teacher for this retreat, discouraged them from even keeping a journal. "Don't clutter up your life," he said. He wanted people to focus on the practice with as few distractions as possible. Radical simplicity is probably not viable for most of us right now. But even in the midst of complexity, some degree of simplicity can be attained.

The fifth recommendation is to maintain pure ethical discipline. The core of Buddhist ethics is to avoid engaging in deeds that are detrimental to your own or others' well-being. In the major Western religions—Judaism, Christianity, and Islam—ethics is imposed on humanity by an outside, divine authority. That is not the spirit of Buddhism. Ethics derives naturally from the pursuit of genuine happiness, from training and refining the mind, and exploring reality. This is similar to scientific ethics, which entails complete honesty in reporting one's research, for if this is violated, the scientific enterprise grinds to a halt. One of the four most important ethical rules for Buddhist monks is "Don't fake the results of your spiritual practice," or, in Buddhist terms, "Don't lie about your attainment." Do not in any way distort or exaggerate your degree of spiritual realization. If you do that, you are no longer a monk.

The sixth and final admonition is "Don't get caught up in fantasies." This suggests that the quality of presence that we emphasize in formal meditative practice can help release us from obsessive thinking in our waking interactions with others, our environment, our work, and in life as a whole.

3

The Awareness of Being Aware

IN THE PRACTICE OF settling the mind in its natural state, we observed the contents of the mind, but in the awareness of being aware, we do not direct our attention to anything. We simply allow awareness to rest in its own place, conscious of itself.

After twenty years of training in developmental approaches to spiritual awakening, as taught in Theravada Buddhism and the Gelukpa and Sakyapa orders of Tibetan Buddhism, in 1990 I came under the guidance of Gyatrul Rinpoche, a senior lama of the Nyingmapa order, who had also received extensive training in the Kagyüpa order. Those are the four main orders of Buddhism that have emerged in Tibet over the past twelve hundred years. Although I had been introduced to the *shamatha* practice of being aware of the nature of awareness by two Gelukpa teachers, Geshe Rabten and Gen Lamrimpa, in the 1970s and 1980s, it was Gyatrul Rinpoche who first made this subtle practice accessible to me. I was especially impressed by the instructions on this practice, called "quiescence without a sign," as explained by Padmasambhava in his book *Natural Liberation*, which I translated under Gyatrul Rinpoche's guidance.

Practice

Before you begin the next meditation, it is worthwhile to spend a minute or so to bring forth your most meaningful motivation for pursuing this practice. You can make this a larger issue. The quality of motivation that you bring to bear on work, vacation, meditating, on anything, filters into the very nature of the deed. The more meaningful the motivation, the deeper and more meaningful the act. Bring to mind your highest aspirations for your own well-being and sense of fulfillment, for the meaning of your own life as a whole. Also include the recognition that no one is isolated. We are interconnected, and therefore, in a broader sense, our most meaningful motivation must encompass and embrace others. So let your highest aspiration be your incentive for pursuing this practice.

Settle your body in its natural state, as you have done in the previous meditations, bringing forth the qualities of relaxation, stillness, and vigilance. Let your body reflect the quality of your mind. The quality of awareness that you are cultivating here is one that is at ease, still, and calm, and at the same time bright, vivid, sharp, and clear.

To help calm the mind, begin with mindfulness of breathing, counting twenty-one breaths as before. Now, as in the previous practice of settling the mind in its natural state, let your eyes be at least partially open. Rest your gaze in the intervening space between the point where you feel you are looking from and the shapes and colors that appear in your field of vision. Rest your gaze in the space itself, not on any visual object. Continue breathing into the abdomen in a natural, unforced manner. Now radically simplify your awareness, not focusing on the breath, or even on the contents of your mind. Settle your awareness in the very state of being aware. Perhaps this is your most primary and reliable knowledge—prior to and more certain than any knowledge that you have of the outside world, even of your own body, even of the contents of your own mind. This is the awareness of the sheer fact of being aware. This is sometimes called *shamatha without a sign*. In this practice, unlike the preceding two, you are not focusing on any object, mental or physical. You are not directing your awareness inward or outward; awareness is equally present both outwardly and inwardly, and prior to making such a division of experience. Simply let awareness settle in its own nature. Thoughts may come and go, but they do not obscure the nature of awareness; they are expressions of it. Rest in that state of awareness, without being carried away or distracted by any contents of awareness, and without grasping onto anything at all.

In the midst of thoughts that compulsively arise and pass in the field of your awareness, do you detect anything unchanging, as still as space itself? It is said that awareness can manifest as all kinds of sensory and mental representations. This quality of awareness to reveal itself in such forms is called its clarity, or luminosity, and that's one of the distinguishing qualities of consciousness. It is like radiant space that illuminates everything that arises in that space, yet its radiance remains even in moments when consciousness has no discernible object. Can you detect in your experience a clarity in the midst of mental imagery that also lingers on, even in the absence of mental imagery, like the face of a mirror with or without a reflection?

Furthermore, awareness is not simply the clarity or luminosity of appearances manifesting. It has a second quality, and that is cognizance. Awareness is imbued with a quality of knowing. Not only do appearances arise to awareness, but awareness also apprehends these appearances, enabling us to report on them afterward. Images arise, for instance, in a mirror, but the mirror doesn't know they are there. In the space of the mind, on the other hand, appearances arise and we know of their presence. Can you discern the event of sheer knowing?

Don't let your mind become so focused that it impedes your breathing. Now and then monitor your breath and see that it is flowing naturally, without any constraints from your concentrated attention. Let your belly remain soft, and continue breathing effortlessly into the abdomen.

Now let's try an experiment within this practice. Continue breathing as you have been into the abdomen, naturally and unforced, such that when you inhale it expands a little bit. As the abdomen expands during inhalation, it takes on a slightly rotund shape. When you exhale, maintain some of that roundness, that vaselike shape. Do this gently, without straining the muscles of the belly. Maintain a bit of the fullness of the abdomen during the out-breath as if it were waiting for the next in-breath. It expands a bit further as you breathe in. See if this has any beneficial effect on the practice. This is called *gentle vase breathing*, and many

Tibetan contemplatives have found it useful for stabilizing the mind. Another experiment you can do is try breathing through the mouth. These two techniques are not crucial to the practice, but if you find either of them helpful, continue. It is crucial, though, to keep the eyes open. This helps to unclutter the mind, enhances the clarity of awareness, and also begins to break down the false duality that there is an outside and an inside to the mind.

Whatever thoughts arise in the mind, they do not obscure the nature of awareness. Awareness is equally present during and between thoughts, so there is no rationale in this practice for trying to quiet the mind. Ascertain the space of awareness that lingers between thoughts, that out of which thoughts arise, that into which they disappear. Rest without expectation, without desire, without hope or fear.

Although you are not specifically attending to the contents of the mind, you are not unaware of them either. By resting your awareness right in the nature of awareness itself, whatever constrictions or perturbations of the mind that arise will release themselves naturally, without applying any remedy. Continue to breathe easily. This is a deeply relaxed state of awareness; it's not constricted.

The quality of rest is so deep and the mind is so relaxed, that when you become proficient in this practice you will feel that you could slip directly into sleep. But if you were to fall asleep you would not relinquish the clear knowing of your awareness but enter into a lucid, nondreaming state, relaxed and nonreferential.

You began by bringing forth your most meaningful aspirations and motivations. As you end this twenty-four-minute session, reaffirm whatever benefit, whatever increase in understanding or clarity has come: may this lead to the fulfillment of your most meaningful yearnings and aspirations for your own and others' well-being.

For Further Contemplation

In this chapter I have introduced the most subtle *shamatha* technique I have ever encountered. You may find that settling the mind in its natural state is subtler than mindfulness of breathing, and the *shamatha* practice of being aware of being aware is subtler still. This third technique of cultivating meditative quiescence is the culmination of this particular line of meditative training. It is the simplest, and potentially the deepest and most powerful as well. In this technique there is nothing to cultivate. We are not developing attentional stability and vividness. Rather, we discover through our own experience whether there is any aspect of the very nature of awareness that is innately stable and clear. Right in the nature of awareness itself there is luminosity and clarity. It might be obscured or covered as a result of conceptual grasping, but it is innate to awareness itself. The practice of *being aware of being* is one of releasing that which obscures this intrinsic stillness and luminosity of awareness. This is a discovery approach rather than a developmental approach, a process of release rather than control. We can check for ourselves to see whether the nature of awareness itself has luminosity, vividness, and clarity. This is not something to be accepted as dogma.

In the previous practice, we set out from the point that Descartes thought was our most certain knowledge: we are aware. His frequently quoted statement "cogito ergo sum" is usually translated as "I think, therefore I am," but the Latin term *cogito* means both *to think* and *to be aware*. So his declaration may be better translated as "I am aware, therefore I am." In Buddhism, we would scale back this assertion to "there is awareness of events." Of that we can be absolutely certain, even if there is no such thing as a self, or an ego, that exists separately from awareness and is the agent that is aware. The Tibetan Lama Sogyal Rinpoche has called this awareness of being aware "the knowledge of knowledge." We can be more certain of the presence of awareness than we can be of anything else. This is a good place to begin meditating.

The technique explored in this chapter goes beyond both directly controlling the mind and "knowing thyself" in personal and specific terms. Rather, in this practice we ask: is knowing yourself as a individual, with a specific location in time and space, all there is to knowing yourself as a conscious being in this universe? Are we defined by the parameters of gender, age, nationality, and personal history? Or is there a deeper, transpersonal level of our existence that is accessible when the conceptually conditioned mind grows dormant?

Here you have a technique for releasing the veils obscuring the ground of the ordinary mind and the dimension of primordial consciousness that lies beyond that, yet suffuses all states of awareness. You rest in that of which you are most certain. Even before the thought "I think, therefore I am," you *know* that awareness is present. In between thoughts you don't black out. Prior to thoughts, between thoughts, and when thoughts have vanished altogether—like when you are dying—you can ascertain that which remains. In this practice, instead of trying to *cultivate* attentional stability and vividness, *release* that which obscures the innate stillness, stability, and vividness of awareness itself. When you rest deeply in that awareness, you cut through the artificial, conceptually superimposed structure of "outer" and "inner." When your eyes are open and your visual gaze is simply resting in the space in front of you and mental awareness is resting in the sheer event of being aware, where exactly are you located? Are you inside your head, outside it, or are these questions no longer relevant? Outer-versus-inner fixations may simply fall away. Subject-versus-object may also vanish, especially if it turns out that the subject/object dichotomy—the way we structure our perceptual and conceptual experience—consists of nothing more than fabrications that we superimpose on experience. If these are artificial superimpositions, then by releasing them we may settle into a underlying state of nonduality. It might be useful to linger there in our final meditation during the dying process. But why wait if we can do it now?

The great eighth-century Indian Buddhist master Padmasambhava described this approach to the refinement of attention as "*shamatha* without a sign." Tsongkhapa, a fifteenth-century Tibetan sage, referred to it as attending to "the sheer awareness and the sheer clarity of experience." He described this practice as a form of nonconceptual attention—there is no focus on any object of meditation. Panchen Lozang Chökyi Gyaltsen describes this method as follows:

Be unrelenting toward thoughts, and each time you observe the nature of any ideas that arise, they will vanish by themselves, following which, a vacuity appears. Likewise, if you also examine the mind when it remains without fluctuation, you will see an unobscured, clear and vivid vacuity, without any difference between the former and latter states. Among meditators that is acclaimed and called "the fusion of stillness and dispersion."

In the dying process, there will come a point when the respiration stops, so mindfulness of breathing will no longer be feasible. But even after the breathing has ceased and the physical senses have shut down, you can continue to meditate, for mental events continue to occur. In this phase of the dying process you can practice the second technique of observing the domain of the mind: images, thoughts, memories, emotions, and impulses. Instead of fearing death, take an interest in the events occurring in the space of the mind and in the nature of that space itself. Your mind is now about to disappear, for the brain is shutting down, but the substrate consciousness will remain. And it's possible to rest in that dimension of awareness with bliss, luminosity, and nonconceptuality. Even when all mental activities cease, you can continue to remain vividly aware of the vacuous space of awareness into which all those activities vanished. That is called the *substrate* (*alaya*), and the basic awareness of that domain is the *substrate consciousness* (*alayavijñana*).

The practice of *shamatha* without a sign, or simply being aware of being aware, results in a vivid experience of the substrate consciousness, which is imbued with the qualities of bliss, luminosity, and nonconceptuality. That is also the state of consciousness that eventually emerges through the previous practice of settling the mind in its natural state. Sogyal Rinpoche calls this the *ground of the ordinary mind*, and it is very easy to mistake it for the ultimate nature of consciousness, variously known as *pristine awareness* (*rigpa*), *primordial consciousness* (*yeshe*), or the *clear light* (*ösel*). There are many subtle differences between the two, but the most important is that simply dwelling in the substrate consciousness does not purify or liberate the mind from any mental afflictions, whereas dwelling in pristine awareness radically frees the mind of its obscurations and opens up an inexhaustible wellspring of spontaneous virtues. Düdjom Lingpa writes in this regard:

> Someone with an experience of vacuity and luminosity who directs his attention inward may bring a stop to all external appearances and come to a state in which he believes there are no appearances and no thoughts. This experience of brilliance from which one dares not part is the substrate consciousness . . . some teachers mistake it for the clear light. . . . In reality, it is the substrate consciousness, so if you get stuck there, you will be cast into the formless realm, without coming even a bit closer to the state of liberation.

With regard to resting the mind in a state of profound inactivity, as is described here, it is reasonable to ask whether this is the culmination of Buddhist practice. Is the ultimate aim to calm all activity and end up sitting serenely under your own *bodhi* tree with a happy grin on your face as you do nothing whatsoever? In this world with all of its suffering, injustices, and conflicts, that would be an anticlimax. Ego-driven, or I-centered, activity is flatlined as much as possible in this kind of meditation, but you don't fall asleep or become dopey. A luminous awareness remains, without activity or movement. Out of that state of fluid, restful awareness, thoughts emerge effortlessly. In normal circumstances, when the mind is involved in grasping, we would call these thoughts distractions, but after the meditation it is possible to maintain at least some semblance of this restful quality of awareness that is not ego-driven.

The goal of meditation is not just sitting quietly. It is sitting quietly and then getting up and moving in stillness, remaining silent, in a sense, even as you are speaking. It is out there in the play of spontaneous activity that the culmination of the Buddha's life took place when he began teaching. The culmination was not in the stillness of sitting under the *bodhi* tree. It was in the service to all beings that flowed out of his experience of awakening.

As you engage in such practice, you may find that the floodgates of your creativity are opened spontaneously. In a state of serene awareness, with the ego dormant, see what arises out of that stillness spontaneously and effortlessly. The stillness is not even lost when the mind becomes active. Likewise, you may find that you do not necessarily relinquish that stillness even when you are speaking or your body is in motion. William James found that all geniuses have a quality in common: they all have an exceptional ability to sustain voluntary attention. He was convinced that it was their genius that led to this enhanced ability to focus the attention for long periods of time, not that their sustained attention made them geniuses. I'm sure there's much truth in that claim, but if we broaden the notion of genius in the sense of acknowledging that everyone has a degree of genius, or innate ability, for something, then I'm convinced that this kind of *shamatha* practice can help to reveal that genius. Once the ego is relatively out of the way, the wellspring of creativity opens up. See whether that's true for you.

In the practice of meditative quiescence there are two complementary models: development and discovery. Common to both is the idea that a serviceable mind is imbued with attentional stability, enabling one to sustain focus on a chosen object. Whether problem solving, listening to or creating music, teaching school, or raising children, you are present in a sustained fashion. It's the opposite of being agitated, distracted, or fragmented. The second quality common to both models is vividness. Stability without vividness is not very useful unless your goal is deep sleep, which has good stability but little clarity. The first two techniques we explored—breath awareness and observing the mind—both follow a developmental approach. While cultivating mindfulness of the breath, we learn to control the wild steed of the mind. We struggle with this unruly mind with the sense of, "You have dominated me, but now I am going to turn the tables and master you. I am going to learn to ride you so that you can't kick me off or bruise me." Without this, one is dominated by an unruly mind, one that moves the body, controls the mouth, and damages others by sarcasm, dishonesty, abuse, harshness, and ridicule.

The practice of releasing into the natural stability and vividness of awareness can be carried beyond formal meditation. Between sessions, if you would like to maintain that quality of awareness and still be able to do what you need to in the world, you may continue to rest your awareness in that space in front of you, even in the midst of a conversation. Focusing your eyes in the intervening space does not preclude seeing what is out there. As mental events appear, don't cling to them. Let them arise and pass. You may find this impractical when writing or doing intellectual work, but at other times when walking down the street or waiting in a supermarket line or in many other situations, this can be practiced. Maintain as much continuity as possible. This is a direct approach to exploring the fundamental nature of our existence, nothing less.

The Five Factors of Meditative Stablization

The Buddha spoke of five factors of meditative stabilization (*dhyana*), which is not a trancelike state but a clear, intelligent, focused, stable awareness that is not subject to compulsive fluctuation or laxity. These five factors are:

1. Applied thought
2. Sustained thought
3. Well-being
4. Bliss
5. Single-pointed attention

Related to the five factors of meditative stabilization are five hindrances to the achievement of such stabilization, obscurations that veil the ground state of consciousness. These are:

1. Lethargy and drowsiness
2. Skepticism
3. Malice
4. Excitation and guilt
5. Sensual craving

It turns out that each of the five factors of meditative stabilization naturally counteracts a corresponding hindrance in the order presented here. The first of the five factors, *applied thought*, entails an initial, voluntary engagement of the mind with an object. This mental activity is likened to striking a bell with a hammer. Among the five hindrances to meditative stabilization, it counteracts lethargy and drowsiness. Simply by directing the mind to an object and engaging with it with intelligence and alertness, the attention is aroused and the obscurations of lethargy and drowsiness are banished.

The second factor of mental stabilization, *sustained thought*, entails an ongoing, voluntary mental engagement with its object. It does not involve compulsive thinking or conceptual associations but is a directed, discerning, focused attention. This is likened to the reverberations that continue on after a bell has been struck. Sustained thought has been found to counteract skepticism—the vacillating, doubting mind that just can't settle down and engage with the task at hand. The mind that comes under the influence of skepticism, or wavering uncertainty, will undermine any task you attempt, whether it is starting a business, getting a college degree, or engaging in spiritual practice. Tibetans say meditating with such a mind is like trying to insert a frayed thread through the eye of a needle.

The third factor of meditative stabilization is a sense of *well-being* that emerges from a profoundly balanced mind, a mind settled in meditative equipoise. It is not referential, not being happy "about" some particular thing or event. Rather, it emerges from the very nature of the mind when it is free of attentional and emotional imbalances. This feeling of well-being naturally counteracts malice—the intent to inflict harm—which is the most disruptive of the five hindrances. Not only does it profoundly disturb the mind, it can also wreak great havoc in the world. Observe your mind whenever it succumbs to anger, hatred, or malice. See if these afflictions don't invariably arise when you are unhappy or frustrated. Malice and well-being are mutually exclusive. One has to disappear before the other can arise.

The fourth factor of stabilization is *bliss*. As you progress on the path of *shamatha* toward the realization of meditative stabilization, a growing sense of bliss will saturate your body and your mind. This does not arise because you are thinking a happy thought or experiencing a sensual pleasure. This crisp and clear bliss arises from the nature of your awareness simply because the mind is stabilized with vividness. Bliss is a symptom of the mind when it is healthy and balanced. Restlessness, dissatisfaction, anxiety, boredom, and frustration are all symptoms of a mind that is unbalanced and afflicted.

Bliss naturally counteracts excitation and guilt. In Buddhist terminology *excitation* doesn't refer to all agitated states of mind, but specifically those that are induced by desire, craving, and attachment. Why do we crave or desire anything? In anticipation that it will bring us bliss! But if bliss is already present, there are no grounds for excitation. In this same category of hindrances is listed guilt. True remorse can be wholesome. It can lead to greater mental balance and harmonious interactions with others. If you have been harsh with another person, feeling remorse afterward and wishing to correct your ways is a good thing. But remorse can also turn into obsessive shame and guilt, and when this happens it obstructs spiritual practice in general, and the cultivation of meditative stabilization in particular. Its natural antidote is bliss. You cannot feel guilt when your mind is saturated with bliss. One of the two has to go.

The fifth factor of meditative stabilization is *single-pointed attention*. Here the mind is relaxed, stable, and vivid, free of the imbalances of laxity and excitation. Such focused attention naturally counteracts sensual craving, which comes from a feeling of desire, inadequacy, a lack of fulfillment. When the attention is perfectly balanced in single-pointedness, desire for sensual stimulation vanishes. Now the mind is so well tuned that it needs no outside source for its well-being or satisfaction. It has become its own source of joy and fulfillment. This is a healthy mind, and it is an indispensable foundation for engaging in insight practices to explore the nature of reality as a whole.

PART II

Insight through Mindfulness

4

Mindfulness of the Body

THE FIRST THREE CHAPTERS of this book were devoted to the cultivation of attention, including mindfulness and introspection. To the extent that you have cultivated mindfulness through the practice of *shamatha*, you are ready to *apply* mindfulness in the practice of *vipashyana*. The first book on Buddhist insight meditation that I studied with care was Nyanponika Thera's classic work *The Heart of Buddhist Meditation*, which gives a detailed explanation of the Four Applications of Mindfulness. This was in 1970, and three years later, I had the good fortune to receive extensive instructions on this practice from the Theravada monk Kitti Subho, who had trained for six years in Thailand. Around that same time, Geshe Rabten also taught me this practice, which is preserved in the Tibetan Buddhist tradition but is not widely taught.

Many people confuse *vipashyana* with *shamatha*, but the two differ qualitatively, leading to different results. The practice of *shamatha* develops the faculties of mindfulness and introspection as a means of enhancing the stability and vividness of the attention. This entails simply focusing the attention upon a chosen object and sustaining that attention, and that is the gist of the practice taught earlier in this book. On the other hand, the practice of *vipashyana* (or *vipassana*, as it is called in Pali) is an intelligent, mindful investigation into the central features of our existence. For example, mindfulness of breathing as explained in the Buddha's primary discourse on this training begins as a *shamatha* practice, but it develops from there into *vipashyana* because of the added dimension of critical inquiry. The difference between the two is not the degree of concentration or mindfulness, but that the element of investigation is lacking in *shamatha*.

This chapter initiates a fourfold series comprising the fundamental modes of Buddhist insight meditation. Called the Four Applications of Mindfulness, they are mindfulness of the body, of the feelings, of the mental states and processes, and of mental objects, including all manner of phenomena. The purpose of applying mindfulness to these four domains of experience is to gain insight into the nature of these elements of our existence. Specifically, we probe the nature of each of these domains to see whether any of these objects of the mind are unchanging; whether they are true sources of happiness; and whether any of them are truly "I" or "mine" by their own nature, independent of our conceptual projections. Through such insights, it is possible to uproot the underlying causes of mental afflictions and other disruptions of the heart and mind that result in so much suffering.

Throughout his forty-five years of teaching, the Buddha strongly emphasized the cultivation of the Four Applications of Mindfulness as a direct path of contemplative insight and liberation. Time and again he praised this combination of practices, saying, "This is the direct path, monks, for the purification of beings, for the overcoming of sorrow and lamentation, for overcoming pain and grief, for reaching the authentic path, for the realization of *nirvana*—namely the four applications of mindfulness." The practice begins with the close application of mindfulness, which has already been refined through the practice of *shamatha*, to the body, the feelings, the mind, and all other phenomena. We start with the body, which in many ways is the easiest to examine.

Practice

Settle your body in its natural state, and bring forth your highest aspiration in terms of what you would like to be, the quality of life you would like to experience, what you would like to accomplish, and also what you would like to offer the world. Holding that vividly in mind, engage in this practice as a means of fulfilling that wish.

With your eyes closed or just slightly open, begin with mindfulness of breathing by focusing your attention on the tactile sensations where you feel the breath coming in and flowing out, and count twenty-one breaths. Continue breathing normally into the abdomen, but now redirect the attention to the crown of the head. Simply observe whatever tactile sensations arise in that area, whether they are experiences of firmness, hot or cold, tingling, or motion. With as little conceptual superimposition as possible, attend to the tactile sensations as they present themselves to your awareness. Do they change as you continue observing them?

Now imagine your field of awareness as a curved surface about five inches in diameter covering the top of the head. Note the tactile sensations you experience there. As you continue, keep that field of awareness, roughly the same size, about five inches across, like a circle of awareness continually in motion. Next, move this field of attention down to the right side of your head, down to the level of the ear and including the ear. Then slowly move it around to the back of the head, sliding over to the left side of the head. If you discover areas of tension, relax into them immediately. Now move the awareness to the forehead, down to the level of the eyes and the nose, down to the mouth and chin, then across the cheeks. Slightly expand the field to cover your whole face and see if you get a mental image of your face. If so, release that image and attend to the tactile sensations alone. Move this field of attention back from the front of the face, right through the head, to the back of the head. Do it slowly, as if you were scanning through your head. Move from the back to the front, then forward to the face, noting whether you can discern any sensations inside the head or whether you pick them up only on the surface.

Thus far we have used a more or less two-dimensional field of awareness. Now expand it to three dimensions. Include the sensations throughout your entire head simultaneously. Maintain this field of awareness down your neck to the collarbone, adjusting its width and size to the contours of the body. Move it along the right collarbone over to the shoulder, noting both the tactile sensations on the surface where your skin touches your clothes, for example, and also inside the body. Keep this field in motion as you move from the right shoulder down to the elbow, then down to the wrist. Let this space of awareness jump over to the left hand, moving from the tips of the fingers up to the left wrist, from the left wrist up to the elbow, maintaining as much continuity of awareness as you can. Go from your elbow up to the left shoulder, then across the collarbone to the base of the neck.

As you continue scanning through the body, divide the torso into nine sections, like a tic-tac-toe diagram, attending first to the upper left region of the chest, the inside of the torso, and the upper left region of the back. Note any sensations of movement associated with the breathing. Shift to the upper central region. Continue to the right upper region. Move down now to the middle right region, focusing on the level of the diaphragm, the bottom of the rib cage. At the very center, focus on the solar plexus, front, inside, and back. Move left to the middle left area, then down to the lower left quadrant down to the level of the hip. Move to the lower central region. Go across to the right lower region. Focus now on the right buttock, noting the sensation of solidity of your buttock against the seat. Move down the thigh on the surface and interior to the right knee, from the right knee down to the ankle, from the ankle to the tips of the toes. Note the sensations that arise in the foot. Move up immediately to the left buttock. Shift the awareness down to the left knee, the ankle, and the tips of the toes. You have to be mentally quiet to experience these sensations vividly.

Very briefly, return to the crown of the head. Taking only a few seconds, rapidly scan from the top of the head down to the tips of the toes. Now come back to the crown of the head. A second time, taking just a few seconds, sweep all the way through the body. Then, for a third and final time, come to the crown of the head and then sweep through the body.

Expand the volume of your awareness to include simultaneously the entire field of tactile sensations from the crown of your head to the base of your thighs to the tips of your toes. Attend closely. If you notice a mental image of what you think your body looks like—this may arise habitually—see if you can release that and focus with bare attention on this field of tactile sensations.

Slowly open your eyes. Without breaking your focus, direct the same quality of awareness, this stillness and bare attention, to another domain of experience; the visual. You have just examined the field of tactile experience; the visual domain is quite different. In this realm of experience you perceive colors, shapes, and the intervening space that seems to lie between yourself and visual objects.

Close your eyes and redirect your awareness to another domain of experience: sounds. Listen just to what is being presented without adding any conceptual overlays.

Shift now to the olfactory sense, another domain of experience. Can you detect any fragrances? Now move to the experience of the gustatory, or taste, sensation. Are there any tastes lingering in the mouth?

Finally, attend solely to the sixth domain, that of purely mental experience, wherein mental images, internal chitchat, emotions, desires, impulses, memories, and fantasies arise. Observe with bare attention.

Bring the session to a close.

For Further Contemplation

While the practice of *shamatha* eventually leads to experiences of bliss, clarity, and inner stillness, this doesn't bring about any irreversible purification or liberation of the mind. It is wonderful to balance the attention so that the mind becomes its own source of well-being, but to heal the mind of its afflictions, we must apply that attention to gaining direct knowledge of our own nature and the rest of the world. This is where the Four Applications of Mindfulness come in.

Techniques for developing *shamatha*, or more broadly speaking, *samadhi*, were well developed before the time of Gautama the Buddha, and many contemplatives took these meditative states as an end in themselves, believing them to be true liberation. Gautama recognized that they did not constitute any lasting freedom from suffering and its inner causes; they merely suppress the symptoms. Anyone who has had a disease of any sort knows that suppression of symptoms isn't bad. But a cure would be far better. That is where we are headed, and this step is one of the great innovations the Buddha brought to India.

We have begun with mindfulness of the body, achieved through a careful scan of our tactile sensations. Many who have practiced such body scanning find that it benefits the health. It is also very good for grounding the mind, bringing awareness back into the body, coming to our senses. We return to the senses instead of being caught like a fly in the spider's web of our conceptual elaborations and automatic responses. By dealing only with what we are given—in this case physical sensations—life becomes simpler, less fraught with the complexities of compulsive fantasies.

I cannot overemphasize how fundamental this group of four practices is to the Buddhist path. Here neither a leap of faith in a creed nor blind devotion to a guru is required. These practices comprise a rigorous, clear, incisive, compelling, and beneficial way to probe into the nature of existence and into what it is to be a human being in this universe.

Regardless of the great diversity in our backgrounds and personalities, I think many of us share some basic motivations, such as the wish to be better people. We aspire to greater virtue, to be more compassionate, more open and more tolerant of others, and to have greater equanimity. A life that excludes such aspirations is certainly not a full one. When the Buddha said of these Four Applications of Mindfulness, "This is a direct path for the purification of beings," he meant we can gradually lighten the burden of mental afflictions that impair virtue and genuine happiness. If we can purify our minds, our speech, and our behavior so that we do less damage to ourselves and others, then we will be of greater benefit to everyone. Furthermore, I suspect that all of us would like to find greater satisfaction and happiness, and a deeper sense of fulfillment and meaning in life. The Buddha said this is a direct path to overcoming pain and grief. Once the afflictions of the mind are dispelled, genuine happiness arises of its own accord. We don't need to find it outside ourselves. This is a direct path to the authentic realization of *nirvana*, to the final cessation of suffering and its source.

In all the years I attended college and university, I never heard of a course specifically designed to help students become more virtuous, happier human beings, less troubled by unnecessary suffering and problems. Much of modern education is directed toward the acquisition of knowledge, but this knowledge has little to do with the pursuits of virtue and genuine happiness. Yet these are key elements in leading a meaningful life. Most of us finish school and do what we must to make a living. Then we do what we can to be happy. This life leads us in the unhealthy direction of escape. Who needs reality when you can have fun? Yet we know very well that happiness can only be found if we are present in our daily lives.

The Buddha suggested that the qualities of virtue, happiness, and understanding reality as it is are deeply interrelated. The Four Applications of Mindfulness contribute to each of these qualities. The quality of mindfulness we are cultivating in the aforementioned practice is sometimes called *bare attention*, a quality of awareness that is relatively free of conceptual prestructuring, filtration, modification, interpretation, and projection. It's not absolutely free of such conceptual superimpositions. It is unlikely that we can just flick a switch, bringing compulsive conceptual activity to a halt. But we can attenuate it, make it less compulsive, by attending more closely so that we have a clearer picture of what is being presented to our six senses. One way we can begin to do this is by scanning the body. Think about the many other situations in which we have the possibility of attending closely. A birdwatcher in the field with binoculars attends closely, trying to see tiny stripes on wings, or listening for a bird song. A chef at work over the stove also attends closely. We have all had glimpses of such modes of attention. Some of us may have developed considerable skill at this from our vocations. The Buddha summed up this ideal:

In the seen there is only the seen; in the heard, there is only the heard; in the sensed, there is only the sensed; in the cognized, there is only the cognized.

In other words, just pick up what is presented and don't conflate it with your projections. Don't mix it with "I like, I don't like, I am

disappointed, I am elated," all those endless, compulsive associations. Cut through that. What is seen, just see; what is heard, just
hear; as you are scanning through the body, just sense; what is cognized in the sixth domain of experience, the mental domain, attend
only to that. There are times when thinking, imagination, analysis, and memory are extremely useful. In fact, it is an important
part of certain Buddhist meditations. But it is not useful when
thinking becomes compulsive.

The Buddha has provided us with alternatives, practices that are
pertinent to everyday life. This is not just for running off to the desert
and sitting alone on a cushion, but for active life with families,
friends, and colleagues—for being in the world. These practices are
especially valuable for engaging with others. Unless you have
already gone through a great deal of purification, upon meeting
someone who is disagreeable you will likely become upset or irri-
tated. The mind starts out in a state of relative calm, then something
causes us to become upset. That which disrupts the inner equilibrium of the mind is called in Sanskrit a *klesha*, a mental affliction. It
would be nice if we could just choose never to be disturbed by such
afflictions, but we don't have the freedom to immediately suspend
obsession, jealousy, and anger. However, if we are mindful of an
affliction when it arises, then we are not fused with it. We can see it
and identify it, and we have a choice, the possibility of responding
in a noncompulsive manner. In the absence of mindfulness we are
out of luck and out of choices. These compulsions are the same
habits that have gotten us into misery, trouble, and anxiety all
along—ruts in the road that just get deeper and deeper.

A Buddhist philosophical system that is especially compatible
with the Four Applications of Mindfulness is called the Sautrantika view, which is one of the four philosophical schools in
Indo-Tibetan Buddhism. According to the Tibetan tradition, this
is not the definitive view within Buddhism, but is to Buddhist philosophy what Newtonian mechanics is to physics. It is the first
philosophical system studied in many of the monastic universities of Tibet. When I became a monk in 1973 and began my training in the Buddhist Institute of Dialectics in Dharamsala, this was
the first subject we studied. All our instruction and texts were in

Tibetan, and for most of my time there, I was the only Western student. The rest were Tibetan monks. In addition to attending lectures, studying the course materials, and memorizing dozens of pages of material verbatim, we also spent about five hours each day in philosophical debate. This was a lively, scintillating activity, filled with humor as well as crisp analysis, and I found it very helpful for honing my intelligence and understanding this system of thought.

Learning the Sautrantika worldview and applying it in meditation and everyday life can be very helpful, despite the fact that some of its basic tenets don't stand up to the deepest analysis. Just as in physics, where classical mechanics is superceded by quantum mechanics and relative theory, so is the Sautrantika view superceded by the more subtle Yogachara and Madhyamaka views. We won't go into these more advanced theories now. For the time being, we'll stay with some of the more basic ideas from Sautrantika.

One of the central assertions of this view is: something is real, as opposed to imaginary, if it has the potential to present itself directly to any of your six modes of perception. Perhaps this "something" is presented to your senses through the aid of a telescope. If it can be apprehended perceptually, without conceptual superimposition, it is considered real. That includes the contents of mental perception, with which we are immediately aware of thoughts, emotions, and a wide range of other mental phenomena. These are no less real than the things we directly perceive with our five physical senses.

Those things that present themselves in your fields of perception are real. Those things that exist only because you have conceptually superimposed them are imaginary, or merely conventional. I could hold up a piece of paper and say, "This is mine," but you could look at it until your eyes clouded over and never see what is "mine" about it. The fact that it is mine is true only because we conceptually project this and agree on it among ourselves. When you find yourself troubled by something, try to see if it is real or imaginary. For example, when you look in the mirror and view the reflected image as your face, examine it closely and see what makes it yours. Observe whether this quality of ownership is really perceived or just conceptually superimposed. This is an application of discerning mindfulness.

A second proposition of the Sautrantika view is that things that are real have causal efficacy. They can do things. They have influence. They, in turn, are influenced in causal sequences. All of these real things exist in a nexus of causal interrelationships—they influence and are being influenced. Science has a similar notion of reality. If you think you have discovered an elementary particle, you want to make sure that it can do something, can influence other entities measured in a bubble chamber, such as other elementary particles. If it has no influence and can't be influenced by anything, it won't be considered real.

From this perspective, *belief* in imaginary things, or matters of convention, is "real," for belief arises in dependence upon causes and conditions, and it in turn influences other things, such as our behavior. Consider, for example, the belief "This paper is mine." The fact of this paper being mine has no causal efficacy of its own. It's not like a hammer or an emotion that can, by its own power, influence other things. But my *belief* that it is mine can influence many things. For example, it may cause me to be upset if someone takes it without my permission. Or I might feel gratified if someone praises the quality of the paper.

Compare this view to the view of scientific materialism that only physical phenomena are real. Your brain is real. Your hormones, body chemistry, and glands are real. Illnesses based on these are real. But subjective events, such as mental images and feelings, which don't evidently have any mass or spatial dimensions, are somehow less real, for they are "only in your mind." The underlying assumption here is that objective phenomena, such as mass and energy, are real, but subjective mental processes are real only insofar as they are identical to, or derivative of, physical phenomena.

Physicists are concerned with understanding the nature of the real, objective world that exists independently of anyone's mind, whereas Buddhist contemplatives are concerned with understanding the world of experience that exists only in relation to the minds of sentient beings, human and otherwise. This is a major difference in the basic orientations of these two traditions. According to Buddhism, mental events influence physical events as well as other mental phenomena, and physical events influence other physical events, as well as immaterial mental events. If we attend closely to the world of experience, this becomes perfectly obvious, even if we can't identify any mechanism by which such interactions between material and immaterial processes take place. They just do. And if no mechanisms can be found to account for this—just as no mechanisms have been found to account for the interactions of electromagnetic fields and elementary particles—maybe that's just a limitation of mechanical explanations.

The Three Marks of Existence

A central theme of the Buddhist worldview as a whole, and one that relates directly to the Four Applications of Mindfulness is the Three Marks of Existence, the first of which is impermanence. As you scan through the body, then later investigate the nature of feelings, other mental states, and all other phenomena, see if anything in these various domains of experience is stable and unchanging through time, including yourself. Is there anything that presents itself to your fields of perception that is causally real, and is also static and unchanging through time? According to Buddhist investigations, the answer is no. All these conditioned phenomena—our bodies, our minds, ourselves, the environment, other people—are in a state of constant change. All these things are subject to "coarse impermanence," in that sooner or later they all disappear. Everything that is born eventually dies. Everything that is accumulated eventually disperses. Everything that is elevated eventually descends. In addition, everything that is produced by causes exists in a constant state of flux, arising and passing with each moment. Hair doesn't suddenly turn gray on birthdays. Moment by moment, individual cells of hair are aging and losing their color. But in the midst of this perceptual reality of constant change, we conceptually superimpose a false sense of durability, stability, and permanence on our bodies, our minds, other people, and the overall environment. Distinguish between what is being superimposed and what is being presented to fields of perception. This will begin to illuminate the actual nature of your own presence in this world and everything around you.

The second mark of existence is that everything that is subject to mental afflictions—including craving, hostility, and delusion—is bound up with dissatisfaction, pain, and suffering. Under the influence of such afflictions, we may identify many things, events, and people as being true causes of happiness, but upon careful inspection, we will find that they merely contribute to our well-being; they are not the source. And all too often, they contribute to our misery. Shantideva sums up the pathos of this human condition: "Those desiring to escape from suffering hasten right toward suffering. With the very desire for happiness, out of delusion they destroy their own happiness as if it were an enemy."

We don't have to be persuaded to desire happiness or to be free of suffering and pain. It is natural, built in. If we haven't given up on this pursuit of happiness, it only makes sense to take a keen interest in real sources of happiness and of pain and suffering. It is very easy to conflate their causes with other factors that are only incidental to the quality of life we seek. We long for happiness and freedom from suffering, and yet we often fixate on other things: "If I can just have that man/woman [job, mansion, vacation, BMW] . . . I will gain the happiness, satisfaction, and fulfillment I want." But you may get that thing only to discover it doesn't bring the happiness you expected. You just got "it" instead. How dismal to spend months or years striving for something that in the end delivers only disappointment, because one thing you can't buy is time.

Before totally investing yourself in trying to acquire something, investigate what the chances are that it will give you true happiness. And when you are seeking the origin of some unhappiness or suffering, check to be sure you aren't pointing to something that was merely a catalyst and not the source at all. Consider the farmer who year after year produces a poor crop. He thinks, "More fertilizer or less fertilizer? More water or less water?" But if the quality of his seed is poor, it doesn't matter how much fertilizer or water he uses. What are the true sources of happiness and what are the true sources of suffering? This second theme points out that many of the things we hope will turn out to be genuine sources of happiness, satisfaction, and well-being don't wind up that way. They may turn out to be one more source of dissatisfaction or at best a desired object that may or may not contribute to happiness.

The third mark of existence is "no-self." Within the world of our experience—as we attend to the body, feelings, mental states, and mental objects—is there anything that presents itself to us as an unchanging, unitary, autonomous self—a "real you"? Is there an enduring entity, the same person you were yesterday or four years ago? Is there anything that appears, by its own nature, as being truly yours, belonging to your personal identity? Or have you merely been conceptually superimposing a sense of "I" and "mine" on various events in your world? Do you ever perceive a real you?

Practice

Begin by establishing a relaxed yet vigilant posture and a degree of meditative quiescence in the manner of the previous practice. After counting twenty-one breaths, let your awareness permeate the entire field of tactile sensations throughout your body. You will now apply discerning mindfulness to five specific elements of the body. Within the field of experience of your body, you can identify five elements that are said to make up the physical world. The first of these is called the earth element, and it consists of anything that is firm and solid. The second is the water element, which has the qualities of fluidity and moisture. The fire element is that which is hot and burning, so the degree of warmth and coldness of things correlates to the intensity of the fire element. The air element has the qualities of lightness and motility, or motion, and the fifth element is space, which has a quality of unobstructedness. These five elements are all there is to the periodic table of contemplatives, which are concerned with gaining experiential insight into the nature of the world of experience, as opposed to a purely objective, physical world existing independently of experience. So view these five elements not simply as subjective sensations, but as basic elements of your experienced body and the surrounding physical environment.

With your eyes closed, apply bare attention to every tactile phenomenon, identifying it as exhibiting the qualities of one or more of the elements. First see if you can detect the earth element. To do so, it is easiest to focus on points of contact where you feel your legs against the cushion or chair, your hands on your knees, and the touch of your clothing.

Now move to the water element. The most obvious place is in your mouth, where you can feel the moisture of saliva. How do you experience the water element with bare attention, as opposed to your ideas about fluidity or moisture?

Focus on the spectrum of heat and cold. Can you tell whether the interior of your body is warmer or cooler than the exterior, whether the top is warmer than the bottom or the front cooler than the back? In this way, closely apply mindfulness to the fire element.

Attend to the air element, any tactile phenomenon that displays the qualities of lightness and motion. As you examine carefully, see if there is anything in this field of tactile experience that is not saturated by the air element. Is everything in motion to some degree? For a minute or two focus on your right hand, and now your right index finger. Slowly set the finger into motion, by raising and lowering it incrementally. Move it a little bit and then stop. Move it and stop. Observe the nature of motion as opposed to relative stillness.

Can you detect the element of space with the tactile, or somatic, sense faculty, or can it be apprehended by means of mental perception? Can it only be imagined? See whether space is something that you can perceive directly, or whether it is only a conceptual superimposition on your perceptual field of tactile experience. At the conclusion of this session, see if there is anything that presents itself to your tactile awareness that is not earth, water, air, fire, or space. Is there anything left over?

After concluding this practice, dedicate the merit. This means bringing to mind whatever is beneficial and dedicating your efforts to the fulfillment of your aspirations for yourself, for others, and for this troubled world.

For Further Contemplation

The purpose of this type of investigation is, once again, to give you a clearer sense of what actually appears to your senses, in contrast to what you are involuntarily, and perhaps unconsciously, projecting on those fields of perceptual experience. When you *think* of something solid—the notions of solidity, firmness, and weight—is that not radically different than experiencing it with bare attention? Likewise for the other elements. What you find when you experience the entire field of tactile sensations is probably very different from your normal experience of your body. This is a theme that runs throughout: attend more closely to what is being presented as opposed to what is being superimposed.

This practice begins by closely applying mindfulness to your own body, but it doesn't end there. The Buddha extended this method of inquiry with these words:

> One dwells observing the body as the body internally, or one dwells observing the body as the body externally, or one dwells observing the body as the body both internally and externally.

Observing the body *as* the body means to examine it with discernment, not with blank, spaced-out awareness. Observing it internally means to inspect your own body from within. As you extend this practice into daily life, you can closely attend to the bodies of others, noting their gestures, facial expressions, tone of voice, and other physical mannerisms. Being thoroughly present with others in this way provides a basis for empathy, which, in turn, is the foundation for the cultivation of loving-kindness and compassion.

Here is one way of going about this practice: First, get a clear perception of your own body, seeing what is presented as opposed to what is superimposed. Then—and this can be fun—attend to the bodies of others. Sit on a bench by a busy sidewalk. Quiet your inner chatter. Watch people's bodies, observing closely the body language, expressions, and tone of voice. After observing internally and then externally, dwell on observing the body *both* internally and externally. Begin with your own body, attend to another person's body, and then to yourself again. As if you were on a merry-go-round, rotate your axis of perspective and imagine looking from the other person's perspective, both internally and externally. Then flip back to your own perspective. Shift around using imagination, not naked awareness. Being able to experience something of this sort is part of the marvel of the human mind. Imagine being present in someone else's body.

Mindfulness of the body can beneficially be extended to daily life, as you attend closely to the postures of walking, standing, sitting, and lying down, as well as during the activities of looking, bending, stretching, dressing, eating, drinking, excreting, speaking, keeping silent, staying awake, and falling asleep. In other words, again and again apply mindfulness to all of life's activities. Observe what factors give rise to an emergence of these experiences, how they dwell, how they linger, and how they dissolve. Attend closely.

Looking ahead a few chapters, after working with the Four Applications of Mindfulness and then the Four Immeasurables, I shall introduce dream yoga, an insight practice done first during the daytime and then at night. If you would like to explore this practice, I suggest some preparation because dream yoga can be quite challenging. To lay the groundwork, begin paying close attention to your dreams. Just be mindful of them, without trying to analyze them. When you fall asleep, do so with the resolve, "Tonight, I will attend closely to my dreams." Then, when you awaken, remember and write down your dreams. Over the course of the coming weeks and months, see if there are any recurrent dream signs: repeated emotions, situations, or people that appear in your dreams. Then, by the time you get to the chapter on dream yoga, you will already know what your dream signs are. In this way, your contemplative practice will begin to saturate all the hours of the day and night. As Atisha's disciple Drom Tönpa counseled, "Let your mind become Dharma!"

5

Mindfulness of the Feelings

AMONG MENTAL STATES, the Buddha identified feelings as a special domain worthy of careful inspection through the close application of mindfulness. Since feelings could have been included within the practice of mindfulness of the mind, why this special emphasis? Feelings are important because feelings of pleasure, pain, and indifference are essential to sentient beings. Our physical movements, decisions as to whether we marry or have children, what kind of job we have, where we live, what kind of possessions we acquire, and so on—all of the choices we make in life are driven by feelings.

From a scientific standpoint, feelings are necessary because they alert us to danger, so that, for example, we don't get too close to fire or become too cold. When we feel hungry, we seek out food so as not to starve. Feelings enable us to survive. They push us, direct us, and prod us in many ways. But once we have survived and procreated, as we have biologically evolved to do, when our bellies are full and we have our jobs and have raised our families, there remains an unfulfilled longing. There is a feeling of something missing. For example, how many people feel neither fulfilled nor happy even though they are successful? People become depressed, they kill time by watching TV, or they lose themselves in thrill seeking. When things are otherwise fine, what are feelings of unrest, dissatisfaction, and depression good for? Pursuing the answer to that leads into very deep territories of contemplation.

When we are experiencing dissatisfaction or depression without any clear external cause for it—no bad health, disintegrating
marriage, or other personal crisis—this could be a symptom or
message to us coming from a deeper level than biological survival.
How should we respond? Antidepressants essentially tell such
feelings "Shut up. I want to pretend you don't exist." But the feeling is emerging for a reason. The aim of the practice of mindfulness of feelings is to understand the origins, nature, and effects of
feelings on our lives and those around us. One of the most common assertions in Tibetan Buddhism is: "All sentient beings are
yearning for happiness, wishing to be free of suffering." What do
we have in common with all sentient beings? Feelings. And not
just feelings, but wanting some things and not other things.
Attending to feelings is the very ground of empathy. Empathy is
a "feeling with," a sense of how another person is doing: happy,
sad, fearful, and so on. The grounds of altruism, of compassion
and loving-kindness, are all about feelings. On the other hand, the
common basis of obsession, jealousy, anger, hatred, conflict, and
strife is also feelings. Feelings exert such an enormous influence
on our lives that it would be wise to know them better. It's a bit
like knowing who is our master, because frequently we are the
slaves of our feelings. This application of mindfulness is designed
explicitly to gain deeper insight into the nature of these phenomena that are so important to us.

Practice

Settle your body in its natural state so that you can be comfortable
for one *ghatika*, and stabilize your mind by counting twenty-one
breaths. Now focus on the field of tactile sensations throughout
your body, head to toes, and especially the torso. Just be present,
mindful of this field of sensations, which you experience as your
body. Note how simple this is. Give your conceptual mind a rest
from its normal exertions. Rest your awareness in bare perception,
quiet attentiveness.

Thus far you have attended to tactile sensations, including those associated with the breath. This is mindfulness of the body. You have also observed the other objects of the physical senses. Now move to mindfulness of the feelings, specifically those you experience in the body. But if you should hear sounds or have any other sensory experience, concentrate not on the content of the experience but on the feelings associated with it. See if you can exclusively attend to three kinds of bodily feelings: pleasant, unpleasant, and neutral. Tactile phenomena, such as firmness, moisture, warmth, and movement, are *objects* of tactile perception, but according to Buddhism feeling are elements of *subjective* awareness, a *way* of experiencing. We painfully experience a sensation of heat or pleasurably experience a sensation of softness. Here we attend to an event or experience—be it pleasure, pain, or neutral—and distinguish between the objective content of the experience and the subjective way we feel it. They are not the same.

Within the field of tactile sensations, pay attention to what feels good or bad. If you feel any urge to move, to scratch or fidget at all, before you do so, identify the feeling that is arousing that desire. When no feelings of pleasure or pain arise, can you identify a feeling of indifference, the neutral feeling? This is not a feeling of nothing, it is just neutral. If we imagine a graph of feelings, positive ones to the right of the vertical axis feel good, negative ones to the left of the axis feel bad, and feelings right in the middle are neutral. Just as Indian mathematicians were among the first to acknowledge the number 0, so do Buddhist contemplatives acknowledge feelings with a magnitude of zero.

As your baseline, maintain mindfulness of the body, attending to the breathing, and from that platform closely inspect feelings as they arise from moment to moment. Do the feelings change when they are observed, or do they stay the same? When you observe the feelings as passively as possible, to what extent does your attentiveness influence them? If you find yourself starting to think about the feelings or identifying with them, how does that affect them? When a feeling of any sort arises, does it remain unchanged for a period of time? Or, when you observe it very closely, do you find that it is in a state of flux? When you concentrate on it intensely, what happens to the feeling?

Now come back to the breath with mindfulness throughout the body. As you exhale, release. Let the in-breath just flow in, relaxing deeply, but still maintaining a posture of vigilance without having to intentionally draw the breath in. Let your body *be breathed* as if the surrounding atmosphere and your body were embracing, the environment breathing you as you breathe the environment. Relax deeply into the out-breath. Relax into the in-breath. Release the out-breath and continue releasing it until you feel the tide of the breath turning and the in-breath comes sweeping in like a wave flowing onto the shore.

Dedicate merit and bring the session to a close.

For Further Contemplation

Some meditations are difficult, either inherently or because at times we don't have enough faith or confidence. This practice is not. You don't even have to focus on subtle tactile sensations around the nostrils. You can feel your body—it's right here. Of course, distractions may come and carry you away, but your body is still present, a platform to which you can always return. When practicing mindfulness of feelings, don't just be generally mindful of them, but scrutinize them with discerning intelligence. We all naturally care about feelings, our own and those of our friends and loved ones. Our scope of caring may be quite broad. What we care about is people's well-being, which has to do with how they are feeling: happy, sad, worried, indifferent, or at ease. If we want to be successful in the pursuit of happiness and freedom from suffering, we need to observe the ways in which feelings arise. Take a scientific attitude toward feelings, inquiring into the causes of the feelings you desire and of those you dislike.

For example, suppose you really enjoy music, but during times when you are tired or wound up, music may not bring any pleasure or satisfaction. Instead, it is overwhelmed by your mood. We can tap into something potentially very deep here: what are the true causes for the happiness, meaning, and fulfillment we seek and what are the causes of suffering? Once we have gone through the easily identified feelings, then we move on to our deeper sense of unrest or dissatisfaction, the yearning for something more, or for something less. What are the causes of that dissatisfaction?

As we analyze feelings in a simple, straightforward way, we discover something that is not immediately obvious: feelings have two aspects. If you are meditating and hear a loud noise, you experience not only the noise that you detect with auditory awareness, but you also experience the noise in a disagreeable fashion. You feel, "That's an irritating noise. I don't like it." The real thing you don't like is the feeling, not the noise. If the unpleasant feeling vanished, you would no longer say that the noise is disagreeable. It would just be a noise. You might then even label it as a pleasant noise. For example, if your neighbors are holding a party and making a racket, you might find this irritating, until they invite you to their party and you're making a racket with the rest of them.

You have physical feelings and you have mental feelings. They're not the same. While your body is feeling fine, your mind may be feeling unhappy, burdened by some trouble, such as having a loved one who is ill or any of the many problems that can beset us all. On the other hand, your body might be in terrible shape while your mind is courageous, cheerful, or optimistic. This can happen during illness. It can happen in contact sports when the body is bruised and yet the athlete gets up and eagerly returns to play. The mind may be elated while the body feels terrible. Sometimes the body and mind feel good simultaneously, or they both feel bad, but they are not the same. Within these two modes of feeling, body and mind, we have three categories within a spectrum: pleasurable, neutral or indifferent, and painful.

When you observed the feelings in the body, did you find that they were altered merely by closely attending to them? Or did they remain just as they were when you first noticed them? Because we do a lot of conceptual superimposing on our experience, distinguish carefully between bodily feelings and your mental responses to those feelings. Conceptual superimpositions are not necessarily false, but they are not the same as perceptual experience. In this meditation we seek to differentiate between perceptual experience and conceptual projections.

Let's review how feelings originate. First you have an immediate contact with a sensory stimulus, and that acts as a basis for a subsequent feeling. For example, you first see a person walking through the door, then you experience the person as an old friend or maybe as a threat; this brings a felt response. Once this feeling appears, it may in turn give rise to desire or aversion toward the object, which is not the same as the original feeling. Then the response of desire or aversion may lead to something else, such as intention. Many desires don't result in intentions. When sitting in meditation you may notice subtle, fleeting sensations, which are then experienced with a certain feeling tone. That may lead either to attraction, aversion, or indifference, and those feelings may or may not give rise to an intention and a subsequent action. Normally, this whole sequence of events is fused together because we semiconsciously identify with them, rather than observing carefully. With the close, discerning application of mindfulness, you can distinguish these events in the sequence in which they arise.

As the psychotherapist Tara Bennett-Goleman explains, this close application of mindfulness to feelings provides us with an alternative to repression, suppression, and compulsive expression of our emotions. Citing the research of the neurosurgeon Benjamin Libet, Bennett-Goleman points out that from the moment that an intention arises, there is a quarter second before the intended action begins. Tara Bennett-Goleman comments, "This window is crucial: it is the moment when we have the capacity to go along with the impulse or to reject it. The will, one could say, resides here, in this quarter second."

As you practiced, did you find that a feeling arose all of a sudden as a singular experience, or did it rise gradually, as a growing continuum of experience? Were the feelings static and enduring or momentary and intermittent? How do feelings subside—all at once, or do they gradually fade out? One of the most common events in meditation is the experience of physical warmth, which may be due to the capillaries opening up and blood flowing to the extremities as one relaxes more and more deeply in meditation.

When heat arises, examine how it is experienced. Is it something agreeable or disagreeable? Move into this second mode of attentiveness to the feelings.

During meditation, if, for example, your knee begins to hurt, you don't have to do a special exercise to pay attention to it. The challenge here is to be aware of the body and mind, watching them closely, rather than simply identifying with them. Instead of falling into habitual thoughts of "my knee hurts" or "I feel rotten," observe the feelings as they arise in relation to the physical sensations. Is it possible to have a mental feeling of pleasure, happiness, sadness, uneasiness, or restlessness that you don't identify with, that you can observe and take an interest in?

If you found the feelings that arose in your body interesting, you'll see that the mind, too, is a fascinating arena of experience. If in the near future you experience a moment of depression or sadness, some disagreeable mental feeling, take an interest in it. Really attend to this unpleasant feeling, not the stimulus that made you feel bad, but just to the resultant feeling. When you watch carefully, is the mind with which you are experiencing the lousy feeling itself feeling lousy? Can you neutrally, calmly experience this feeling? Can you nondepressively experience depression? When you do, you may well find that this emotional imbalance vanishes under your gaze.

Another very important point is to be attentive to when feelings arise—pleasant, unpleasant, and neutral—and recognize the chain of feelings *they* give rise to. In Buddhism there is a universal principle: anything that is an effect is also a cause. Anything that is a cause is also an effect. This means that every event is in interaction with other events prior to it and with events following it. They form a chain of interdependent origination. There are no dead-ends in causality—nothing that is an effect and not a cause. Feelings are no exception. They arise from prior conditions. Attend closely to what a feeling leads to. Did it give rise to aversion or desire? What then? There's nothing wrong with desire, like the desire for water, in and of itself. The desire leads to an intention to find some water, and we take a sip. There is no disruption of the mind. No mental affliction has intruded. But often our desire doesn't stop there, and it ends up disrupting our mental equilibrium.

In Buddhism we speak of the primary mental afflictions, those mental processes that result in internal suffering and conflict in our relationships with others. These include variations on the affliction of craving—obsession, desire, and attachment—and varieties of aversion: hatred, aggression, anger, and hostility. These are mental processes that throw us off balance time and again. Traditional Tibetan medicine makes the same point. These afflictions disrupt not only the mind, but also the balance of the constituents of the body, leading to ill health. This is being recognized more and more in modern medicine. Negative emotions damage your health, both physically and mentally. It is not merely these feelings but also what flows from them that is the problem.

Craving and aversion are two of the three primary afflictions of the mind. The third is ignorance and delusion. Ignorance manifests as inattentiveness and stupor, and it commonly leads to delusion, which entails an active misapprehension of reality. Our response to indifferent feelings commonly leads to these mental afflictions. We don't succumb to stupor if the mind is aroused in a pleasurable or in a painful way. We slip into it when nothing much is happening. Then a kind of mindlessness, or "ignore-ance," can take over, in which we're behaving on autopilot. And in such a state it is very easy to misconstrue what is happening to us and within us. This is where delusion sets in, and this primes us for falling into all other kinds of mental afflictions. Delusion fundamentally lowers the psychological immune system, making us vulnerable to mental imbalances and unhappiness.

Now let's consider wholesome mental states, because feelings don't lead only to afflictive mental states. All of us share something fundamental: we are striving for happiness. We have different motivations and different desires and yearnings, but the sense of wishing for fulfillment and greater happiness, greater contentment, is common to us all. The wish that others may encounter happiness and the causes of happiness is called *loving-kindness*. If you are aware of people who are suffering, you may spontaneously empathize with them, and yearn that they be free of that suffering. That yearning is called *compassion*. Then there is *empathetic joy*—taking delight in others' joys and the causes of happiness—and finally, *equanimity*, the calm, clear, equal plateau of even-mindedness, free of attachment and hostility toward those near and far. These four qualities of the heart are known in Buddhism as the Four Immeasurables, and they are supported by the wisdom gained from the Four Applications of Mindfulness.

Practice

Settle your body in its natural state and count twenty-one breaths. Now bring attention into the domain of experience of the mind, with its thoughts, imagery, fantasies, memories, and dreams. How do you feel mentally? Mental feeling can be aroused by sensory experience; you may mentally feel good about how your body feels or looks, but feelings can also be catalyzed by thoughts.

Go into the laboratory of your mind and run some experiments. Bring to mind a very pleasant memory, drawing one out of your past. Observe the nature of the feeling that arises as you experience this memory. Does the feeling have a location?

Now think of a sad experience. It could be personal or perhaps something from the news. Observe the feeling that arises with this experience. When you observe it, does it change?

Now release your mind to free association. Allow anything to appear, be it the sound of traffic, or your imagination about future events. Closely apply discerning mindfulness to your feelings as the mind alights upon an event or an object, one experience after another. Closely observe the subjective feelings themselves, rather than fixating on the objective phenomena that catalyzed them.

You may recall in an earlier practice, as you settled the mind in its natural state, you simply observed events with as little superimposition of "I" and "mine" as possible, just watching them as mere events within the sphere of the mind. Now see if you can observe feelings in the same way, without the identification of "my" feeling. Can you be so at ease, so inwardly at rest, that the tentacles of grasping are withdrawn and you simply observe the feelings arising and passing?

For the last couple of minutes come back to the breath. Be fully present in your body, in the field of tactile sensation. With each in-breath, breathe into those areas that feel tense or knotted or dense. With each out-breath, release any undue tension in the body and the mind.

For Further Contemplation

This is a simple practice you can apply in the midst of your daily activities. When there is nothing you need to do with your mind, during a break at work, or when you are just walking or standing in line, bring your awareness into the body, attending lightly to the breath. Rather than falling into the habitual inner chitchat, with one vagrant thought leading to another, rest in quiet mindfulness. The key to success in meditative practice is continuity. Let the thread of mindfulness run through the course of your day. It won't be all you do, but it can be something that comes back as a friend, a resting point, a point of orientation, of being present, of being sane. It can be done in any position, and just about any setting. As you are falling asleep you might want to try this. Some meditations so arouse the mind that you cannot fall asleep. This one is so soothing you can slip into sleep with mindfulness. You will find this practice very useful when we come to dream yoga, lucid dreaming.

Having attended to the feelings in ourselves, we can then focus on others' feelings, much as we did with the bodies of others in the previous chapter. The Buddha returns to this threefold scheme of practice: "In this way, one abides contemplating feelings as feelings internally, or one abides contemplating feelings as feelings externally, or one abides contemplating feelings as feelings both internally and externally." The psychologist Paul Ekman's writings on attending to and understanding others' facial expressions can be very helpful in this regard. This is a matter both of discerning observation and imagination. We can be more sensitive to others' feelings if we ourselves are feeling calm and centered. If we want to attend closely to our own feelings, we must stop grasping onto compulsive thoughts, so that we can attend more clearly to whatever arises in our minds. We all know that when we are on the edge of our seats wanting to tell someone something, sometimes we just interrupt, without really listening to others in the meantime. That is one way of engaging with other people. Another way is to be present and let your mind be calm and silent so you can be attentive to what others are saying and also the quality of the voice, their body language, and the environment. You can pick that up only if your mind is fairly quiet. In this way, you attend to feelings within yourself, and in others.

Are we doing something more here than just making our own suppositions about how others are feeling? Do we know others' feelings solely by means of logical inference, like inferring fire from smoke? Or is there something more immediate, more intuitive, taking place—something not so cerebral as figuring things out by inference. Attend to feelings within yourself, attend to feelings within others, then attend to feelings in both. Switch perspective occasionally so your mind becomes malleable and you can attend to feelings from multiple perspectives. That is mindfulness of the feelings in a nutshell.

6

Mindfulness of the Mind

IN THE FIRST THREE chapters we examined three different techniques for calming the mind to bring greater stability and vividness to awareness, and now we have begun to apply mindfulness to fathom the nature of our existence in relation to the world around us. The introductory methods of *shamatha*, or meditative quiescence, are a salve for the mind and especially helpful for people living in the modern world. This is because of our lifestyles. I have lived with Tibetans for many years, including former nomads and farmers whose lifestyles are relatively calm and uncluttered. Many of them come to Dharma practice with a lot more equilibrium and poise than we do. We Westerners arrive with a rapid pace of life, a lot of concerns and activities, and many things to remember.

When we practice *shamatha*, it may happen that we remember all the things we have to do, our day's agenda. The mind opens up and these things pop out. For a lifestyle that is filled with activity, quiescence is like an untangling of knots. It soothes the mind and gets us back to simplicity. It is not, however, a panacea. Quiescence alone will not bring about irreversible transformation, immunity from getting caught up in the same snags that we are habituated to. If this were the case, we could just do *shamatha* all the time. But as the Buddha found out twenty-five hundred years ago, techniques that are designed just to calm, center, and still the mind will inhibit, but not eliminate, the mental afflictions, the turmoil, and the turbulence of the mind. These problems have just gone underground for a while, ready to spring forth as soon as we return to active life and the bombardment of stimuli we receive in our hyperactive society. If we are interested in actual transformation and not just maintenance, then we need something more than *shamatha*.

For transformation, the Buddha taught the Four Applications of Mindfulness. Among them, perhaps the most fascinating and profound is mindfulness of the mind itself. In Theravada Buddhism, there is said to be a dimension of consciousness called the *ground of becoming* (*bhavanga*) that manifests in deep sleep, in a coma, and at the very last moment of consciousness prior to death. This is the dimension of consciousness to which the Buddha referred when he declared, "Monks, this mind is brightly shining, but it is defiled by adventitious defilements. Monks, this mind is brightly shining, but it is free from adventitious defilements." All mental activities arise from this luminous, empty domain of consciousness, and it is very easy to mistake it for enlightenment itself.

Contemplatives in the Dzogchen tradition of Tibetan Buddhism access this same ground state of individual consciousness, which they call the *substrate consciousness* (*alayavijñana*). Although the Theravada and Dzogchen interpretations of this vacuous state vary in some respects, I am convinced that they are referring to the same experience, which results from the cultivation of *shamatha*. Düdjom Lingpa describes it in this way:

> When you fall asleep, all objective appearances of waking reality, including the inanimate world, the beings who inhabit the world, and all the objects that appear to the five senses, dissolve into the vacuity of the substrate, which is of the nature of space, and they emerge from that domain.

According to Buddhism, mental phenomena are *conditioned* by the body in its interaction with the environment, but those physical processes are not sufficient for producing any state of consciousness. All mental activities arise from the substrate consciousness that precedes mind-brain interactions, and at death, all such activities are withdrawn back into that substrate.

We can demarcate two realms of experience that both come under the umbrella of *chitta*, the Sanskrit word commonly translated as "mind." Within the realm of *chitta* there is the mind at work, engaged in emotions, thoughts, memories, imagination, mental imagery, and dreams—all the events and activities of your mind. This is like the kinetic energy of the mind. Also within the realm of *chitta* is the substrate consciousness, the luminous, relative ground state of the mind, out of which all mental activity emerges.

This is not metaphysics; no leap of faith into the abstractions of Buddhist cosmology is required of you here. Rather, it is based on the meditation experiences of generations of Buddhist contemplatives. In practicing mindfulness of the mind, you will examine both the contents of the mind and the space from which those contents emerge, the substrate. When you are practicing *shamatha*, as opposed to *vipashyana*, you just place your attention upon the breath or otherwise settle the mind in its natural state. But with *vipashyana* you actively inquire into the nature of the object of awareness, examining the causes that produced it and the conditions in which it vanishes.

A central Buddhist hypothesis is that we suffer unnecessarily as a result of ignorance and delusion that can be eliminated from our mind streams. If we find we are suffering, especially mentally, then there are reasons for that, what the Buddha called the Second Noble Truth: suffering has a cause. The cause can be identified experientially. And the extraordinary Buddhist hypothesis is that it can then be rooted out. The underlying premise here is really startling and also quite alien to our contemporary Western civilization, with its roots in the Greco-Roman and Judeo-Christian traditions. The afflictions of the mind, our tendencies toward hatred, belligerence, greed, selfishness, jealously, conceit, arrogance, and so forth, are not hardwired; they are not intrinsic to our very being. Despite hundreds of thousands or even millions of years of evolution, we don't have to suffer these afflictions. Those who follow developments in neuroscience know the brain has recently been found to be far more malleable than previously assumed. To a considerable extent—and it's up to us individually to discover exactly to *what* extent—our minds and brains have a quality of plasticity.

How can you utilize this psycho-neural plasticity? Here the twenty-five-hundred-year-old Buddhist tradition and the hundred-year-old neuroscientific tradition are in agreement. If you would like to bring about transformation, what's required is sustained, continuous effort. You must accustom yourself to a new way of engaging with reality. Sustained, continuous effort can actually reconfigure your brain to a considerable extent. Psychologically you develop new habits, new ways of viewing reality that over the course of time become effortless. This is really promising. The Buddhist premise, going further than what cognitive scientists have come up with thus far, tells us that we are not fundamentally, intrinsically prone to delusion or any other mental affliction, despite the influences of biological evolution. We have the potential to be free.

Let's find out if this is true. We will have two guided meditation sessions, each one *ghatika* in duration. The first session will focus on mental events, and in the second one we will explore the substrate consciousness.

Practice

Rest your body in a suitable posture imbued with the qualities of relaxation, stillness, and vigilance, and let your mind come to rest with those same three attributes. Count twenty-one breaths as a preliminary *shamatha* exercise. Rest in a nondiscursive, nonconceptual mode throughout the course of the in-breaths and the out-breaths.

As the mind has been made serviceable with some degree of stability and vividness, move from the mode of quiescence, or simple calm, to the pursuit of insight, specifically into the nature of that extraordinary phenomenon we call the mind, or *chitta*. Attend specifically to whatever events arise in the domain of the mind, as opposed to the five physical sense fields. It might seem a little odd to think of observing the mind. But just as you can direct the attention to the five sensory fields of experience, you can direct it to the experiential realm in which thoughts, mental images, emotions, feelings, memories, fantasies, and desires—a whole host of mental events—take place.

First, direct the attention to the proper domain. Sitting quietly, consciously think a thought, for example, "What is the mind?" Generate that thought, but instead of identifying with it or trying to answer it, observe the event itself, the phenomenon of the thought "What is the mind?" Consciously generate another thought. Observe this event arising into the field of mental experience. Watch it appear, play itself out, and vanish. Keep your attention right where it was after that thought disappeared. Again place your attention in the domain of the mind. What's the next event to occur in this domain of experience? If you identify with the mental events that arise, they are difficult to observe. You become fused with them, and in this way, you are brought under their control. See if you can observe these events without intervention or judgment. Without grasping, without identification, inspect whatever arises and observe it as it passes. This is a first step on the path to freedom.

So far, this exercise is similar to the *shamatha* practice of settling the mind in its natural state. Now let's move to insight meditation, involving inquiry into the nature of the mind. For a few minutes, survey the range of the mind. Examine any impulses of desire, images, thoughts, memories, and the degree of calmness, agitation, clarity, or dullness that are present in the mind. Is the mind disturbed or serene? If the mind is silent for a while, what interrupts the silence?

Now let's pursue a deep question experientially—not simply speculatively or analytically. When you hear your own voice, you may have a sense of "my voice" or "my sound." If you hear someone else's voice, you might have a sense that there is sound or "I hear a voice," where the sense of "mine" is not present. Likewise, if you look in the mirror and see an image of your face, you may think "my face." If you see the reflection of someone else's face, then it seems to be just an image. You may touch something and just feel it as the texture of a book, or the feel of cloth. If you feel a tactile sensation inside your body, you may feel "my sensation," "my warmth," "my tingling."

Those experiences pertain to three fields of perception: the visual, the auditory, and the tactile. When it comes to mental phenomena, we apply another mode of perception (not imagination or memory), that Buddhists call *mental perception*. With this mode of observation as your basis, you are ready to begin posing questions to your mind. To begin, observe whether all events that emerge in the domain of the mind are experienced as *yours*. For some of the thoughts, emotions, and other mental events, are you simply a witness? Do you have the sense that some are yours and some are merely events that are taking place within this particular private domain of experience? Observe closely.

If you experience some mental processes as yours, what makes them yours? Are they objectively yours? Is there something in the nature of the events themselves that makes them your possessions and puts them under your control? Or is it more a matter of how you engage with them? What happens when you release grasping? When you release the tentacles of identification and simply observe these as events, like a flock of birds flying through the sky of your mind, are any of these phenomena intrinsically, objectively yours? Which aspects of these mental activities are really under your control? How do you know?

See if you can voluntarily relinquish control, the sense of possession. Imagine that the mind is like a television screen and you are relinquishing the remote control. Voluntarily give it up. Now observe as precisely as you can just how the mental events, thoughts, mental imagery, and memories, come into existence. How do they emerge into the domain of experience? Do they come in all at once, from the left or right, or above or below? Do they come from any direction at all? If you think nothing is there, look more closely. Perhaps you will see something subtler that had previously slipped beneath the radar screen of your attention. Watch more closely by arousing the vividness of attention.

When a mental activity has emerged into the field of mental experience, how does it persist? How long does it last, five or ten seconds? Is it static or is it effervescent? What is its nature? Finally, how do they disappear, all at once or gradually? Do they fade out or suddenly stop? Watch closely.

Now dedicate merit and bring the session to a close.

For Further Contemplation

This way of investigating mental phenomena provides insights into more than the mere images and sensations themselves. As an analogy, if we direct this type of discerning, inquisitive intelligence to, say, the field of visual experience, we learn more than simply the nature of colors and shapes, more than something about the nature of our own visual perception. We learn about things in the surrounding world that somehow relate to or engage with our visual impressions of the world. Galileo gazed at Jupiter through a telescope and discovered it had moons. A skeptic might say that all he really discovered was white specks in his visual field. But he made some important discoveries based on those white specks. If we listen closely, we can do likewise with our auditory field. Wildlife biologists have to learn how to listen with discerning intelligence. Only in that way can they understand the nature and significance of the sounds they hear in nature. The same goes for the senses of taste and touch, which are highly developed by people such as wine connoisseurs and massage therapists. We are not living in a self-contained world, our own personal fishbowl, with access only to our own individual, subjective impressions. We are learning about the intersubjective world by way of those impressions. Just as we make discoveries about the nature of physical reality through the five physical senses, we can also learn about mental reality by way of appearances that arise to the field of mental experience. In other words, there is no reason to believe that events in the domain of mental experience are uniquely personal and isolated from the rest of the world, whereas all of our physical senses are engaged with the world around us. The mind is not imprisoned inside a skull, impervious to outside influences.

When it comes to exploring the extraordinary phenomena of the mind, there is no technology that provides us with immediate access. If we are to refine and extend our exploration of the nature of mental phenomena themselves, the only tool that we have available to us is mental perception. Unlike our physical senses, mental perception can be extraordinarily enhanced with training. The Dalai Lama has worn glasses since he was a child. There is no ocular refinement meditation that can solve his eyesight problem. And there are other highly realized lamas who need hearing aids. They don't say, "Forget the hearing aid. I'll just do the ear mantra." I don't know of any meditation to make the ears or eyes better. They are not very malleable to training. Mental perception, the only mode of observation that cannot be enhanced with technology, is the one kind of perception that can be greatly enhanced through training.

When we inspect the wondrous realm of the mind, we see immediately that some events arise only within this field of experience. We see directly, not through analysis or memory, that a given event is taking place here and now in the mind. In the realm of mental activities and processes, did you not find that some experiences seemed to occur spontaneously, uninvited, and once they came in, they didn't seem to be yours? Or do you feel that you own everything that comes into your space? If so, I would be very hesitant about entering your house or flying over your country.

We have a strong habitual tendency to own whatever comes into our mental field. How many emotions have you had that you felt weren't yours? What makes an emotion yours? They are really up close and personal. Then again, at other times you may have experienced thoughts like a flock of birds just winging through your mind, as if you were overhearing a conversation in which you were not participating. You may have had an image that just appeared, maybe some memory, without any sense of its being *yours*. You just experienced it. But if a desire pops up like, "I really want to move my leg," chances are that you grasp onto it as "mine." When you start getting disappointed or upset, or if you start feeling happy or uplifted, you probably have a sense of owning that feeling. Is there anything in the nature of these activities themselves that tells you, "You have to take possession of me, I am yours," like a little kid saying, "I am your kid. You have to own me"? Do any of these events beckon from their own nature, demanding your proprietorship over them, whereas other ones are merely casual visitors? Could it be that mental events, by their own nature prior to our conceptual projections, are merely phenomena, some of which we habitually grasp onto and identify with, while others we do not?

At the beginning I suggested that you bring forth a thought consciously—"What is the mind?" Because you intended to do that, you may have had a strong sense of, "That thought was mine because I made it," a sense of identification, grasping, of my-ness.

Most thoughts don't come voluntarily, otherwise we would all achieve *shamatha* the first time we tried. We could all simply decide, "I will now have a perfectly silent, focused, stable mind for the next twenty-four minutes," and it would be so. If your mind is really yours, if the domain of mental activity belongs to you, like your computer or your hand, it should do what you want it to do. What makes you think your mind is yours if you can't control it? Maybe it's only on loan. Or maybe it doesn't have any owner at all. This is one of the big issues the Buddha raised: the meaning of "I" and "mine."

When we are looking at mental events, how do they arise? Do they occur because we want emotions, thoughts, mental images, and desires to arise, as if we were the captain who orders, "Make it so"? If this were the case, we would really be in command of the starship of the mind. But we know perfectly well it doesn't work that way at all. A lot that happens in the brew of mental activity is just taking place of its own accord. From the Buddhist standpoint, it takes place not out of chaos with no causality whatsoever, and also not under the dominion of a "lord of the mind," namely an "I" or ego. I can't just tell the emotions and memories to jump and have them ask, "How far?" To a large extent, they seem to act on their own, under influences over which I have little or no control. But that is not the whole story. When you decided to think, "What is mind?" the thought came out. Five seconds later, something else may be happening that is out of your control again. So it is a strange mix. The mind is not completely out of control, otherwise we couldn't get any work done, we couldn't be employed or function in this world. But it is not totally under control either. The events that take place in the mind are not uniformly under control and not uniformly out of control. So where are the demarcations? What makes something yours?

As you observe the mind and probe the range of experience of mental events, you'll discover that they aren't anything more than simple phenomena arising in a chain of causes: neurological causes, previous mental events, and environmental stimuli. The brain is in a state of flux, our engagement with the environment is in flux, everything in a state of momentary rising and passing, as causes and events appear and vanish, stimulating other mental events that flower, come into bloom, then vanish back into the space of the mind. That is the Buddhist view: none of these are intrinsically under the control of an autonomous ego, self, master, homunculus, or "lord of the mind." On careful inspection, even emotions, thoughts, and desires that really do feel like they are yours, and over which you do feel you have some control, turn out to be otherwise. When you check closely, you see that the appearance of intrinsic ownership is misleading. These emotions and thoughts that you feel are yours; even the feeling, "I really am in control of this body," is false.

The possibility of controlling one's own mind when in fact there is no autonomous "I" is an intriguing paradox in Buddhism and one of its central themes. A Buddhist aphorism states, "For one who has subdued his mind there is happiness; for one who has not, there is no happiness." And the Dalai Lama often comments, "You are your own master." Be master of your own mind. You have a mind that is malleable, and you can use it for your own and others' benefit. But a mind that is out of control, obsessed, warped, dull, or unbalanced gives rise to suffering.

In this close application of mindfulness to mental activities, we are bringing intelligence to our observation. Recall that when we practiced meditative quiescence, we just quietly observed whatever came up and passed away without intervention, judgment, or reaction, without identification. That was sweet and simple. But here we need to take the next step and investigate the nature of our existence, because unfortunately the ignorance that lies at the root of suffering and mental affliction is not just an ignorance of not knowing, not merely an ignorance of not being aware. If that were the case, the direct antidote would be knowledge, and having that, we would be done.

The ignorance that influences the way we behave and engage with the world is active. We actively misconstrue and distort our experience of the world, both internally and externally. This is obviously true of our engagement with other people. All too often we find our evaluations don't correspond to reality, and we act out of what we believed to be true, which leads to unnecessary conflict and suffering. But the antidote is not just bare attention. The antidote is intelligent, discerning mindfulness. It is recognizing where we are deviating from reality, where we are falsely superimposing. A common theme throughout the Four Applications of Mindfulness is watching for conceptual projections upon what is actually being presented to us by perception. We superimpose many assumptions, desires, and expectations not only upon other people—on what they think or feel or are imagining or planning—but we are also very vulnerable to false superimpositions about ourselves.

For example, what kind of person do you think you are? A kind person? Unkind? Patient/impatient? Smart/stupid? Calm/agitated? Hyper/lax? Hard working/lethargic? Friendly/aloof? Where do you fit in? If you were to write a brief summary of the kind of person you are, this would be a depiction of what you have been *attending* to, not necessarily what is real. But there is more to it than that. Ignorance that lies at the root of suffering goes beyond not paying attention. Ignorance is also superimposing our conceptual constructs, then mistaking them for reality. Eventually we act on that basis, and that's when things really start to go awry.

Therefore, with intelligent discernment, as we observe mental events arising throughout the course of the day, not only in a twenty-four-minute session, we can pose some important questions. Among the wide array of mental events that emerge from moment to moment, we can begin to recognize types. First, recognize times when the mind is poised, balanced, in equilibrium. See for yourself what it is like. At those times we can say that mind is relatively unafflicted. Then as you observe the events that surge into the mind, notice those occasions when the equilibrium is shattered, when you get thrown out of kilter. At one moment you have access to clear intelligence, imagination, creativity, and memory, but then the balance gets lost, and there is disruption. In his book *Emotions Revealed*, Paul Ekman calls such an episode of internal disequilibrium a *refractory period*, during which "our thinking cannot incorporate information that does not fit, maintain, or justify the emotion we are feeling," and this "biases the way we see the world and ourselves."

These moments that disrupt our equilibrium are toxins of the mind because they afflict us by disturbing the body and the mind. When they contaminate our speech, our words become instruments of pain, for they are used in ways that are abusive, cruel, misleading, devious, or manipulative. When mental afflictions, or *kleshas*, pollute our physical behavior, we may do things with the body that are destructive or harmful to ourselves and others. But we must always be aware that such harm starts in the mind.

Can you recognize afflictive mental tendencies and see for yourself that they are destructive for your health? On the other hand, can you encounter qualities that enhance mental well-being, so that when they influence your words, you speak with clarity, gentleness, and intelligence? We can make people very happy with our voice and likewise with physical actions. Recognize what is wholesome and what is unwholesome. Fundamentally, there is nothing moralistic about this. It's a pragmatic issue.

Practice

Settle your body and mind in a state that is at ease, stable, and vigilant. Take a deep breath through the nostrils, down into the abdomen, slowly expanding, filling the diaphragm, finally breathing up into the chest. Then release it in a long gentle out-breath. Do this three times, feeling the sensation of the in- and out-breaths throughout the body. Then count twenty-one breaths as you have done before.

Now apply mindfulness to the domain of the mind, once again consciously bringing forth the thought "What is the mind?" (or it could be any thought). From what did that thought emerge? Wait until the next thought comes along. When a mental event arises, once again emerging of its own accord, don't regard it as an obscuration. Instead, examine: where is this mental activity coming from? We say that thoughts come from the mind. What is that mind from which thoughts emerge? What are its qualities? Is it static or in flux? Is there anything about it that suggests it has an owner?

Continue attending closely, intelligently, inquisitively, into that ground of the mind that is prior to any type of mental activation, mental constructs, images, or impulses.

Next, once some mental activity has occurred, observe where it is taking place. Does it have a location? Attend not to the foreground, the activity, or the players on the stage, but to the background, the stage itself. Thoughts now arise as an aid to the practice because they help you identify, once again, the domain in which mental events play themselves out. Attend closely. We say thoughts and feelings occur in the mind. What is the mind in which mental events take place?

If grasping occurs, if you find yourself identifying with a certain mental activity, simply observe that grasping itself. Does the space of the mind contract at times, gravitating in on the grasped object? Does the mind become small, as it were, filled by the object? When grasping subsides, does the space of the mind remain open, without contraction, creating no friction with the mental events that arise and pass through it? Observe the space of the mind. Is it static, or is there warp and woof to the space of the mind? Is it the real you, or is it really yours? Or is it simply a natural phenomenon, like physical space?

Finally, once a mental event fades out, take not so much an interest in the event itself, but in the *bhavanga* into which it vanishes. Attend not to the process of dissolution of the mental event but to that into which it vanishes.

In this practice, stray thoughts are not obstacles. As you attend to the mind, if at times no thoughts or other mental activities arise, observe the space of the mind itself. If something is starting to emerge into the mind, good. Observe that *from which* it is emerging, and examine where it is then located. If something is vanishing from the mind, good; observe that into which it is vanishing. The mind is always present. The substrate consciousness is always present and only our lack of attentiveness obscures it.

For Contemplation

What we are approaching in this exercise is something William James calls *pure experience*. In his intriguing essay entitled "Does Consciousness Exist?" he writes, "The instant field of the present is at all times what I call the 'pure' experience. It is only virtually or potentially either object or subject as yet. For the time being, it is plain, unqualified actuality, or existence, a simple *that*." Many meditators aspire for such nondual experience, which is commonly experienced as one of bliss and luminosity, in which grasping onto "I" and "mine" vanishes, as does any sense of a subject/object duality. Some people call that *nirvana*, others call it *ultimate reality, pure consciousness,* or *pristine awareness*. But most likely they are gaining a glimpse of the substrate consciousness, in which grasping has temporarily subsided.

Merely lingering in such a state does nothing to purify or liberate the mind of its afflictions. It's more like a contemplative holiday resort—a nice place to hang out, but it's not transformative in any profound, enduring way. One Theravada Buddhist text called the *Milindapañha* compares it to the radiance of the sun, for it is naturally pure and luminous. It is the resting ground state of consciousness that is withdrawn from the senses, and it is the state the mind returns to when not doing anything else. This is the natural, unencumbered state of the mind, and while the normal functioning of the mind is like light, which may get cut off, the substrate consciousness, which naturally manifests in dreamless sleep, has a radiance that exists whether or not it is obscured.

When we consider that the world of experience exists only in relation to minds that perceive it, it becomes easy to understand the declaration in the renowned Pali text *The Dhammapada*: "All phenomena are preceded by the mind, issue forth from the mind, and consist of the mind." The Mahayana *Ratnameghasutra* goes further in stating, "All phenomena are preceded by the mind. When the mind is comprehended, all phenomena are comprehended. By bringing the mind under control, all things are brought under control." And finally, another Mahayana discourse attributed to the Buddha, called the *Ratnachudasutra*, declares:

The mind, Kashyapa, is like an illusion, and by forming what is not, it comprehends all sorts of events. . . . The mind, Kashyapa, is like the stream of a river, unsettled, breaking and dissolving as soon as it is produced. The mind, Kashyapa, is like the light of a lamp, and is due to causes and contributing conditions. The mind, Kashyapa, is like lightning, cut off in a moment and not abiding. The mind, Kashyapa, is like space, disturbed by adventitious afflictions.

The mind described in this passage is to be fathomed by posing the questions: Is this relative ground-state of consciousness unchanging, or does it exist in a state of flux? Is it a true source of happiness, or does it provide only a respite from the dissatisfaction, misery, and pain? And finally, is there anything in the nature of the mind that is truly "I" or "mine," or is this simply an impersonal phenomenon like space, time, and matter? Only when we venture into these crucial features of the mind can we find true freedom from mental afflictions.

7

Mindfulness of Phenomena

THE BUDDHIST PURSUIT OF understanding is not confined only to the body and the mind. It is aimed at fathoming the nature of all phenomena. The object of this fourth application of mindfulness is known in Sanskrit as *dharma*, which in this context means simply *phenomena*. This is not to be confused with the capitalized form of the word, *Dharma*, which refers to the teachings and practices that lead to liberation and spiritual awakening. We now expand the scope of mindfulness to inspect all manner of things and events—all dharmas—including both subjective and objective phenomena. The result of such inquiry is called *prajña*, a kind of insight and knowledge that irreversibly heals the mind of both its inborn and acquired afflictions and obscurations.

After living in Sri Lanka and practicing as a monk under the guidance of Balangoda Anandamaitreya from 1980 to 1981, I came to the conclusion that the Theravada and Tibetan Buddhist traditions have far more in common with regard to the nature of *shamatha* and *vipashyana* than first impressions would suggest. This becomes clear when you rely on the most authoritative scholars and meditation masters in both traditions. During the months that Anandamaitreya trained me in the practice of *shamatha*, I found nothing in his instructions that was incompatible with the teachings I had earlier received from my Tibetan lamas, including the assertion that when you achieve access to the first meditative stabilization (in Pali, *jhana*), you can remain in single-pointed *samadhi*, free of even the slightest laxity and excitation for at least four hours. I asked Anandamaitreya how many people he thought there were in Sri Lanka at that time who had actually accomplished access to the first meditative stabilization. He replied that among the thousands of monks and laypeople in Sri Lanka who were then devoting themselves to Buddhist meditation, you could count on the fingers of one hand the number who had achieved such a level of *samadhi*. If that's true, a degree of skepticism is warranted with regard to the claims of many contemporary Western meditators—with far less theoretical and practical training than most Sri Lankan monks—who believe they have achieved the first meditative stabilization and higher degrees of *samadhi* and realization in the practice of *vipassana*.

Practice

At the outset of this one-*ghatika* session, settle your body and mind at ease, in stillness, and in a state of vigilance. Take three luxurious breaths, slowly and deeply, expanding the abdomen, filling the diaphragm, breathing up into the chest, and releasing the breath gently and fully.

Return to normal respiration and for a few moments bring forth the most meaningful aspiration you can for this session. What are your highest goals as an individual, and also for your life in relation to those around you? What would you like to achieve, to experience, to become? What would you like to offer? Wherein lies your greatest happiness? Let the fulfillment of your aspiration be your motive for continuing.

Having cultivated a meaningful motivation, prepare your attention and make your mind serviceable by calming the tendencies of agitation and laxity. Bring awareness into the field of tactile sensations of the body, from the soles of your feet, to the thighs, the buttocks, up through the torso, through your limbs, and up to the head. Maintaining this field of awareness of tactile phenomena, attend to the breath as a preparatory exercise. Rest in a purely witnessing mode, not being carried away by memories, fantasies, or speculation. During the in-breath, arouse the vividness of your attention, and during the out-breath, relax and release any extraneous thoughts or other distractions that may have arisen. Count twenty-one breaths as you have done before.

Now proceed to the mindfulness of phenomena. Recall the counsel given by the Buddha: "In the seen there is only the seen; in the heard, there is only the heard; in the sensed, there is only the sensed; in the cognized, there is only the cognized." Begin by directing awareness, with eyes at least partially open, to the phenomena of shapes and colors: everything that appears nakedly to your visual perception. Just be present with that.

With your eyes closed, attend just to sound.

Can you now detect any odors? The challenge is to abide simply in a mode of witnessing, without judgment, without attraction or aversion, without mental grasping of any kind. Abide in a mode of pure receptivity that is fluid, not rigid.

Are there any tastes lingering in your mouth?

Now apply mindfulness to the fifth domain of sensory experience, tactile phenomena. Be aware of your body with respect to what is being immediately presented to your tactile perception.

Notice that you may identify with or grasp onto objects in any of these fields of experience. If, within visual awareness, you see the shape of your legs or hands, you latch on and think "mine." You hear your own voice, just a sound, but you recognize it and think "mine." You may even latch on to "my smell," "my taste," and certainly "my bodily sensations." But when you observe closely, do you see anything intrinsically "I" or "mine" in any of the contents of the five fields of sensory experience? Or are these merely events arising in dependence upon causes and conditions?

Finally, move to the sixth domain of experience, the realm of mental phenomena, where you experience thoughts, images, feelings, emotions, and memories. Observe this domain as you have done with the others.

Now try something new. Release control of your mind. Let your mind, your attention, be free from any control. Then rest in choiceless, undirected awareness. Let your attention float in the space of awareness, carried by the winds of stimuli so that it soars to the sensory—the visual, the tactile, the auditory, and so forth—and to the mental, like a butterfly alighting from flower to flower. Let your attention go where it will, as you remain motionlessly, choicelessly, in the space of awareness, neither controlling your mind nor being controlled by it.

Bring the session to a close.

For Further Contemplation

I said before that mindfulness of the mind may be the most fascinating of the Four Applications of Mindfulness because it goes so deep, right into the very nature of awareness itself. But what could be more fascinating than *everything*? That's what we have here; nothing is excluded. Everything that arises to perceptual modes of experience, immediate impressions, mental imagery, sight and sound; whatever arises to the conceptual mind (thoughts, images, memories, fantasies, speculations about the future) all of these are dharmas. All that exists is included in the category of dharmas. They are all appearances, objects of the mind.

This raises fascinating and important issues, especially for our culture. One is intuition. I often think about various forms of traditional medicine—ancient Greek, Indian, Tibetan, Chinese—where did they learn what types of herbs and other natural compounds alleviate specific diseases? The Chinese have a vast, complex system that takes years to learn and master. In traditional Tibetan medicine, one pill can contain thirty-five to a hundred ingredients in specific proportions. How did they come up with this? I once heard a Native American describe the medicinal properties of one plant after another, all in considerable detail. Considering the fact that there are a lot of poisonous plants, I asked her, "How did they discover the healing ones?" Her answer was the same answer that I know is true for the Tibetan tradition, and suspect is true for the Ayurdevic tradition of India, as well as Chinese medicine: intuition. In the case of Native Americans, it is said that the plant tells the practitioner what it is good for. In the Tibetan Buddhist tradition, the Medicine Buddha tells the advanced practitioner what compounds of herbs and minerals are effective for treating a wide range of diseases.

Because many of these medications work, I cannot discount what these practioners say about where they get their knowledge. It is unlikely they secretly ran double-blind experiments on thousands of mice, let alone human beings. What I am getting at is that intuition is another mode of knowledge, one that is different from analytic thinking, designing experiments, and developing better technology. In modern English "intuition" is a vague, touchy-feely kind of term, but intuition is important not only in contemplative practice but also in science, which history has shown to be not purely rational and analytical. This mode of knowledge that is immediate and inexplicable in terms of logic can be cultivated. In an earlier chapter I asked the question: how do we sense what other people are feeling? Is it a rational process of reading and interpreting body language, comparing it to our own experience, and then superimposing it? It doesn't feel like that. It seems immediate. Intuition can be wrong, but this does not preclude the possibility that it is another mode of knowledge.

For example, how does a Native American hear a plant talking? Or a Tibetan Buddhist hear the Medicine Buddha tell him during meditation how to treat a certain disease? This is a type of mental perception, whether it comes by way of the physical senses or from the mental domain of experience. As mentioned earlier, mental perception is the only one of our six modes of perception that can be greatly refined with practice. Among the six modes of perception, this is the one we can enhance as we get older and the other senses get dimmer. To do so requires that we cultivate an inner stillness and clear receptivity to what is being presented from moment to moment. And to achieve that, we have to diminish our habit of grasping.

Grasping is a term heard frequently in all schools of Buddhism. On the one hand, we have the way reality is presented to our senses. Some of the things that reality dishes out to us are painful and disturbing. Others are pleasant or neutral. But most of us are not just flowing with the appearances that arise. Rather, we are actively interpreting them. Some things irritate us. When we want it to be silent, reality gets noisy. This interpreting and preferring is called grasping. When that happens, a sound is not just sound.

If your meditation is disturbed by a sound, it is not the sound that is doing the disturbing, it is the grasping at the flow of appearances. Grasping often entails either aversion or attraction. We want it to go away, or we want it to stay as it is or get stronger. All of this is grasping—going beyond appearances to what is imagined as the sources of the phenomena.

A coarser, delusive mode of grasping objectifies things, imbuing them with a more tangible, independent existence than they actually have. Nothing exists independently. All conditioned phenomena are arising from moment-to-moment as dependently related events. So grasping onto things puts us at odds with reality. It also sets us up for a host of mental afflictions, of craving, hostility, envy, pride, and so on. This is where grasping, in the form of delusion, shows how toxic it can be. When I was being taught how to ride a motorcycle, my instructor told the class: in any collision between you and anyone or anything else, you lose. Likewise, in any collision between reality and us, we lose. Reality never loses. Reality doesn't suffer. We do. There are three common ways this can happen.

One way we collide with reality is by grasping onto that which by nature is in a constant state of flux—impermanent, moving, transforming, passing, gone—as being stable and permanent. Everything that arises in our fields of perception is in constant flux. Whether it is subjective or objective, or a combination of the two, it is all topsy-turvy, flowing, always effervescent. When something rotten happens, we grasp onto it as being eternally rotten, when in fact the situation we encounter is constantly in flux and sooner or later disappears altogether. Bad neighbors, we feel, will live forever and be irritating every day for the rest of our lives. It's not so much that we can't stand them in the present moment; what we really can't stand is that they seem permanent.

The same goes for positive events. Something nice happens. The classic case is romance. It seems like such attraction will endure forever, whereas sexual infatuation is notoriously fleeting. We may project the same quality of permanence on a new acquisition, hoping, and even expecting, that it will look and function indefinitely as it did the day we bought it. But things don't become defective and fall apart because they're made wrong. *They become defective and fall apart because they are made at all.* You can count on it. All the dharmas that originate and appear to the mind will persist for a while and then end. If we could somehow wrap our lives around that reality, it would serve us well, because that's what is true.

The crucial point here is that under the influence of such grasping, our perception of reality is distorted, and when we act in accordance with that distortion, we suffer. This is the essence of the Second Noble Truth, the origins of suffering. We can avoid a tremendous amount of unnecessary suffering by recognizing the coarse and subtle impermanence of all conditioned phenomena, and by taking that into account as we lead our lives.

A second way we collide with reality is by grasping onto that which is not a true source of happiness as being the real cause of the joy and satisfaction we seek. Consider this: is there anything that arises as an appearance or object to your mind—anything whatsoever—that is itself a true source of happiness? Or a true source of suffering? There are countless things that may arouse pleasure, and a lot more of them that can arouse suffering. Freud observed, "We are so made that we can derive intense enjoyment only from a contrast and very little from a state of things. . . . Unhappiness is much less difficult to experience." Consider this statement as you reflect on the temperature range at which you are comfortable, the range of foods you can digest, and the range of situations in which you can be relaxed and happy.

Yet here we are, caught up in the pursuit of happiness. This pursuit is even built into the U.S. Constitution as a *right*. But in this pursuit, what exactly should we pursue? Are great jobs, fine salaries, and beautiful homes sources of happiness? What the Buddha deduced from his own exploration is that we grasp onto things and other people that are not by nature sources of happiness as if they were. We invest our lives in them, and then demand the payback of happiness. Grasping onto something that is not by nature an actual source of happiness, yet considering it as such, is an immense problem. Some people are single and are convinced that having a partner would provide them with true, lasting happiness. Is having a spouse a true source of happiness? A lot of married people think their spouse is the source of their suffering. So being single is not a source of happiness and having a spouse is not a source of happiness either. How often do we invest ourselves in a job or in obtaining a certain kind of house? We invest deeply in the hope and vision: "Therein lies my happiness." But happiness doesn't dwell in the objects around us. Remember, an object may catalyze happiness, but the same object may also lead to suffering.

According to Buddhism, this human life with which we are endowed is precious beyond any possible evaluation. Given our ability to pursue virtue, happiness, and truth, our lives are priceless. But is that how you view your life from day to day? How much is a day of your life worth? How much would you want in return for dying one day earlier? One hundred dollars? How about a thousand dollars? More? And yet so many of us think we have time to kill. The capital of our lives is limited. This is especially true of the prime time when we are in good health, have enough to eat, without having to spend all of our time just trying to survive. Consider how you are investing your precious time. What are you doing in the pursuit of happiness?

The third and perhaps deepest way we collide with reality is by grasping onto that which is not "I" or "mine" as being "I" or "mine." As we apply mindfulness to the whole range of phenomena, we detect nothing but appearances arising to the mind—emotions, memories, feelings, physical sensations, and thoughts—mere appearances. We are habituated to grasping onto many of them as "mine": my friends, my family, my spouse, my material possessions, my reputation, my body, my emotions, my desires, my thoughts, my memories, and so on. And we grasp onto our own sense of personal identity as a real, autonomous "I," which owns and frequently tries to control all those things that are deemed "mine." In their pursuit of self-worth, many people try to control as many things and people as they can, demonstrating to themselves and the world at large that they *really* exist, they're really in control. But when you apply mindfulness with discernment to outer and inner phenomena, observing them with as few conceptual superimpositions as possible, none of these objects of the mind present themselves as either "I" or "mine." According to the experiential exploration of Buddhist contemplatives, this deeply ingrained tendency to grasp onto anything at all as inherently "I" or "mine" is deluded: it sets us on a collision course with reality, and the result, once again, is that we suffer.

For example, imagine cultivating a business relationship with somebody who, unbeknownst to you, is devious, manipulative, and self-serving. Eventually this person ruins your business. You lose money not simply because he was a crook and a liar, but because you thought he wasn't. Compare that to mistaking that which is not "I" and "mine" for that which is "I" and "mine." If you mistake a crooked associate for an honest person and do business with him, that may harm you for a certain phase of your life. But it will pass, and you can recover. But if you misapprehend the nature of your very existence, that will infect everything you ever do. Your whole life will be based on this fundamental error.

A Mahayana *sutra*, or discourse attributed to the Buddha, addresses this point eloquently:

> The aggregates [comprising the body and mind] are impermanent, unstable, naturally brittle like an unbaked pot, like a borrowed article, like a city built in the dust lasting for a time only. By nature those conditions are subject to destruction, plaster washed away by the rainy season, like sand on a river's bank, dependent on contributing conditions, naturally weak. They are like the flame of a lamp, their nature is to be destroyed as soon as they arise, unstable as the wind, sapless and weak like a clot of foam.

The significance of naming things is not confined to one's own identity. In a discourse recorded in the Pali language, the Buddha comments, "These are merely names, expressions, turns of speech, designations in common use in the world. Of these he who has won the truth makes use indeed, but is not led astray by them." And in another Pali discourse, he declares:

> Just as when the parts are set together
> There arises the word "chariot,"
> So does the notion of a being
> When the aggregates are present.

On this same theme, the Buddha is recorded as saying in a Mahayana *sutra*, "Nameless are all conditions, but illuminated by name." As you attended quietly in the previous meditation, moving from one domain of sensory experience to another, or resting in choiceless awareness, did any one of these events rise up and name itself? We name something, we conceptually designate it, and then it arises out of the smooth fabric of appearances to meet us. We name ourselves. Our name illuminates how we are demarcated from others and this is a meaningful convention. A name arises, crystallizes something, and illuminates it. This is very useful, but how seriously do we take these names? As soon as we name something, grasping takes place. Grasping is not by nature delusional, but it opens the door to objectification. It is like a Pandora's box to a myriad of delusions.

Practice

Settle your body and mind in a posture that is at ease, still, and vigilant. As you relax the muscles of the shoulders and face, keep the eyes soft and the forehead relaxed. Take three deep slow breaths though the nostrils. Then, with just twenty-one counted breaths, corral this wild stallion of the mind so that you can ride it in comfort.

Let's pursue the kind of truth that is valid for everyone at all times. These are truths across all cognitive frames of reference. What is constant and invariable? First rest in choiceless awareness, in which you utterly surrender control, giving your sense of ego, the controlling "I," a rest, letting it become dormant for a while. Let the mind go free, and yet don't allow yourself to be controlled by the mind. Don't be carried away by the mind or oppressed by the mind. Let it go where it will; let the appearances arise as they may.

This is a superb preparation for dying consciously, when we are compelled to relinquish control and the facades of control, but retain the option not to be controlled by our emotions of fear, anxiety, or sorrow. There is a saying, "This is a free man, the lord of no one, but lorded over by no one." Here and now be free, as you rest in the very nature of awareness, which is luminous and transparent. Rest there choicelessly, without grasping.

In terms of mindfulness of the mind, you will recall that there are the contents, the events, and the processes of the mind. Then there is the substrate consciousness, the ground from which those appearances arise. You may come to rest in the substrate, reposing there and then observing without intervention whatever activities arise within this sphere of the mind, the domain of mental experience. Now cast this open to the whole of reality, not just the domain of the mind. Open up to the domain of all experience, all appearances. Once again you have the appearances, the contents, the events—the objects that arise to consciousness. Then there is that out of which these appearances manifest, that in which all of these appearances occur, and that into which these appearances vanish. That is the space of awareness. What is this ground from which all appearances arise, this space in which the appearances occur, and that into which they vanish? What is this luminous ground, this luminous space? Closely apply mindfulness to the whole range of phenomena and to the space from which they emerge, in which they abide, and into which they vanish.

Bring the session to a close. We began with the cultivation of a meaningful motivation. Whatever benefit there may be from your practice—what Buddhists call *merit*—dedicate this to the realization of your most meaningful aspirations and motivations. May the merit of this practice lead to the fulfillment and realization of your deepest yearnings.

For Further Contemplation

In this practice, I raise the possibility that there are truths that are invariable throughout space and time. To elaborate, I propose that there's a spectrum of truths, ranging from the very personal to the very general. Is my improvising on the piano the best music in the world? The answer may be yes for one individual. This statement may be just as true as $E = mc^2$ in the very narrow context of a one-person universe. You could say that such a person is ridiculously self-centered, operating out of only one perspective on truth. Insofar as our minds are dominated by self-centeredness, we feel, "My well-being is the most important thing in the world. The second most important thing is the well-being of people whom I care about most." You could stack the rest of sentient beings like a pyramid down to those "people who should be hit by trucks and don't deserve any happiness because they rub me the wrong way." This is a perfectly self-centered perspective, where truth is true for only one person.

Let's push this idea into a broader context. Imagine a nomadic culture where families are separated because their herds need plenty of space to graze. Here the family nucleus is the center of the universe. Apart from occasionally trading with other family units, all you want from them is that they not overlap into your territory. You can have a family-centered worldview that has beliefs that are true only for your family and not for other families. We can progress then to a city-centered mentality in which truth-claims apply to the inhabitants of a city like Sparta or Athens, where some claims are true for Spartans but are not necessarily valid for Athenians. This can also be applied more broadly to ethnocentricity or nationalism. There may be truths that are only valid for a single ethnic group. There could also be language-centered frames of reference. Truths could be valid in English but not true in German or Sanskrit.

What I'm getting at is this: there are dimensions of your existence, here and now individually, that are not locked into your specific persona, which includes your gender, age, ethnicity, nationality, and species. And those dimensions can be experienced. That is what this practice is about. Regardless of our cognitive frame of reference, there are universal truths—not purely objective ones, but ones that are true regardless of your perspective. The three marks of existence of such truths are:

1. All conditioned phenomena, all those that arise in dependence upon causes and conditions are subject to impermanence, as they arise and pass from moment to moment.

2. As long as our minds are subject to mental afflictions, all our experiences will be unsatisfactory. No objects of perception or thought are true sources of happiness.
3. Nothing that we experience is truly "I" or "mine," by its own nature. These concepts are merely superimposed on mental and physical phenomena, none of which is an inherently existent self.

Recognizing these crucial features of existence—through personal experience—leads to the realization of nirvana, the ultimate freedom from all mental afflictions and their consequences. The path to that freedom consists of the practice of ethics, *samadhi*, and the cultivation of wisdom. In this way the pursuits of virtue, genuine happiness, and truth are thoroughly integrated. This is the path to liberation.

PART III

Cultivating a Good Heart

8

Loving-Kindness

WHEN WE BEGIN TO experience the benefits of *shamatha* meditation, with the serenity and clarity it brings to the mind, it's tempting to focus exclusively on such practice. But the Buddhist tradition encourages us to extend our spiritual practice beyond the borders of inner calm. A few years ago, when I was interpreting for one of the Mind and Life conferences with His Holiness the Dalai Lama and a group of cognitive scientists, Tsoknyi Rinpoche, a highly respected Tibetan meditation master, was one of the invited guests. One evening, he and I sat together and discussed the spread of Buddhism to the West, and he commented on some of the drawbacks of becoming fixated on *shamatha*. Some students, he said, would become so immersed in such practice that they wound up becoming detached from everything around them, thinking, I feel totally nonattached toward other people's problems! I'm doing fine myself. The result of their spiritual practice was a kind of aloof indifference to the plight of others, while they enjoyed the relative calm of the inner sanctuary of their own minds. This he saw as a real impediment to spiritual growth.

Only insight into the nature of reality can truly heal the mind of its afflictions, so we progress from *shamatha* to the Four Applications of Mindfulness, the foundations of Buddhist insight practice as a whole. These practices have been covered in the first two parts of this book. Many people find the cultivation of mindfulness to be very effective in bringing about greater clarity and insight into daily life, and I have met a number of people who say they are Buddhist simply because they practice mindfulness. Some even equate this with Buddhist meditation as a whole, and claim that meditative practices other than the cultivation of bare attention are misguided. There's a kind of dogmatism in this attitude that is unfortunately common among religious believers of all faiths: we have the only way, and anything other than what we believe and practice is wrong and harmful. But there is a theme in the Buddha's teachings that bears directly on this: wisdom without compassion is bondage, and compassion without wisdom is bondage. This is a profound truth. The path of awakening is marked with many potholes and ruts, and it's easy to get trapped in a narrow, exclusivist view, even regarding excellent practices. I've heard the Dalai Lama comment on some teachers he's met whose years of practice centered on the Four Applications of Mindfulness. While they exhibited a deep sense of calm and equanimity, he also found a kind of stern and joyless quality in them, with no apparent warmth or empathy with others. Wisdom without compassion is bondage.

The Buddhist path of spiritual awakening is not only one of unveiling the innate bliss, luminosity, and purity of awareness. It is also one of cultivating wholesome qualities of the heart and mind and expressing these through our everyday conduct. So to complement the profound wisdom that can be realized through the practice of the Four Applications of Mindfulness, we turn now to the cultivation of the Four Immeasurables: loving-kindness, compassion, empathetic joy, and equanimity. Each of these is a vital element in the pursuit of genuine happiness. In our day-to-day lives, we tend to oscillate between hopes and fears, joys and sorrows, all of which arise in dependence upon prior causes and conditions. Many, if not all, of these causal circumstances are beyond our control. Genuine happiness, the pursuit of which is the very meaning of life, is not simply a pleasurable feeling aroused by contact with objective, agreeable stimuli. Rather, it emerges from inner causes and conditions, arising out of the center, that midpoint between the vicissitudes. Cultivate an open heart, filled with immeasurable loving-kindness and compassion, and happiness naturally emerges from within.

Practice

Let's first make our minds serviceable. We have little control over our surrounding environment—a mere semblance of control, which often collapses on our heads. And when we turn inward, we may find that the mind too is often out of control. But perhaps we can learn greater control, greater mastery, over our own minds—we can make this mind serviceable so that it becomes our ally.

Assume a posture that is conducive to practice, with the body at ease, still, and vigilant. Relax the muscles of the shoulders and the face, including the jaw. Relax the eyes and the muscles around the eyes. And now take three slow, deep, full inhalations, breathing into the abdomen, followed by a full release of the breath through the nostrils.

Seek, first, the subtle joy of serenity, an inner calm. Release the worries of the day, release anticipations of the future, and settle into the only reality there is now: the present. Release your awareness into a mode of simple witnessing, bringing it into the field of tactile sensations throughout the body. Let the breath proceed without intervention. Don't try to breathe deeply. Just leave your abdomen loose so that when you do inhale, it expands easily. If it is a deep breath, let it be deep; if a shallow breath, fine.

Now radically simplify your mind. Let your body be filled with mindfulness and your mind be present in the field of these tactile sensations, of in- and out-breaths felt throughout the body. If you find it helpful, try counting just twenty-one breaths—one count at the beginning of each inhalation. Besides that, give this troubled mind a rest, this mind with all of its concerns, plans, memories, hopes, and fears. Let it rest simply in the awareness of the gentle rhythm of your breathing.

We now move to a thoughtful mode of meditation, in which we fully use our powers of imagination, intelligence, and intuition. This type of practice is called discursive meditation, and it is an important complement to the nondiscursive practices of *shamatha* and bare attention.

Do you yearn for happiness? You are most likely seeking something beyond the mere desire to survive or to achieve fame and material prosperity. Otherwise you wouldn't be doing this practice. So what is the source of this yearning and what might be its fulfillment? What is it that you really want? Can you envision it? It might be easiest to start off by recognizing what you are not seeking, that which will not suffice, will not bring you the happiness you seek. Scan your memory to find examples of things that you thought would bring you genuine fulfillment, but in the end let you down. They shouldn't be hard to find.

For millennia, with their lives and their words, the great teachers in the Buddhist tradition have been encouraging us to recognize that our yearning for genuine happiness is not in vain. Can you imagine a way of life that is realizable, a way of life conducive to pursuing such happiness? Are you living it already? And if not, what would be necessary? What change would be needed to so alter your life that you could steadfastly pursue genuine happiness, tracing it to its very source?

Now consider your life as it is. You are surviving, and you have encountered the Dharma. Perhaps you have spiritual friends and teachers. The door is open to follow this path to enlightenment. Such circumstances occur only rarely. Such a life is called "a precious human life of freedom and opportunity." Opportunity to do what? To pursue genuine happiness and trace it to its source. Is it possible to direct all our efforts toward finding such happiness for ourselves and for all of those around us? That would be a life of loving-kindness.

So bring forth loving-kindness for yourself, wishing for the realization of your deepest yearnings. And imagine a way of life that allows you maximum freedom to pursue that which is of greatest value. This requires faith. It's not so obvious as we view the world, watch the evening news, watch what happens from day to day, that genuine happiness is even a possibility. There are so many causes of suffering, of conflict, of sadness and pain. But faith in our innate goodness and the possibility of happiness is an option. And choosing that option opens the door to this pursuit. It brings us back to the core theme. The Christian tradition says, "The kingdom of heaven is within." And Buddhism says, "The buddha-nature is the very essence of your being." Here is the source of joy, the source of compassion, the source of wisdom—the source of all good. Here there is hope and the platform for cultivating loving-kindness for ourselves and for others. How can we nurture and guide ourselves so as to lead lives that are conducive to the manifestation, the flowering, the realization of this buddha-nature, such that it becomes more than an article of faith?

Imagine your buddha-nature—the essential purity of your own awareness—symbolically as a pearl of radiant white light at your heart. And all of that incandescent, radiant white light is of the nature of joy, of loving-kindness that has always been within you. Then, with each in-breath, imagine drawing from this inexhaustible source of light at your heart, as if you were drawing water from a well. With each in-breath imagine drawing out the light from this source, a source that can be so easily obscured while we attend to others things, as our priorities become lost in distractions. With each in-breath imagine drawing this light out, like drawing from a deep well. Then with each out-breath imagine this light of well-being, this light of loving-kindness, suffusing every part of your body, your mind, your spirit. Then think: May I experience genuine happiness and the very source of happiness itself. May I be well and happy.

As this light expands, imagine it dispelling all kinds of conflicts, afflictions, imbalances in your body and mind, all that may bring suffering to your being. Vividly picture these afflictions being dispelled by this radiant light, and imagine it saturating and filling your entire being. Begin this practice of loving-kindness by yearning for your own well-being, bearing in mind the Buddha's comment, "One who loves himself will never harm another."

As it fills your own body to overflowing, imagine this field of light around your body filling your room, then extending to the outer world such that it suffuses everyone around you, near and far. As your light expands out to the world, omitting no one, think: May all beings like myself, above and below, in all directions, may each one find happiness and the sources of happiness.

Then, for just a moment, release your imagination, release your yearning. Utterly at rest, settle your awareness in its own nature. Simply be aware of being aware.

Bring the session to a close.

For Further Contemplation

Loving-kindness, called *maitri* in Sanskrit, is the first of the Four Immeasurables, and it means a heartfelt yearning that others might experience happiness and the sources of happiness. In response to the question "What is the meaning of life?" many of the great contemplatives, saints, and religious leaders of the past—East and West—have answered that life's meaning is just that: the pursuit of happiness. That's pretty good news. We wanted to do that anyway, and if that is also the meaning of life, great! But on further investigation, the quest for happiness brings up some provocative and also disturbing issues. When we think of the pursuit of happiness, what kinds of things do we have in mind? How do we envision spending the days of our lives striving for it? Of course one relevant issue is simply survival. It's hard to be happy if we can't even survive, if we feel our very lives are imperiled. Then once we have taken care of survival, we want security, and with that we would also include health. Those would certainly be basic to our pursuit of happiness.

But beyond these essentials we are often involved in pursuing mundane pleasures instead of genuine happiness. In the Buddhist tradition there are many references to the Eight Mundane Concerns. To review this list of concerns, the first two are the yearning for gaining new material acquisitions and avoiding the loss of those we have already obtained. Some people evaluate their own self-worth and their degree of success in life on a purely quantitative basis: how much money and material goods they have been able to acquire. Such people have equated the pursuit of happiness with the pursuit of wealth. The second pair of mundane concerns is the pursuit of stimulus-driven pleasures of all sorts—sensual, intellectual, and aesthetic—and the desire to avoid any kind of suffering or pain. The third pair is the concern for acquiring others' praise and avoiding their disparagement, abuse, and ridicule. The last two concerns have to do with achieving the high esteem, affection, acceptance, and respect of others, and avoiding their contempt, dislike, rejection, and indifference. These eight concerns can occupy every waking moment of our lives, so it's worthwhile to take a close look at them to see if they warrant such single-minded dedication.

The neuroscientist Richard Davidson, a friend and colleague of mine who has begun to conduct rigorous scientific studies of the effects of meditation on emotional well-being, uses the term "hedonic treadmill" to characterize a life centered on the Eight Mundane Concerns. The pursuit of happiness and mental health is gaining more and more attention among cognitive scientists who are asking: What really leads to happiness? One of the more remarkable books recently published on this topic is *The High Price of Materialism* by the psychologist Tim Kasser. With regard to the first of the Eight Mundane Concerns, his research concludes that people who strongly value the pursuit of wealth and possessions report lower psychological well-being than those who are less concerned with such aims. Such fixation on material acquisitions not only undermines our own happiness, it also warps our way of engaging with other people. Kasser comments in this regard, "When people place a strong emphasis on consuming and buying, earning and spending, thinking of the monetary worth of things, and thinking of things a great deal of the time, they may also become more likely to treat people like things." The scientific evidence he has accumulated suggests that beyond having enough money to meet our basic needs for food, shelter, and the like, attaining wealth, possessions, and status does not yield long-term increases in our happiness or well-being. Even the successful pursuit of materialistic ideals typically turns out to be empty and unsatisfying. He sums up this point: "People who are highly focused on materialistic values have lower personal well-being and psychological health than those who believe that materialistic pursuits are relatively unimportant. These relationships have been documented in samples of people ranging from the wealthy to the poor, from teenagers to the elderly, and from Australians to South Koreans."

In Buddhism a clear distinction is drawn between a life devoted to the true causes of happiness and a life devoted to the outer symbols of happiness—namely, the Eight Mundane Concerns. A meaningful life is one oriented around genuine happiness, and that necessarily entails the pursuit of virtue and understanding. Navigating our way through life by focusing on the constellation of the Eight Mundane Concerns is a meaningless and, upon careful scrutiny, an ineffective strategy for finding what we have been seeking all along: happiness. I am reminded of Shantideva's poignant comment: "Those desiring to escape from suffering hasten right toward suffering. With the very desire for happiness, out of delusion they destroy their own happiness as if it were an enemy."

Our modern, consumer-driven society is being constantly bombarded by the advertising industry, the media, and other institutions with the message that if we only try harder, earn more, and spend more, we can find the satisfaction we seek. We just need to be more effective in reaching our materialistic goals, then that elusive prize of happiness will be ours. Of course, the very people who promote this ideal are themselves mesmerized by it, otherwise they would never try to delude others into embracing it. According to Kasser's findings, these attempts at mass, global hypnosis are proving effective:

> The percentage of students who believe that it is very important or essential to "develop a meaningful philosophy of life" decreased from over 80 percent in the late 1960s to around 40 percent in the late 1990s. At the same time, the percentage who believe that it is very important or essential to "be very well off financially" has risen from just over 40 percent to over 70 percent. Society's value-making machine is an effective one.

If we ponder the ends we have pursued, the ways we have expended our energy over the course of our lives, we may find that an enormous amount of effort has been directed toward the pursuit of these Eight Mundane Concerns. But aren't these pursuits merely skating on the surface of happiness? Isn't there also a kind of happiness that has to do with our very way of being present in the world? If we feel we have very little self-worth, even if we are surrounded by a lot of nice things and nice people, it is very difficult to be happy. Ah, but notice also that there are people with extraordinary high self-esteem who are not happy. And for all the other sources of mundane happiness I've mentioned, there are people who have some or all of them, yet genuine happiness eludes them. If we carefully inspect these means of pursuing happiness, we'll see that none of them are either necessary or sufficient. Over the years, I have known many people with no financial security, poor health, and none of the other trappings of the "good life," and yet they have found happiness and meaning in their lives.

If all of those mundane things are neither necessary nor sufficient for the actualization of happiness, what's left over? What is necessary and sufficient? The Buddhist answer is Dharma, which can be defined as a way of viewing reality and leading one's life that results in genuine happiness. Does this mean that all mundane concerns are worthless, and everything aside from the cultivation of wisdom and compassion is irrelevant? If we pursue happiness in ways that are unrelated to virtue, genuine happiness, and understanding, I would answer yes. Even when we turn to spiritual practice, this too can be used in the pursuit of mundane concerns. We may meditate, for example, simply for the immediate sense of relaxation, inner peace, or happiness it may bring. In this way meditation serves as little more than a spiritual proxy for the array of drugs the pharmaceutical industry has created to chemically alter the brain. We may also engage in acts of service in order to win other people's praise, love, and respect, which means we are still pursuing mundane concerns with a thin veneer of Dharma. During the spring and summer of 1980, I lived in solitary retreat in a cabin in the mountains above Dharamsala, India, with a loose-knit community of Tibetan yogis as my neighbors. That was when I first met Gen Lamrimpa, who had been meditating in solitude for about twenty years at that time. He told me that even seasoned recluses could fall into the trap of trying to impress their benefactors with how austere and pure they were as meditators. That wish to gain the admiration of others, he said, is one of the most tenacious of all the mundane concerns.

Some Tibetan lamas go so far as to declare that if any aspect of your spiritual practice is tainted by mundane concerns, it is a waste of time. But it's important not to feel overwhelmed by this ideal. One friend of mine, on recently hearing such a statement, phoned me saying that he felt demolished: "I feel now my whole spiritual practice is worth nothing because I still like movies and I still like to go out with women, and I still like a lot of mundane pleasures." But then he brought these concerns to his lama, and the gentle response was: "Slowly, slowly."

What *are* these mundane things are good for? They are good for *supporting* spiritual practice by providing us with the necessities and simple pleasures of life. We get derailed only when we take them as ends in and of themselves. We must be careful because when life is going very well, when we are prosperous and "the living is easy," spiritual practice can easily seem like a luxury, not a necessity. As the philosopher Alfred North Whitehead observed, "Religion is tending to degenerate into a decent formula where-with to embellish a comfortable life." Devoting oneself to spiritual practice, to the very meaning of life, can appear to be a luxury that we try to insert in the midst of very busy and generally agreeable lives.

Buddhists have an antidote to the obsession with mundane concerns and the mesmerizing slogans of our materialistic society: be satisfied with that which is merely adequate. But how do we determine that? What is adequate in terms of material possessions? How much entertainment is enough? How much luxury? The answer emerges from the very nature of spiritual practice. It is the pursuit of enlightenment; that is the guideline to our desires. By meditating on what we desire above all else, what is paramount in importance, we can discover what is adequate and what are only ephemera.

Cultivating loving-kindness has everything to do with the pursuit of enlightenment. And in Buddhist practice one begins with loving-kindness for oneself. This is a very deep practice, one that requires a kind of vision quest: what is your vision of happiness? What is genuine happiness, which yields "the good life," and also the possibility of dying well—"the good death"? And if there is continuity of individual consciousness beyond our present life, what does that entail? What is your vision of happiness in the long-term? It is the Dalai Lama's view that loving-kindness and compassion are inborn, not something we acquire just from the environment, from good training or education. They are intrinsic to our very identity, to the nature of awareness itself. Nevertheless, these innate qualities can be and often are muted and obscured. Accepting that premise, you can resort to them in times of difficulty, as you would take refuge in trustworthy friends.

Practice

Our first meditation session was a personal vision quest, posing the question: Wherein lies my happiness? Now let's extend ourselves a little further. In preparation, settle your body and mind in a state of relaxation, stillness, and clarity, and follow your breaths for twenty-one counts, with your eyes partially open.

Once again symbolically imagine the purity of your own pristine awareness, your own buddha-nature, as an orb of radiant, purifying light, a quarter-inch in diameter in the center of your chest. Imagine this light to be one of boundless, unconditional love and of happiness. With each in-breath, imagine drawing forth this light at your heart as if you were pumping water from a well. And with each out-breath imagine the light suffusing all aspects of your being, every cell of your body.

Now, in your mind's eye, in the space in front of you, bring to mind as vividly as you can a person whom you hold dear, in whom it is very easy to find loveable qualities. Recall the wonderful qualities of this person that are exhibited day in and day out, time and time again. Vividly picture a person who displays such goodness.

Now bring to mind and empathetically engage with this person's yearnings. What does this person hope for from life? What is this person's vision of happiness? And just as you wish for your own happiness, your own fulfillment, so include this person in the sphere of your loving-kindness with the yearning, "May you find the fulfillment you seek. May you find happiness and the sources of happiness." And with each out-breath, imagine light emanating from your heart, flowing out—a light of bounty, a light of loving-kindness. From breath to breath, imagine this person's dearest longings being fulfilled. Picture this person, or a community of such people, finding the happiness that they seek.

Now bring vividly to mind another person whom you know well, but for whom you have no special attachment or aversion, no special sense of closeness or distance. If this person were to move away, it would have very little impact on your life or your thoughts. You might even take this person's death with equanimity. It would be a little ripple in your own life, nothing more. Bring this person vividly to mind. How easy it is to see others, especially those to whom we are indifferent, as mere surfaces, as ciphers, as things. But now imagine being this person. Imagine this person's life, this person's hopes and fears, every bit as textured, as multilayered, as rich and diverse—the yearnings just as passionate, the fears just as poignant—as those of your own and your closest friends. Recognize the profound similarity between yourself and this person. With each out-breath, send forth the light of loving-kindness and the heartfelt wish: "May you, like myself and my closest loved ones, find the happiness you seek. May you tap into the very wellsprings of happiness itself." And with each out-breath, as this light from your heart embraces and saturates this person, imagine this individual finding the happiness and fulfillment he or she seeks.

Next bring to mind a person who has done you harm or even taken satisfaction in your misfortune. At the same time realize that all such harmful attitudes and behaviors, motivated by mental afflictions such as malice, fundamentally stem from ignorance and delusion. See if you can include this person too in the field of your loving-kindness, wishing with each out-breath: "May you be free of these sources of sorrow and pain. And may you too, like myself, be well and happy. May you discover for yourself the wellsprings of genuine happiness."

Now expand this field of light from your body and your heart, expand it in all directions evenly, all-inclusively. With each out-breath send forth this light of loving-kindness with the yearning: "May all beings like myself experience happiness and the sources of happiness." And with your Dharma-vision imagine it to be so.

Finally, release the imagination, release all objects from the mind with a sense of complete abandon, of profound relaxation. Let your awareness come to rest, settling in its own nature.

For Further Contemplation

Our culture is very action-oriented: "Get out there and *do* something!" This is a society that values efficiency, speed, and productivity, with constant references to the "cash value" of things and even the "financial worth" of people. While there's a lot to be said for pragmatism and efficiency, another tradition that persists to this day—Buddhism—suggests that the very best offering you can make to the world is yourself, as a person who embodies loving-kindness and expresses this open heart in daily life.

Milarepa, one of the great contemplatives and saints of Tibet, spent most of his life as a solitary yogi living in radical simplicity in the Himalayas, possessing none of the mundane trappings of happiness; he simply *found* happiness itself. So one day Milarepa was meditatively cultivating loving-kindness in his cave. Drawing it from the depths of his being, he created a field of loving-kindness all around him. As he was meditating there quietly, a hunter nearby was tracking down a deer, his dog in hot pursuit. The deer, running for its life, almost on its last legs, saw Milarepa, ran to him, and took refuge in his gentle presence, collapsing at the yogi's feet.

The dog, probably one of those savage Tibetan mastiffs, came running up to the cave behind the deer. But as it drew near to Milarepa, it slowed and then lay down calmly next to the deer. Then in came the hunter. When the hunter saw what this holy man, Milarepa, had done—ruined a perfectly good hunt—he became enraged. Drawing an arrow from his quiver, he shot it at the man who spoiled his hunt, but his arrow mysteriously veered away. Coming closer to get a better shot, he let fly a second arrow, but this one, too, missed its mark. The hunter was astonished. Why weren't his arrows flying true? Finally, he too drew nearer and his wrath subsided. He experienced the loving-kindness of another and thus his Dharma practice began. As the Buddha declared, "Animosity is never quelled with animosity. Animosity is quelled only with the absence of animosity. This is an ancient truth." This may sound like a fable, but I have met people who could immediately transform people's lives with their love. Maybe you have as well. It is a quality we can all cultivate, and there is no greater gift we can make to the world.

But how does one determine what is genuine loving-kindness as opposed to mere facsimiles, or counterfeits, of loving-kindness? Whether you call it *loving-kindness*, or *love*, the genuine item always arises in relation *between* beings, subject to subject. It involves engaging with the subjective reality of another person—with his or her joys and sorrows, hopes and fears, similar to your own—and then yearning, "May you, like me, be happy." In contrast, the mental affliction of attachment, as it is defined in Buddhism, entails a subject-to-object relationship, what the Jewish existentialist Martin Buber called an "I-it" relationship. In Buddhism *attachment* also implies viewing another sentient being as a means to one's own gratification. Let me define this more precisely: attachment is an attraction for an object on which one conceptually superimposes or exaggerates desirable qualities, while filtering out undesirable qualities. This has various manifestations including craving, obsession, addiction, and self-centered desire.

It is important to recognize that the Buddhist notion of *attachment* differs from the way the term is used in modern psychology, where it often has positive attributes, as in the sense of the bonding exemplified in the close and nurturing parent-child relationship. In the Buddhist context, attachment is the counterfeit of loving-kindness. It often takes on the guise of loving-kindness, or presents itself as the real thing. It will often call itself *love*, and it will mimic love. And we can delude ourselves and others into thinking it is love, whereas in fact it is tainted by a mental affliction: our attachment. In contrast, genuine love, or loving-kindness, taps into the source of happiness itself.

Attachment, insofar as it dominates the mind, is a radical disempowerment of the individual experiencing it. If we are feeling attachment for another person as an object, we are superimposing or exaggerating that person's attractive qualities, then desiring and craving her, while filtering out her other qualities. This is a process of dehumanization. We turn the person into a desirable object, as so often happens in romantic relationships. When we do this, we are hinging our happiness, our well-being, the fulfillment of our hopes, on something over which we have little or no control. This sets us up for anxiety and fear, and primes us for hostility, aggression, jealousy, and possibly violence—more misery for everyone involved.

The crucial distinction to be drawn between loving-kindness—a profoundly beneficial, innate quality of our own awareness—and attachment, which is an affliction that obscures the deepest nature of our being, is that the former is based on reality and the latter is rooted in delusion. We commonly observe how attachment can so easily flip over into anger and aggression. Loving-kindness doesn't do that. Love doesn't easily turn into hate.

The opposite of loving-kindness is hatred. While loving-kindness is defined as the heartfelt yearning that others experience happiness and the sources of happiness, hatred is disengaged from everyone's happiness, including our own. It is troubling even to think that we experience this at times. It is even sadder to see it dominate the mind and realize that we would actually take satisfaction if someone experienced humiliation, loss, misery, and disgrace. Hatred is diametrically opposed to loving-kindness, its exact opposite, and in fact is an obstacle to the genuine happiness we seek.

As you cultivate loving-kindness, are there any road signs indicating your success, giving you encouragement? The most reliable sign is seeing that your tendencies toward hostility and hatred decline even when you are treated badly. It is easy to be free of hatred when people are treating you well. But when you are treated with thoughtlessness, duplicity, or even malice—when you are the recipient of injustice, pettiness, selfishness, spitefulness, jealousy, and so forth—if you can respond without hatred, that is an indication that your heart is growing in loving-kindness.

When cultivating any of the Four Immeasurables, including loving-kindness, the challenge is to do so evenly, to have our loving-kindness flow out to others like water over an even surface. Our loving-kindness doesn't flow just to the nice people and skip over those whose behavior is disagreeable. It is easy to feel loving-kindness for friends and close relatives. But what do we do when we encounter people exhibiting profoundly unlovable behavior? Why not start with ourselves? Can we love ourselves when we see our own displays of unlovable behavior? In those moments it is time not for unrealistic optimism or mere realism, but for Dharma vision. Can you love yourself—the one who is acting in unlovable ways, acting out of hurt, acting out of confusion, yet at the same time yearning for happiness, wanting to be free of suffering—can you love that one? Why not accept this possibility as a working hypothesis and see what happens? Our lives are so terribly limited when we assume otherwise.

The cultivation of loving-kindness succeeds when it makes animosity subside, and it fails when it produces afflictive attachment. We begin by learning to love ourselves, with clear awareness of our limitations and imperfections, and in so doing, we release self-hatred and low self-esteem. Such animosity toward ourselves, with which we can never forgive ourselves for our own failings, is abandoned. Yet it is not replaced by attachment, or an inflated sense of self-worth and self-importance. We come to relate to ourselves with gentle, nonjudgmental acceptance, and we extend this loving heart to all those around us, who, like ourselves, wish to find happiness.

9

Compassion

COMPASSION IS THE ROOT of the Buddhadharma. This was the motivating force that aroused the Buddha from his solitary meditation under the Bodhi Tree and inspired him to lead others to a lasting state of genuine happiness. Immeasurable compassion is the aspiration, "May all beings be free of suffering and its causes." With this cultivation of compassion, called *karuna* in Sanskrit, we address the second of the Four Immeasurables. The Buddhist *mudra*, or hand gesture, symbolizing meditative equipoise is one in which the left hand, palm facing upward, symbolizing wisdom, supports the right hand, also with palm facing upward, representing compassion. The two hands join at the thumbs, making for the union of wisdom and compassion. In this *mudra* of meditative equipoise the compassion is not just a sentiment, a friendly feeling; it is the natural expression of wisdom.

I have experienced such compassion from my Buddhist teachers many times over the years. When, at the age of twenty-four, I felt the urge to withdraw from the philosophical training I was receiving in a traditional Tibetan Buddhist monastery in Dharamsala, the Dalai Lama kindly encouraged me to pursue my wish to devote myself wholeheartedly to meditation. Years later, when I was finding life as a Buddhist monk in the West untenable, he gently gave his permission to return my monastic vows, with the option of becoming a monk later in life if I chose to do so. Time and again throughout the decades of my spiritual practice, I have found my teachers to be consistently understanding, nonjudgmental, and compassionate in guiding me along the path to genuine happiness. It has been their unwavering kindness as much as the wisdom of their teachings that has provided me with a constant source of inspiration and confidence in this path.

Practice

Before meditating, bring forth your highest motivation, your most meaningful goals and yearnings. Now settle your body in a posture of ease, stillness, and vigilance. Remember the sequence. For this session, lasting one *ghatika*, let your body be still. You'll be bringing images to mind, like reflections in a pool of water. Reflections are clear only if the water is still. Take three luxurious, deep, full breaths, breathing through your nostrils, breathing down into the abdomen, then expanding the diaphragm and finally breathing up through the chest. Exhale through the nostrils, slowly, deeply, and fully, three times.

Now let this mind, which has been driven so hard through the day, come to rest and settle back into a mode of simple awareness. Feel the tactile sensations throughout your body. If thoughts come, just let them float away without sticking, without your grasping. Release them as if with a sigh of relief, thinking, "I don't need to catch that particular train." Be aware of breathing. At the beginning of the next in-breath, mentally and very briefly count "one." Then, in a mode of simple awareness, continue to attend to the breathing, counting to twenty-one.

Now let's again call into play the power of the imagination. Move out of this mode of simple awareness, away from stilling the mind, and bring forth your powers of creative thought. Let's begin with the body. Affirm to yourself if you will—as a working hypothesis, if not something you've experienced directly—the essential purity of your awareness. This dimension of consciousness is conceptually unstructured, primordially pure, and of the nature of sheer luminosity. And imagine it now, in symbolic form, as an orb of inexhaustible, radiant white light at your heart in the center of your chest. In Indian thought this area—not in the heart organ, but in the center of your chest—is called the heart *chakra*.

Imagine this light to be one of compassion, of goodness, of joy—utterly and primordially pure. Imagine rays of white light—purifying, soothing, and calming white light—emanating from this orb at your heart and saturating your entire body, right out to the pores of your skin, dispelling all mental and physical afflictions and imbalances.

Now extend the imagination outward and bring to mind, as vividly as you can, another being—this could be one or more persons, or it could be an animal or some other sentient being—someone about whom you care very deeply. Direct your attention to someone who is going through a very difficult time right now. It could be because of physical afflictions or disease, a life situation of conflict, depression, anxiety, or pain. Bring that person to mind.

Now imagine you are this person. Picture yourself undergoing these same problems. Imagine taking on this person's burden. Now return to yourself and then again attend to this loved one. As the Buddha counseled, attend to this person internally, externally, and both internally and externally. Then, with a sincere, natural, effortless yearning, bring to mind the wish: "May you be free of this suffering and the true sources of this suffering." Allow compassion to rise from your heart. Then, as you inhale, imagine taking in, in the symbolic form of a dark cloud, the problems, the disease, the mental turmoil, whatever it may be that troubles this person. Imagine this as a dark cloud, and with each inhalation draw in this cloud as if you're siphoning it off. Draw it in, breathe it down to this incandescent orb of light at your heart, and let this darkness be extinguished there, without leaving a trace behind. Imagine the dark cloud dissipating with each in-breath, lightening. Imagine this person's burden, sorrow, illness—whatever it may be—lightening as well. Imagine the person's relief.

With each in-breath let this yearning arise: "Just as I wish to be free of suffering and the sources of suffering, may you too be free of this pain, free of this distress and its causes. Imagine the person actually experiencing this transformation, feeling the burden lighten, and breathing more easily. And if there is fear, imagine that fear being calmed.

Then imagine the cloud utterly vanishing, the darkness dispelled, not transferred but drawn in and extinguished. Just as when you turn on a light in a dark room, the darkness doesn't go anywhere; it simply vanishes. Imagine this person free of affliction and experiencing a sense of complete ease and profound relief.

Now expand the field of your awareness, recognizing that if this person is a loved one for you, so the entire world is filled with individuals who are loved ones for others. Recognize that all beings are worthy of love. Bring to mind in this broad, all-encompassing way all the countless individuals like yourself who are beset with troubles and anxieties, fears, and physical suffering. Expand your awareness without limit to exclude no one, from all sides, from above and below, with each in-breath. Let your yearning arise: "May each individual in the world, like myself, be free of suffering and the sources of suffering." With each in-breath draw in the misery and distress, the pain and the fear of each sentient being. Draw it into this infinite light, this inexhaustible source of light that can hold the suffering of the world and not be dimmed. Draw it in and extinguish the darkness in the light of your own heart. The nature of compassion is just this: the heartfelt yearning that others might be free of suffering and the sources of suffering.

Now, for a few moments, release your imagination, release thoughts and aspirations, release all objects of the mind. Rest in the simple nature of your own awareness. Be at ease from your very core. Rest your mind in its own pristine and luminous nature. Simply be aware of being aware.

For Further Contemplation

In his book *The Art of Happiness*, the Dalai Lama defines compassion as "a state of mind that is nonviolent, nonharming, and nonaggressive. It is a mental attitude based on the wish for others to be free of their suffering and is associated with a sense of commitment, responsibility, and respect toward the other." It arises from a feeling called in Tibetan *tsewa*, for which the closest translation may be simply "heartfelt caring," which he views as the most fundamental of human emotions. When compassion fills our hearts, we cannot bear the suffering of others, for we feel it as if it were our own. What we attend to is our reality, and if we truly attend to the reality of others' suffering, a compassionate sense of caring arises spontaneously. Just think of your own immediate response if you see someone being carried helplessly down a raging river, calling out for help. Your heartfelt wish to come to this person's aid isn't acquired by learning. It's innate. It's your deepest impulse, one of caring.

The Buddhist tradition recognizes three levels of compassion:

1. For those experiencing suffering and pain
2. For those fixated on mundane concerns in their pursuit of happiness
3. For those grasping onto a false sense of "I" and "mine"

One thing we all share in common is our experience of pain and suffering, and recognizing this can bring us together, caring about others' difficulties as we do about our own. The Dalai Lama comments:

> In the same way that physical pain unifies our sense of having a body, we can conceive of the general experience of suffering acting as a unifying force that connects us with others. Perhaps that is the ultimate meaning behind our suffering. *It is our suffering that is the most basic element that we share with others, the factor that unifies us with all living creatures.*

The notion of a unity underlying all beings is a theme that runs through all the great spiritual traditions of the world. Shantideva expressed this in terms of the metaphor of the one body of all beings:

> Although it has many divisions, such as its arms and so on, the body is protected as a whole. Likewise, different beings, with their joys and sorrows, are all equal, like myself, in their yearning for happiness.

It is so hard, though, to open our hearts to the suffering of others, for we can easily feel overwhelmed and helpless, especially with the exposure we have to the world's suffering by way of the media. But Shantideva grappled with this same issue more than a millennium ago and came to this conclusion:

> I must eliminate the suffering of others because it is suffering, just like my own suffering. I should take care of others because they are sentient beings, just as I am a sentient being.
>
> As there is no owner of miseries, there are no distinctions among them all. They are to be dispelled because they are suffering. What is the use of restrictions there?

A second level of compassion arises for people who may not be experiencing suffering right now, but who, out of delusion, are leading their lives in ways that can't possibly result in genuine happiness, only in more dissatisfaction, misery, and fear. These are people who still believe that the happiness they are seeking can be found in fulfilling their materialistic aims of greater wealth, power, luxury, praise, and respect from others. All too often they express no qualms about engaging in the most selfish, devious, and heartless acts to gain the success they strive for. Rather than responding to such people (including ourselves at times) with contempt, dismissal, or hatred, a more realistic response is compassion: may they be free of suffering and the causes of suffering.

The third and deepest level of compassion attends to the reality of all unenlightened beings falsely grasping onto a deluded sense of "I" and "mine," as we struggle to acquire all kinds of material, aesthetic, intellectual, and even spiritual goods for ourselves in this dog-eat-dog, every-man-for-himself world. We seek our own happiness as something independent of everyone else's well-being. But we don't exist independently of others, so how can our happiness possibly be independent? When we attend to the reality of other beings as subjects like ourselves, we enter into an "I-you" relationship with them, as opposed to the manipulative, exploitative "I-it" relationships that are driven by mental afflictions. Beyond that, in the terminology of Martin Buber, we may ascend to an "I-thou" relationship, in which the distinction between "self" and "other" is transcended. This is where compassion is fully united with wisdom, and our false sense of isolation is overcome.

A spiritual practice based exclusively on either wisdom or on compassion is like a bird fluttering about in circles with only one wing. With the Four Applications of Mindfulness we cultivate wisdom, and with the Four Immeasurables we cultivate compassion, the two "wings to enlightenment." I have met many people working in service to others, and many of them—including health-care professionals, teachers, environmental activists, and social workers—become overwhelmed by the suffering and evils they encounter. In such a situation, how can we care deeply, and how can we continue to serve without burning out? When asked this question, the Dalai Lama has responded with one word: wisdom. Wisdom is what enables us to go back to the source, to bear the suffering and regain the power of the spirit, strength of mind, and strength of heart, called in Tibetan *semshuk*. A life of compassionate service needs the strength and support of wisdom, which allows us to draw from the deep source of genuine happiness within each one of us. The kinds of wisdom and insight I am referring to are those explained in parts two and four of this book.

At times, we may find it difficult to love our fellow men and women, for they don't always act in lovable ways. How do we bring forth genuine love and compassion for people who behave badly? We seem to hit a brick wall there. But this obstacle is located not in other people's attitudes or conduct, but in our own hearts and minds. We fail to view others with compassion because our own minds have come under the influence of *kleshas*, those poisonous mental afflictions. A fundamental premise of Buddhism is that the natural state of your mind is one of pure luminosity. But when afflictions infect the mind, they cause the mind to become contorted or twisted. The trigger may be the memory of someone treating us badly. Or it may be greed or craving. Fear often plays a part. These are *kleshas*. A mind that malevolently inflicts suffering on others is always under the domination of *kleshas*. Let's take a daring step and see if we can imagine cultivating compassion for those who are sowing the seeds of suffering and not just for those who are reaping the harvest of suffering.

Practice

Begin by settling the body and mind in their natural state, and direct mindfulness to the respiration, counting twenty-one breaths to make the mind serviceable. Now symbolically affirm the essential purity of your own heart, your own awareness itself: undisturbed, uncontaminated by mental afflictions, primordially pure, filled with a truth-given joy, a joy rooted in reality itself. Again imagine this symbolically as a ball of radiant, pure, glistening white light, a light of purity and purification, a light of compassion, a light of forgiveness. Imagine this light suffusing your body and mind. Imagine it purifying, dispelling—in the way light dispels darkness—all the impurities in the body and all afflictions and distortions of the mind.

Think of an individual or group of individuals who are right now subject to mental afflictions, whether delusion, anger, selfishness, greed, or stupidity. Think of people who may be bent on acting from these mental afflictions, thinking they are doing the right thing while being dead wrong about it. Rather, they are actively bringing harm to those around them, maybe even taking delight in doing so, thinking that it is somehow justified.

Imagine yourself being this person or group of people. Slip into his or her skin, then back into yours. Imagine being subject to the same mental afflictions that are at the source of these streams of harmful behavior. Imagine being a person who is sowing the seeds of his or her own grief and misery in pursuit of happiness.

Now move back to your own body and reengage with this other human (or group) who, like yourself, is looking for happiness and wishes to be free from suffering and fear. Imagine, with each in-breath, taking in this cloud of delusion, this cloud of whatever the evil may be, and the afflictions behind it. With each in-breath and with the yearning "May you be free," think: Whether right now you feel well or miserable, may you be free of the source of suffering. As you, like myself, wish to be free, so may you be free.

With each in-breath, as you did before, imagine drawing this darkness into your heart. With each inhalation draw it in, and as you exhale, imagine it utterly vanishing, consumed like a feather in a bonfire, extinguished. Imagine the sources of suffering disappearing. Imagine the cloud being dispelled, breath by breath. And imagine his or her relief as the mind is healed, returning to a serene equilibrium, a state of balance, a state of tranquility and well-being.

Now expand the scope of your awareness to embrace every individual in this world, everyone like yourself, yearning for happiness and freedom from suffering. Think of how you have often erred in your pursuit of happiness and how deluded you can become in trying to free yourself from suffering and fear. Imagine the darkness, the ignorance and delusion and all other mental afflictions to which we all succumb. And with each in-breath and with the yearning, "May we all be free, may all sentient beings be free of suffering and the sources of suffering," take in and extinguish this darkness in the fathomless light of the utter purity of awareness. Imagine the world's burden being alleviated and imagine all beings are truly free, not only from suffering, but from the underlying sources of suffering.

Now, just for a moment, release the yearning, release the imagination, release your mind, and rest in a simple state of awareness that is prior to the mind's arising. Come deeply to rest in the nature of your own awareness.

Bring the meditation to a close. As you began by cultivating the most meaningful motivation you could, now close the practice with this dedication. May whatever benefit has been produced by this practice be dedicated to the fulfillment of your most meaningful aspirations for yourself and for all those around you.

For Further Contemplation

In 1992, I was working with a group of neuroscientists collaborating with Tibetan yogis in the mountains above Dharamsala in northern India, studying the nature and effects of compassion. The most senior contemplative we visited was Geshe Yeshe Thubtop, aged sixty-nine, who had been meditatively cultivating compassion while living in retreat for the past twenty-three years. We asked him, "When you experience compassion, do you experience sadness?" If he did, it would imply that the deeper the compassion you experience, the greater the misery. And if you experienced boundless compassion, this would be accompanied by boundless misery. The yogi replied, "When you first witness a child who is suffering, your immediate experience is one of sadness. But then this emotion is displaced by the yearning, 'How can I help? Does the child need food? Shelter? What can be done to alleviate the child's suffering?' This is when true compassion arises, and when it is present, the previous sadness vanishes." Sorrow comes with empathy, sadness at feeling the suffering and sources of suffering of another person. That is not compassion, but it can be the catalyst for compassion. That is the fuel that may give rise to the light of compassion.

Without empathy, there is no compassion. There may be some external semblance of compassion, but it may be nothing more than pity. Empathy is a shared experience of others' joys and sorrows, their happiness and pain. Perhaps even the duality of self and other vanishes and you merge with the other person, feeling his or her suffering as if it were your own. This empathetic suffering can stir your compassion. Compassion calls for a kind of courage, or inner strength. The lion of compassion is aroused from its den by the suffering of empathy, and it strides forth in its majesty with this yearning: "May you be free of suffering and the sources of suffering."

But compassion doesn't stop there. It's more than an emotion; it asks, "And what can I do?" In some cases there is something tangible you can do to relieve someone's suffering. But in those cases where there is little or nothing you can do on an immediate, practical level, you can go back to your meditation and cultivate compassion. In this way you can move toward enlightenment, which will enable you to become more and more effective in your abilities to alleviate the suffering of the world by fully tapping into your inner resources of wisdom, compassion, and creative energy. That's the reason to become enlightened, not so you can walk on water or achieve clairvoyance. When you are aroused to relieve the suffering of others, the lion of your heart comes out of its den, transcends the sadness of empathy, and works to relieve the distress of others.

What are the impediments to compassion? At what point do we decide that certain people are excluded from our compassion? I think many of us reach the limit of our compassion when we see people who are subjecting others to suffering—by malice, cruelty, selfishness, greed, stupidity, and so on. We look at these perpetrators of suffering, people harming other beings in myriad ways, and we feel, "Sorry, this is where I draw the line. These people are not worthy of compassion." Here is where insight is crucial. It doesn't require much insight to cultivate compassion for children who are suffering, or the victims or survivors of a disaster. But wisdom and insight are indispensable in order to cultivate compassion for those who are inflicting suffering on others. Without compassion for them, our hearts remain bounded by our own ignorance and delusion.

This gives compassion a broader meaning. It isn't just a warm, cuddly feeling. It doesn't mean mere sympathy. In our society, we commonly equate compassion with feeling sorry for others. We feel sorry for AIDS victims and those suffering from genocide, ethnic cleansing, terrorism, poverty, and all the other adversities. But feeling sorry for someone is not compassion. Feeling sorry is just feeling sad, with no drive to action. We don't go on from there to a heartfelt yearning: "May you be free of suffering and the sources of suffering." Sorrow alone, then, is a poor facsimile of compassion, counterfeit compassion.

As we cultivate compassion, a sign of success is seeing that our capacity for cruelty, which is the opposite of compassion, subsides. When any inclination toward cruelty, any yearning to inflict pain, any inkling to rejoice in the misery of other people (the people we don't like), subsides, that is a sure sign that compassion is increasing.

A step beyond that is to feel genuine compassion for those who are cruel. What if we can yearn for the ethnic cleansers and terrorists of the world to be free of the inner sources of the suffering, which cause them to inflict pain upon others and on themselves? If so, we have penetrated a deeper level of compassion. To my mind the fastest route to cutting through the mental afflictions that stifle compassion is to ask, "Why is the person behaving this way?"

When we understand deeply that people engage in evil due to their own ignorance and delusion, we open the floodgates of forgiveness. Compassion then flows all the more powerfully to racists, terrorists, and others who passionately devote themselves to vicious acts of cruelty. How on earth could they do that if they really knew what they were doing? On several occasions I had the privilege of interpreting for a Tibetan monk named Palden Gyatso, who was tortured in prison by the Chinese Communists over a period of thirty-three years. He described his extraordinary life in his book *The Autobiography of a Tibetan Monk*. It was clear from his descriptions that the people who were torturing him felt this was for the greater good. They did not feel that they were doing something essentially evil. No, it was justified for them: "It may look bad, but you don't see the bigger picture. It's just one of those tough jobs that must be done, and this job has fallen to me." Those who perpetrate such cruelty lack knowledge of the true sources of happiness and the true sources of misery and grief and conflict. Out of that unknowing, that lack of clarity, lack of wisdom, comes delusion—the misapprehension of reality—and all the evils of the world stem from that.

Although we may not be ethnic cleansers, there are times when we injure those around us through our thoughts, our speech, and our physical behavior. We often do those things out of delusion catalyzed by fear—fear of losing our livelihood, fear of losing our comforts, fear of losing things that provide us with imagined security. We fear, and out of delusion we retaliate. No one chooses delusion or ignorance. No one deliberately chooses stupidity over intelligence, delusion over wisdom. When asked, "Would you like to be fearless, courageous, and bold, or would you like to be timid, filled with anxiety and fear?" no one responds, "Fear looks pretty good." We don't choose such things; we succumb to them. So it is crucial to distinguish between mental afflictions and the mentally afflicted, rather than lumping them together, identifying people with their mental afflictions. With empathy and compassion we can see, as a doctor sees: here is the patient, and here's the disease. They are not identical; otherwise patients could never be healed, they could only be quarantined. Distinguish between mental afflictions and the mentally afflicted, beginning with yourself. By relinquishing our judgmental tendency to condemn others and ourselves for our limitations and defects, we open up our innate capacity for compassion that excludes no one. Only then do our hearts become immeasurable.

10

Empathetic Joy and Equanimity

SHORTLY AFTER I MOVED to Amherst, Massachusetts, following a four-year period primarily devoted to solitary meditation, I had the privilege of serving as interpreter for Tara Rinpoche, a senior Tibetan lama who was teaching at the American Institute of Buddhist Studies, founded by Robert Thurman. He was a wise and loving man, and a great help to me as I began to integrate my years of studying and practicing Buddhism with life in the modern West. I especially remember his comments on two ways of cultivating unconditional love and compassion, free of bias toward those who are near and far. One way, he said, was epitomized in the monastic ideal, where the monk disengages from his biological family and seeks to view all beings equally, as if they were his mothers and fathers, brothers and sisters. He begins with the even view of seeking to care for everyone in the same way, relinquishing the attachment of thinking, These people are my family and these are my close friends, whereas the rest are outside my inner circle of loved ones. With that starting point of impartiality, the monk's challenge is to care more deeply for everyone, viewing them all as his kin.

The second way, Rinpoche taught, is to begin with the ideal of being a loving spouse and parent, with unconditional love and compassion toward your own family. Even if your spouse or children occasionally behave in harmful ways, instead of distancing yourself from them, you lovingly care about them all the more, seeing ways you can help them back to the path of Dharma. This approach begins with special concern—it may well be mixed with attachment—for your own family. But as your spiritual practice deepens, you extend this quality of nonjudgmental affection for an ever-growing circle of people whom you encounter. You begin to view your colleagues at work and even total strangers with the same love that you feel toward your own family and friends. They too wish for happiness and freedom from suffering, and are therefore equally deserving of having their deepest yearnings fulfilled. So in this way, you begin with greater closeness to your family and friends, but over time the field of your love and compassion becomes immeasurable, embracing all beings equally, with no sense of attachment or aversion toward anyone. While the starting point for the monk and the layperson is different, the end point is the same.

Practice

Let's begin this session following the important tradition of first bringing to mind our highest aspirations. What do we seek from life? What do we seek from our spiritual practice, for ourselves and for those around us?

Then settle your body and mind, as you've done so many times previously, by establishing a proper posture. Learn the routine well: find a posture in which you can quietly sit at ease. Your chest is raised, your shoulders are relaxed, the muscles of your face and your eyes are soft. To complete this process, take three slow, deep inhalations, breathing through the nostrils and down into the abdomen. During the inhalation first expand the abdomen, then the diaphragm, and finally let the breath rise into the chest. When you reach almost full capacity, release through your nostrils, freeing the breath luxuriously, releasing with it the tensions of the body and the mind.

For this session let's go back to the basics, back to cultivating balanced attention, meditative equipoise, quiescence. Arouse your awareness and allow your attention to suffuse the entire field of tactile sensations throughout the body, from the top of your head down to the soles of your feet. Be physically present. Continue breathing, but now normally, with unforced respiration. Let your abdomen be soft and relaxed so that even with a shallow in-breath you have the sense of the air going down deep, slightly expanding the abdomen, then deflating during the out-breath. Let the respiration go at its own pace, without conscious intervention. It is unimportant whether your breathing is deep or shallow, whether the in-breath is longer than the out-breath or vice versa, whether on occasion there is a pause after the out-breath. Allow your nervous system—or in Buddhist terminology, the system of vital energies within your body, closely associated with the breath—to balance itself. And let your awareness rest in this field of tactile sensations, shifting from moment to moment in relation to the rhythm of the in- and out-breaths.

Now, as you begin to cultivate empathetic joy, the third of the Four Immeasurables, you will once again engage your discursive intelligence, memory, and imagination. Direct your attention first to your own life, focusing especially on those circumstances that bring you joy and contentment. If you enjoy good health, loving relationships with those around you, meaningful and satisfying work, or anything else that gives you happiness, in a spirit of gratitude, take delight in your own good fortune.

Then attend to the virtues of the heart and mind you have cultivated, and to moments when your speech and deeds have brought benefit to others. Such qualities and actions of the body, speech, and mind are the seeds of genuine happiness, and it is meaningful to rejoice in them. Encourage yourself in leading a meaningful life, and take satisfaction in those moments when you have lived your ideals.

Now bring to mind a dear friend who exudes a sense of good cheer and joy of living. Empathetically enter into his or her joy, taking delight in this person's happiness. Recall specific moments of delight in this person's life, and share them.

Recall now someone whom you know personally or only by reputation who embodies virtues you wish to emulate. Think of someone who expresses warmth and affection, whose mind is clear and bright, who is altruistically devoted to helping others, even in the smallest ways. Attend to several people, each exemplifying the practice of humility, kindness, generosity, and wisdom, and rejoice in the virtues that inspire us all.

Extend the scope of your awareness to include strangers and people with whom you have been in conflict, and in your mind's eye seek out their virtues, which are so easily overlooked or dismissed. Take delight in how seeds of virtue create the fruit of well-being. Once the field of your awareness has expanded without limit, release all thoughts and images and simply rest for a moment in the empty, luminous space of consciousness. Then bring the session to a close.

For Further Contemplation

Once you have begun to develop the first two of the Four Immeasurables—loving-kindness and compassion—you will find that empathetic joy and equanimity come quite naturally. Empathetic joy in particular is pertinent to our society and to the modern world we inhabit. This is due to our unprecedented access by way of the news media to the state of the world, especially to aspects that can give rise to sorrow, anxiety, depression, cynicism, fury, and despair. I saw recently a bumper sticker that read, "If you're not feeling outraged, you're not paying attention." It takes little imagination to realize what that driver was thinking. If we're wandering through life in a continuous state of outrage, however, we're probably more a part of the problem than we are a part of the solution. Recall the words of William James: "For the moment, what we attend to is reality." This goes for the view of the world we absorb through the media, for our experience of the immediate world around us, and also for our understanding of ourselves. How then can we possibly live with a realistic sense of well-being in a world in which there are so many causes for despair, fear, and anger?

One possibility is through the cultivation of empathetic joy, known as *mudita* in Sanskrit. In this practice, we are *looking* for specific people and events in which to rejoice. Because none of us can take in the whole of reality, we are always selecting our experienced reality by the kinds of things we look at and by how we look at them. We're always editing in and editing out, choosing what will be real for us, or having those choices made for us by the mass media and other powerful institutions.

Take the example of biases in the news media. The news tends to focus on all-too-familiar tragedies, crises, miseries, and evils in the world; that's what sells. In a world where there is so much conflict and suffering, exceptional acts of wisdom and compassion are the real news, but they receive scant coverage. So, as a result of the myopic media, we lose sight of the many virtues and joys in the world. They appear less real to us. In this practice, we seek to balance that out.

When cultivating empathetic joy, we deliberately choose to venture out with a *vivid attentiveness* to discover, "Where is there happiness and virtue in the world?" Of course it is relatively easy to experience empathetic joy with regard to someone close to you. If your child achieves a cherished goal or a friend is promoted to a fabulous job, empathetic joy comes naturally. But in this practice we try to expand the field of our delight in other people's happiness, in the joys and successes of strangers. As long as empathy is limited, and our joy is for some but skips over others; as long as our compassion and loving-kindness are only for a select few, these qualities of the heart are tainted by the afflictions of attachment and aversion. So what we're looking for here is *boundlessness*. When loving-kindness becomes immeasurable, excluding no one, that's what we call *unconditional love*. And when compassion becomes immeasurable, embracing everyone—the evil-doers and the victims—that's called *unconditional compassion*. Likewise, when empathetic joy reaches out like water spreading evenly over a plain, without bias, without prejudice, that's unconditional, boundless, empathetic joy.

Look around. It's not hard to find happiness. You can take delight in something as simple as a child walking down the street enjoying an ice cream cone, or munching contentedly on a pretzel. Rejoice in that child's happiness, and then you can rejoice in the happiness that has spread to you; there's nothing wrong with that. And don't exclude yourself from any of the Four Immeasurables, because then they wouldn't be immeasurable. Probing a little deeper, we notice that if it is meaningful and beneficial to rejoice in the *fruits* of happiness, then of course it is worthwhile to delight in the *seeds* of happiness.

Just as loving-kindness and compassion deepen when integrated with wisdom, so does empathetic joy. We can all remember times when we've experienced a sense of well-being not caused by any apparent outer stimuli. At those times the heart is full and warm. We laugh easily. There's a sense of gladness. We may ask, "What caused that?" With wisdom we can recognize that if the cause isn't outside, then it must be in the one place left over: our own minds.

Buddhist psychology is primarily concerned with understanding mental states that by their very nature give rise to happiness, as well as those that result in misery and conflict. The former are said to be wholesome, and the latter are afflictive. This is a question of causality within the context of human experience, not morality imposed on humanity by an outside, moral authority. When the mind is wholesome, it leads to a sense of happiness that arises from the mind's very nature. So when we witness people exhibiting wholesome mental states, speech, and physical conduct, we can take delight in that. And, if we wish, we can tell them, express our delight.

It doesn't take a dramatic event to trigger empathetic joy. Something as commonplace as simple courtesy could do it. This happened to me once on a plane trip from Mexico. I had misread the seating arrangement and took someone else's seat. Of course the person who had reserved the seat eventually showed up. When the flight attendant explained the mix-up, the person whose seat I had taken apologized quite sincerely for any trouble *he* might be causing *me*. And I, naturally, was sorry to have been the cause of the mix-up. It was no big deal, but the friendliness and courtesy I experienced was genuine and something to take joy in. Those kinds of things happen all the time. So when you run into them, do yourself a big favor: don't pass them by; pay attention to them. *If you're not taking delight in the good of the world, you're not paying attention.*

It is vital also to take delight in our own virtues. Whether your acts of kindness and wisdom are deliberate or spontaneous, take joy in the goodness you bring to the world. Many people have a tendency to downplay their own goodness, thinking that they should remain humble rather than be, or appear to be, self-satisfied. As such, they may overlook their own positive deeds and attributes. But Buddhism says this is inappropriate. After all, if it is worthwhile rejoicing in someone else's wholesome qualities and actions, then it is just as valuable for ourselves. In Buddhism it is said that the easiest and fastest way to empower our spiritual practice is to take delight in our own virtues.

By taking delight in virtuous actions, you empower the potency of that action so that it will bear greater fruit. The same applies to negative actions. When you consciously take delight in something harmful to others, it empowers that negative act. For example, if we enjoy making clever, sarcastic remarks to put others down, we empower the tendency for sarcasm. Likewise, feeling remorse about something, whether it was wholesome or unwholesome, attenuates the power of the action. So taking delight in our own happiness and in the causes of happiness for ourselves and others is a crucial element of spiritual practice. Only when our practice is filled with enthusiasm will it flourish over the long term, and the path to such joyful practice is to take delight in it from moment to moment.

We can take delight in those who devote themselves to spiritual practice, including those who withdraw temporarily into solitude, whether it's for a weekend retreat, one hour in meditation per day, a six-month retreat, or a twenty-five-year retreat. Why rejoice in that? If people withdraw from social interactions simply out of aversion or exhaustion, there's no particular value in that. But how about a person who occasionally withdraws for whatever period seems meaningful and appropriate in order to cultivate virtue, such as attentional balance, discerning mindfulness, love, and compassion? In the short term, it doesn't look like this person is doing anything for society. But such practice leads to psychological balance and spiritual maturation. Clearly that's worth something. When such people tap into their deepest inner resources of virtue and then return to "active duty" with greater kindness, clarity, and insight, they show the rest of us by example that we have everything we need within us right now to find the happiness we've been seeking.

I have known a number of Tibetan yogis who have spent decades in solitary meditative retreat. Yet many people in today's society look askance at such a reclusive lifestyle. When I entered my first sustained *shamatha* retreat in 1980, the Dalai Lama told me of one monk, living in retreat in Bhutan, who had fully accomplished *shamatha*. The monk then continued on to the practice of *vipashyana*, and one of the by-products of his practice was that after some time he found he could heal people of various diseases by his sheer presence. Soon he had to interrupt his meditative practice because people were lining up outside of his hut to be cured. I presume that his original motivation for practice was to heal his own mind of all afflictions, but—lo and behold—he found that his presence could spontaneously heal others of their physical afflictions. We admire people who go to medical school for years on end in order to heal the ill, and we can likewise rejoice when others devote themselves to rigorous, sustained contemplative practice in order to heal the mind of all its afflictions.

When practicing the Four Immeasurables, the focal point is neither the self nor others. Rather, the pervasive theme is "as for ourselves, so for others." There's a complete equality, a total evenness there. The cultivation of empathic joy is a wholesome, meaningful, satisfying practice, with no downside at all. Whether we consider ourselves or others, we take delight in the virtuous *action* itself. So the solution to the problem of selfishness is really pretty straightforward: none of the virtues that we occasionally embody or the wholesome activities in which we participate arise from a self-sufficient, autonomous ego. Such an ego doesn't exist in the first place. All of these virtues arise in dependence upon causes and conditions as dependently related events.

Consider your own most excellent qualities and ask yourself where they came from. They arose in relation to people who cared for you as you were cultivating these qualities. What was supporting you in all of this? What was preventing these qualities from being swept away or submerged? As we start to attend to that which gives rise to our virtues of body, speech, and mind, we find that *all of them* arise due to causes and conditions. In short, all virtues and joys depend on the kindness of others.

As we begin pondering that, we notice two things that go hand in hand. First, we can rejoice in those aspects of our own behavior that bring happiness to ourselves: "How wonderful that my way of life brings happiness to me and to those around me." Then we take a second look, asking where this all came from, starting with our parents, teachers, friends, and others who have assisted us. All of them together helped us cultivate whatever is good in our lives now. So we simultaneously take delight in the wholesomeness of our lives, and, with *gratitude,* rejoice in those who have supported it. And there's the antidote to any arrogance that might arise from our delight in our own virtues.

Choose for yourself the kind of reality you wish to inhabit. If you don't, bombardment with stimuli from the news media and so forth will force you to internalize a perspective that someone else has chosen for you. And that vision of reality is not necessarily in your best interests. When you see causes of happiness in others—some kindness here, a bit of courtesy there—pause and delight in that.

The poor facsimile, or false pretender, of empathetic joy is a kind of shallow, frivolous happiness that fixates on mundane pleasures. Instead of being perceived with empathy, others are viewed as objects who make us happy, who provide us with a "contact high." The opposite of empathetic joy is envy. If empathetic joy is taking delight in another person's success, virtues, and talents, then the opposite is being disgruntled, cynical, and envious of them. In this case, we look at other people's virtue and don't see it as such. Instead, we wonder, "What's their angle?" We're back to the idea of an "I-it" relation with others. This is an attitude that starts and ends in defeat. As the Dalai Lama has said, if you lose hope—if you fall into despair, which is another word for cynicism—then there's no chance of success, because you fail through your own attitude.

The proximate cause of empathetic joy is simply the awareness of other people's virtue and joy. So this practice is mainly one of learning to pay attention. If we really attend to other people's sorrow, compassion arises naturally. And if we attend to their happiness and success, empathetic joy is a natural response. The cultivation of empathetic joy succeeds when its opposites decline. We become less cynical, less envious. Rather than being disgruntled, we become, as P. G. Wodehouse quipped, "gruntled."

Practice

Begin this session, as before, by first settling your body, speech, and mind in their natural state, and then counting twenty-one breaths to help stabilize your mind. As you then proceed to the cultivation of equanimity, or impartiality, bring to mind your innate wish to be free of suffering and pain and to find happiness. We all care for ourselves and yearn for our own well-being, regardless of how we lead our lives. And when we pursue our own happiness at the expense of others, this is invariably due to mental afflictions that temporarily dominate our minds. We harm others, and finally ourselves, out of ignorance and delusion.

Now turn your attention to someone you know well or meet frequently, but about whom you care little. This person's success or adversity wouldn't likely have much effect on you. Let that sense of indifference emerge. Experience it and acknowledge it. Then attend closely to this person, not as an object, but as a subject, a sentient being like yourself. Imagine being this person and experiencing his or her hopes and fears, joys and sorrows. Knowing him or her to be fundamentally like yourself, regardless of all the superficial differences, empathetically yearn that this person's innermost desires be fulfilled, as if they were your own. Moving back and forth from your own perspective, viewing this person as "the other," and his or her perspective, viewing yourself as "the other," wish for this person's happiness and freedom from suffering and its causes.

Now bring to mind a person for whom you feel a strong attachment. Perhaps this is someone who has proven to be your strong friend and supporter, someone who has helped you find success or has given you much joy and comfort. Perhaps you simply admire this person for his or her own fine qualities, physical or mental, and find joy in being with him or her. This person is an object that brings you happiness, and so you respond with attachment. Let that sense of attachment, of self-centered desire, arise, noting how much this person means to you as a support for your own well-being. Now shift your perspective to this person's perspective; imagine being him or her and experiencing his or her hopes and fears, successes and failures. Imagine this person's wish for happiness and security and empathetically embrace that desire as your own. Then return to you own perspective, viewing this person as a human being like yourself, and yearn for his or her well-being, independent of your own self-centered desires.

Finally turn your attention toward someone who has harmed you, wishes you ill, or exhibits qualities that you find repugnant. This person appears to be an impediment to your own happiness and it's unpleasant even to be in his or her presence. He or she seems to be a source of your unhappiness, and you may feel that the world as a whole would be better off without the person. Let your fear, aversion, or hatred for this person manifest as you sit quietly in meditation. Now shift your perspective to this peron's, imagining what it would be like to be him or her, with his or her own hopes and fears and ideas about how to find happiness and security. Some of those ideas may be deluded, but if so, the person doesn't know that yet and is convinced that's the best way to find what he or she is looking for, no matter how many other people are harmed in the process. Without embracing his or her attitudes, behavior, or ideas, attend to this person's fundamental yearning for happiness and freedom from suffering. At heart, it is no different from your own. So experience it as if it were your own, and long for his or her happiness. Bring forth the wish that he or she achieve clarity as to the true causes of happiness and suffering and live life accordingly. May he or she be well and happy, free of fear and suffering, as you wish to be. Attend to this person once again from your own perspective, now viewing him or her not as a disagreeable, threatening object, but as a sentient being like yourself, worthy of happiness.

Now expand the scope of your awareness, encompassing all beings, human and otherwise, who long for happiness and freedom from pain and suffering. Visualize, as you did before, the essential purity of your own awareness in the form of a radiant orb of white light at your heart. As you breathe in, imagine drawing in all suffering of the world, together with its underlying causes, and dissolve this dark cloud of misery in your heart, where it is extinguished without a trace. And as you breathe out, let the light from your heart flow out equally to all beings, fulfilling their deepest desires, bringing them joy and happiness, as they nurture the true causes of their own well-being. May all beings, like ourselves, be free of suffering and its causes. May each one find happiness and the causes of happiness.

As we bring this session to a close, let us dedicate the benefits of such practice: whatever merit may have come from engaging in these practices, may this lead to the blossoming of lovingkindness and compassion, of empathetic joy and equanimity, in our own lives. May we become an example for others. May we embody these Four Immeasurables. Then may we kindle these same qualities in others. May we teach them to our children, and they to their children. May we live well and happily together. Before you conclude this session, release all mental images, thoughts, and desires, and rest for a moment in the unstructured nature of your own awareness. Simply be present, aware of being aware.

For Further Contemplation

Every time you encounter misery in the world, whether you perceive it directly or by way of the media, you may enter into the practice of *tonglen*. The word has the connotation of "taking in" the suffering and evil of the world, and "giving out" joy and virtue to all beings. Whenever you observe evil in the world—the greed, the delusion, and the hatred that generate so much suffering—rather than thinking you are superior and criticizing the "evildoers," practice *tonglen*. We all know firsthand what it is like to be greedy, deluded and hateful. Breathe in and purify that negativity with the yearning "May you, like myself, be free." In other words, the whole world can be a catalyst for your Dharma practice. Instead of reacting with grief, sorrow, or depression, respond with compassion.

One of the best times to practice *tonglen* is when you're watching or listening to the news. If your situation leaves you little time for formal meditation, when you attend to the news, make that your meditation period. *Tonglen* can encompass all the drama of the world—all its miseries and conflicts. Practicing it daily can be quite transformative. But you have to become a kind of quick-draw artist: during the course of the day, if you meet someone who displays disagreeable behavior, whip out your *tonglen*. When you see somebody experiencing misery, do the same thing: quick-draw. When you notice someone actively seeking happiness, join them with your practice of *tonglen*. Do it for one minute here, fifteen seconds there. It's a marvelous practice, one of the crown jewels of the hundreds of meditations Tibetans have preserved and developed over the centuries.

In the year 2000, I helped organize and served as an interpreter for a conference on destructive emotions hosted by the Dalai Lama, which was later described in Daniel Goleman's book *Destructive Emotions: How Can We Overcome Them?* During this five-day meeting, the philosopher Owen Flanagan cited studies indicating that people who are unrealistically optimistic are happier than realists, who commonly tend toward depression. If true, this seems to leave us with only two options. We can be unrealistically optimistic, hoping against hope things will turn out for the best. Or, as the second option, we can be sober realists, dealing only with the facts, which are often dismal and depressing. But is there another alternative?

I think such an alternative can be found in what might be called Dharma vision, a vision of loving-kindness. I don't disagree with the results of those studies. The Buddhist alternative, the vision of loving-kindness, is optimistic, but not in the sense of expecting something over which we have no control to turn out a certain way, with attachment to a desired result. Nor is loving-kindness pessimistic, fixed on the limitations of the present. It is easy to get stuck there, given the suffering and frustration we are exposed to as we survey the repetitive miseries and traumas of our global village. Here Dharma suggests that we not fixate on that, but go deeper. Dharma vision entails a view of happiness that is devoid of attachment, one not based on expectations that things will turn out one way as opposed to another. It cuts through optimism and pessimism to another kind of happiness, one based, in the Dalai Lama's words, on "faith in the truth."

The lesson is that people who are on the whole happy, who maintain a sense of good cheer, of buoyancy and well-being, are those who find many little things throughout the day to delight in. In contrast, occasional episodes of dramatically positive experiences, such as winning the lottery or achieving an important goal, such as cashing in big on an investment, have very little impact on people's overall sense of well-being. So developing empathetic joy, bit by bit, can effectively suffuse your life with happiness.

Equanimity, also referred to as even-mindedness and impartiality, should not be confused with indifference, or as merely a feeling devoid of pleasure or pain. The inner quality to be cultivated here is more than a feeling; it is a stance, an attitude—a way of attending to others that involves neither attachment to those who are near, nor aversion to anyone who might impede our happiness. So equanimity—in the context of the Four Immeasurables—balances our perspective on others. We transcend attachment and aversion, attaining a sense of even-mindedness. This is based simply on the recognition that every sentient being, human and otherwise, is, like ourselves, seeking happiness, wishing to be free of suffering.

However, all of us, except for those who are very, very far along the path, are subject to mental afflictions. When we see someone under the spell of anger, craving, jealousy, and so forth, in all honesty we have to admit, "There, too, go I." Equanimity taps into that reality and breaks down barriers, evens out our notions of "close" and "distant." The wish we cultivate here is: "May I dwell in equanimity, free of attachment and aversion to those near and far." Develop this even concern, even loving-kindness, even compassion, the even caring for others, regardless of their conduct. This kind of equanimity is indispensable. Without it, love, compassion, and empathetic joy will always be conditional, tainted by self-centered attachment. So, equanimity, this impartiality, is an essential component of the Four Immeasurables.

When I first began learning meditation from Geshe Rabten in Dharamsala, India, in 1971, he counseled me to meditate at length on equanimity, viewing all beings as if they were my own mothers and fathers, brothers and sisters. Our attachment to those near and dear to us, our aversion to those who impede our desires, and our indifference to the rest, who seem irrelevant to our well-being, all come from the delusion of self-centeredness. Like a compassionate doctor attending to all patients equally regardless of the severity of their illnesses, Buddhism considers all beings equally deserving of happiness. Such impartiality is the foundation for all further spiritual practice.

Geshe Rabten explained how wisdom supports such impartial, loving concern for the well-being of others:

> When we feel hatred for someone we regard as an enemy, we apprehend the existence of that person very strongly, as if he existed in himself, in a very real and vivid way. . . . But if we investigate the actual manner of existing of the person in question, we find that if we analyze his body into its constituent parts we will be unable to find anything we can call a truly existent base for the label "enemy." Neither is there anything inherent in the person's feelings or his mind which will withstand our investigation, and reveal itself to be the real base for an "enemy.". . . We can also apply this kind of reasoning to an object of strong attachment, someone to whom we feel strong attachment. . . . Our love, concern, and compassion for others must extend equally to all and this is only possible when equanimity is developed. Developing this kind of even-mindedness will naturally give rise to greater mental peace as we free ourselves from the extremes of hatred or attachment. It is this peace of mind which is necessary as a basis for further development.

The indifference we feel toward some people really has nothing to do with their personal qualities or behavior. Likewise, the attributes "friend" and "foe" are not innate to anyone. We project these labels on people on the basis of our relationship with them, specifically in terms of how they have affected or may affect or own well-being. But these relationships inevitably change over time. Someone whom we regard as our dearest friend may grow distant or even turn against us. People who were strangers turn into loved ones, while others become our most feared enemies. And even those whom we have feared and loathed may become faint memories or even cherished friends. Others are not the true source of our own joy or sorrow. Classifying and reifying people as "friend," "enemy," and "stranger" is based on a deluded sense of "I" and "mine." These mistaken attributes arise from an attitude of self-centeredness, the conviction that the well-being of others is significant only insofar as they are contributors to our own happiness. That most people believe that is proof of its invalidity, for each of us is a "friend, " "enemy, " or "nonentity" in the eyes of others.

According to Buddhism, the proximate cause of equanimity is taking responsibility for our own conduct. To appreciate the full significance of this assertion, we need to understand at least the rudiments of the Buddhist theory of karma. The essence of this theory appears in many of the great spiritual traditions of the world: "As you sow, so shall you reap. " In Buddhism, this principle is interpreted within the context of reincarnation, in which our conduct in previous lives influences what we experience in this life. If we have sown the good seeds of virtuous behavior in past lives, we may reap a harvest of good fortune in this lifetime. When others treat us with kindness, this comes in part as a reflection of the kindness we have shown others in the past; and when we are treated harshly, this can be viewed as a ripening of our own past treatment of others.

The counterfeit of equanimity is aloof indifference—simply not caring about anyone. The "distant enemy" of equanimity, that which is diametrically opposed, is clinging and attachment to our loved ones, and aversion to anybody who gets in the way of our perceived happiness. That raises an important point for those of us who are not monks and nuns, those of us living in the world with families: how do we maintain impartiality with regard to our family, loved ones, and so on?

On a practical level, if we are responsible for supporting a family, we have a finite amount of money for fulfilling that responsibility. We don't have infinite funds to help all other families in the world. How then can we both be realistic and practice equanimity? What would it be like to be a *bodhisattva* parent? Take as an example the situation of the Dalai Lama. In a way he is like a father, even though he's been a monk since he was a small child. And we could say his family consists of all sentient beings, but his particular family is the six million Tibetans who look upon him as their leader and inspiration. He knows that these people see him in a special way. And so, much of his busy schedule is devoted to working for the sake of Tibetans and teaching Dharma to Tibetans, his family. True, he takes time to travel throughout the world and meet with others who want his help. And he prays for all sentient beings. But in large part he works for Tibetans. Is that because he thinks Tibetans are more worthy of his concern than the Bolivians, the Australians, or the Ethiopians? No, he devotes himself to them more conscientiously and is more available to them, because they look to him in way that others don't. It's that simple.

From having observed the Dalai Lama in many situations, sometimes while serving as his interpreter, I don't believe he loves Tibetans more than other people. Nor do I think he feels greater compassion for the Tibetans who have suffered due to human rights violations by the Chinese communists than for other people who have suffered genocide under other totalitarian regimes. I don't believe he even feels greater compassion for the Tibetans than for the Chinese, who have oppressed his people. It appears to me that his compassion is truly impartial.

From seeing him in action, I know even such compassion is possible. So, too, can we be good parents and good friends and good siblings and good children to our parents and still have even, unconditional loving-kindness. The cultivation of equanimity is possible. And the boundlessness of the Four Immeasurables hinges entirely upon it.

Before we bring this discussion to a close, let's review the false pretender of each of the Four Immeasurables and see how these practices balance one another. When the cultivation of loving-kindness goes awry, it results in self-centered attachment, and this can be balanced by meditating on equanimity. When compassion succumbs to its false pretender, grief, we can restore the balance of our hearts by cultivating empathetic joy, attending to the joys and virtues of others and ourselves. When the practice of empathetic joy falls into frivolity, this can be overcome by cultivating loving-kindness, in which we yearn that all beings may experience genuine happiness and cultivate its inner causes. Finally, when equanimity yields to aloof indifference, we can counteract this by meditating on compassion, in which we focus on the plight of sentient beings, as they suffer and continue to sow the seeds of their own misery. In these ways, each of the Four Immeasurables serves to balance out the deviations in one of the others. Here, truly, is a path to fulfillment for ourselves and our fellow humans.

PART IV

Exploring the Nature of Consciousness

Bodhichitta:
The Spirit of Awakening

FOLLOWING THE DEVELOPMENT OF the Four Immeasurables, and just before the cultivation of wisdom, comes the crown jewel of all of Mahayana Buddhism. In Sanskrit it is called *bodhichitta*, which I translate as the *spirit of awakening*. If you could read and practice only one chapter of this book, this would be the one. That's because *bodhichitta*, the spirit of awakening, starts with *shamatha*, making your mind serviceable, continues on to loving-kindness and compassion, and then crests in Dzogchen, the Great Perfection. It covers the whole of the Buddhadharma; nothing is left out.

Among all the spiritual teachers with whom I have trained over the years, none more clearly embodies the qualities of *bodhichitta* than His Holiness the Dalai Lama. This was especially evident to me in 1979, when I had the privilege of serving as his interpreter during his visits to Switzerland and Greece. He seemed to radiate a sense of kindness and humility, and I felt suffused by his warmth. In Athens, we were given lodging in a private home. The front door opened onto a sitting room that led to a hallway to all the bedrooms in the house. His Holiness was given the bedroom at the end of the hall, and when he went for a shower, he had to cross the hall to the nearest bathroom. One hot afternoon, walking to his shower, wrapped only in a towel, he looked down the hall at those of us gathered in the sitting room and greeted us with a happy wave and a chuckle.

A couple of days later, we visited a Buddhist center founded by Kalu Rinpoche, a highly respected lama of the Kagyüpa order of Tibetan Buddhism. Earlier Kalu Rinpoche had instructed his novice students to engage in the traditional "preliminary practices," preparatory to venturing into the esoteric meditations of Vajrayana Buddhism. But after his short visit to Greece, he returned to India, leaving his students with no one to guide them in their daily practice. The preliminaries he taught them include the recitation of many mantras and other devotional practices, such as performing 100,000 prostrations to the buddhas. These new students told the Dalai Lama that they had a lot of resistance to performing these practices, despite the instructions of their revered lama. His Holiness replied that these preliminaries are designed specifically in preparation for advanced Vajrayana practice, but they are not basic to Buddhism as a whole. He encouraged them to emphasize above all the cultivation of *bodhichitta*. "If you perform even one prostration with the motivation of *bodhichitta*," he told them, "this is more valuable than doing 100,000 prostrations with a selfish motivation. So let *bodhichitta* be the heart of your practice."

Practice

Sit comfortably, resting your body in a way that is conducive to meditation. To help maintain the coherence of your attention, remain as still as you can. And whether you are on a chair with your feet on the ground or are seated cross-legged, assume a posture of vigilance, with your sternum slightly raised so that you can breathe effortlessly into the abdomen. See that your belly is relaxed, so that it expands when you inhale. Are the muscles of your face relaxed and soft, especially the muscles around the eyes and the eyes themselves? If you find areas of your face tightening up, release them. Now take three slow, deep breaths, inhaling down into your abdomen, fully and deeply, then exhale naturally and freely.

Begin by calming your mind in the practice of mindfulness of breathing. Withdraw your awareness from the external world and rest your attention in the field of tactile sensations throughout your body. With each inhalation and exhalation, note whether the breath is long or short. Rather than tightening your concentration, simply let go of wandering thoughts. Give your discursive mind a rest for the duration of this twenty-four-minute session. With each inhalation, breathe into areas of tension in your body, and with each out-breath, sense the knots in the body and the mind unraveling as you relax more deeply.

Especially at the end of exhalation there is no need to apply your will to the in-breath. Rather, let it flow in like the tide. You can even let go so deeply that you relax into the in-breath, then continue relaxing into the out-breath. Find a sense of inner calm by releasing the tension of your mind, not by constricting but by releasing your attention, so that the stillness emerges from a sense of inner calm.

This practice will lead you to an ever-deepening sense of quiescence that slowly transforms into a sense of well-being. Potentially this is an avenue to profound insight into both the nature of consciousness and the world around us. But for the time being, rather than going deeper into this practice, let us expand the scope of our awareness by using another wonderful faculty of the human mind: the imagination. Let us return to the practice of *tonglen*, giving and taking, which is a principal method for cultivating *bodhichitta*.

Begin by imagining a person who is close to you—a loved one, a sibling, a relative, a friend—a person you know very well and care about greatly. Bring to mind such a person who is encountering special adversity, whether economic, social, psychological, or physical. Vividly picture this person and bring to mind, as well as you can, the causes of his or her suffering, outer and inner. Next symbolically visualize the fundamental purity of your own awareness, your *buddha-nature*. This is your capacity for enlightenment, which becomes obscured by mental afflictions. Imagine this now in the symbolic form of an orb of light at your heart—radiant white light, inexhaustible, brilliant, a light of joy and purification. Imagine this as the ground of your being, your true nature.

Now, taking up the practice of *tonglen*, imagine the suffering and the sources of suffering of your loved one in the form of a dark cloud, obscuring this person's true nature. With each in-breath, imagine inhaling this darkness, drawing it into the orb of light at your heart, where it vanishes without trace. Do this not simply as a visualization exercise, but with each in-breath, bring forth this wish: "May you be free of this suffering and its underlying causes." With each in-breath, imagine this person's misery and its underlying causes dissipating until they vanish completely.

Once more bring this person vividly to mind, but this time focus upon the person's yearnings, and desires for happiness. And with the wish "May you find genuine happiness and embrace its source," with each out-breath imagine this light from your heart flowing directly outward as a gentle, soothing glow of loving-kindness. Imagine this light flowing outward, filling this person with the light of joy. Imagine this to be true here and now.

Now bring to mind someone who has brought you misery and who may still harbor ill will against you. As you bring this person to mind, question whether the reprehensible qualities you perceive in this person are real or imagined. Might they be in part real and in part projected by you? Out of aversion, you may augment your perception of the negative qualities of the other. In any case, you find here a troubling person, and the trouble seems to come from outside. With each in-breath, draw in the qualities that trouble you. Imagine breathing in these causes of suffering, be it in that person's life, in your life, or in the relationship between the two. Draw this to your heart in the form of a cloud of darkness, and extinguish it there. With each in-breath, imagine the dispersal of all these qualities or types of behavior that you find so difficult. Imagine all the afflictions and obscurations of the mind vanishing, extinguished in the light at your own heart.

Now with each out-breath, visualize all goodness, all compassion, and all wisdom flowing out from the inexhaustible source at your heart. With each out-breath bring this thought of loving-kindness: "May you be truly well and happy, endowed with the causes of genuine happiness." Imagine this person being suffused with this light of goodness, experiencing the joy of this realization of loving-kindness and compassion. Picture the light saturating this person growing brighter, and imagine his or her joy increasing.

Now expand the field of your awareness to embrace all beings, who like yourself yearn for happiness and freedom from pain and anxiety. With each in-breath, draw in their suffering, together with its underlying causes, in the form of a dark cloud. With each out-breath, imagine blessing the world with the light of genuine happiness.

Then release your imagination, release the objects of your mind, and effortlessly settle your awareness in its own nature, without subject or object; just let go.

Dedicate merit and bring the session to a close.

For Further Contemplation

Each week during the summer and autumn of 1972, a year after I began my studies in Dharamsala, India, I hiked up the mountain above the village to meet with my teacher Geshe Rabten. He was in meditative retreat at the time, living in a rustic cowshed overlooking the hill station of McLeod Ganj, where members of the British Raj had moved their families during the sweltering Indian summers. At my request, he related the story of his life, beginning with his childhood as a farm boy in the wilds of eastern Tibet. As he described to me the course of his spiritual training and development, he emphasized the cultivation of *bodhichitta* as the most important of all practices, for it is the framework of the *bodhisattva* way of life as a whole. Meditative quiescence, the Four Immeasurables, and the Four Applications of Mindfulness lay a foundation for the development of the spirit of awakening. The practices taught of the Buddha, he told me, consist of just three types: "the ground for *bodhichitta*," "the actual cultivation of *bodhichitta*," and "the harvest of *bodhichitta*," which refers to the qualities of enlightenment that emerge from this practice. In this way, the spirit of awakening reflects the essence of Buddhist practice in the beginning, middle, and end.

Bodhichitta is the heartfelt aspiration to achieve spiritual awakening for the sake of all beings, an aspiration fusing the two noblest goals. The first is to seek enlightenment. But pursuing this aspiration for oneself alone ignores something fundamental about the nature of our existence: none of us lives in isolation, independent of those around us. Our existence is one of interrelationship. We have survived in dependence upon the care of our parents and our relationships with our siblings, friends, and teachers. Society has provided us with sustenance, clothing, and lodging. Each of us has always lived in dependence upon a network of others extending outward, through time and space, without end.

Thus, our aspirations must include the welfare of others. If we are pursuing truth, our aspirations must be rooted in the reality that we exist interdependently. Each of us is striving for happiness and freedom from suffering and anxiety. Yet so often our efforts fail. Recall once again Shantideva's comment in *A Guide to the Bodhisattva Way of Life*: "Those desiring to escape from suffering hasten right toward it. And with the wish for happiness, out of delusion they destroy their own well-being as if it were their enemy." How accurate a picture that is of our own lives and the world at large! This brings us to our second noble aspiration: "What can I do to help?"

Over the years since I was first introduced to these teachings on *bodhichitta*, it has become progressively clear to me that the cultivation of compassion is primarily a matter of paying attention to others, rather than trying hard to care about them. As we have discussed before, compassion is not pity; instead it is seeing suffering and automatically yearning that it may be alleviated. For example, if you have driven by the scene of an accident, you may have spontaneously hoped that no one was seriously injured. That kind of compassion doesn't require a great deal of spiritual practice. It was the natural outcome of paying attention to the plight of others.

When we observe the magnitude of suffering in the world, and the way we foolishly perpetuate the sources of our own suffering, compassion is a natural response. This brings us to the question: How can we be of service—not just to attenuate some of the symptoms, but to remove the core causes of suffering for everyone? To approach this question from a practical perspective, it makes sense that the more we heal ourselves of mental afflictions and the more we develop virtues such as wisdom and compassion, the more effective we can be in serving others. In the words of Shantideva, "Those who long to overcome the overwhelming miseries of existence, those who wish to dispel the hardships of the world, and those who yearn to experience a myriad of joys should never part from the spirit of awakening."

We have both the challenge of *discovering* our buddha-nature and of *waking it up*. This is not a passive state of awareness. Rather, there are steps we can take to arouse our own buddha-nature so that it becomes activated in our physical, verbal, and mental behavior. The key is the cultivation of "great compassion," or *mahakaruna*. Recall the theme of boundless compassion as the second of the Four Immeasurables. This is a kind of compassion that does not fixate on the demarcations between friend, enemy, and neutral person, but embraces all beings, self and others, unconditionally. But *mahakaruna* goes a step even beyond this. It entails taking upon ourselves the responsibility of alleviating the suffering of others and of bringing each of them, without exception, to a state of enduring joy.

When Geshe Rabten was explaining the difference between boundless compassion and great compassion to a small group of students in our monastery in Switzerland, he gave the analogy of different ways of responding to a cow that had gotten bogged down in a sewage pit. A person who had cultivated boundless compassion would view the cow as if it was his dear friend, and he would try to free it with ropes and the assistance of other people helping out from the firm ground outside the pit. But a *bodhisattva* with great compassion, taking personal responsibility for the cow's rescue, would do everything possible to free it, including jumping down into the pit. When one of his students asked whether we should regard ourselves as being like the *bodhisattva*, Geshe Rabten told us bluntly, "You're the cow!"

Great compassion is the motivating force that inspires the *bodhisattva*'s entire way of life. With great compassion we take personal responsibility for the well-being of the whole world. By cultivating this dimension of compassion, we experience a feeling of such profound interrelatedness that the well-being of every other person becomes just as important as our own. Thus, great compassion expresses itself in this wish: "May all sentient beings be free from suffering and the sources of suffering, and may I bring this about."

Three Dimensions of Consciousness

With great compassion we aspire to liberate all beings from suffering and its source, and with the spirit of awakening we seek a way to fulfill this aspiration. In order to give this undertaking a firm footing in reality, we must fathom the nature of awareness. Here is a model of three dimensions of awareness, each of which can be tested through experience. They are:

1. The psyche
2. The substrate consciousness
3. Primordial consciousness

The psyche is the realm of the mind studied by psychologists. It includes the whole range of conscious and unconscious mental processes that are conditioned by the body, especially the brain, in interaction with the environment. These processes are specific to our gender, ethnicity, age, and so on. A major reason for taking an interest in the psyche is to learn to distinguish which of our mental processes are conducive to our well-being and which are not. Buddhist psychology is experiential and pragmatic, encouraging us to answer those questions by observing our own minds and the influences of specific mental states and activities. As our introspective skills improve, we shine a brighter and brighter light on a domain that was previously obscure.

As Buddhist contemplatives have probed the origins of the psyche, they have discovered that it emerges from an underlying dimension called the *substrate consciousness*, an individual continuum of consciousness that carries on from one lifetime to the next, storing memories and other personal character traits over time.

Comparing this view to that of current neuroscience, your psyche is *conditioned* by brain synapses, neurotransmitters, and other neural processes, but it is not located in the brain, nor is it an emergent property of the brain and its interaction with the environment, as neuroscientists now believe.

The existence of the substrate consciousness is not simply a metaphysical speculation, but a hypothesis that can be put to the test of contemplative experience. This is not an easy task, and it is not a hypothesis that can be tested by studying the brain alone. It is a challenge that can be taken on by seasoned contemplatives who have already achieved meditative quiescence. Through such practice you turn your attention into a powerful beam of refined, focused, luminous awareness, cutting like a laser through the turbulent, superficial strata of your psyche. As the murkiness and perturbations of discursive thoughts calm, the space of the mind becomes increasingly transparent. Many Buddhist contemplatives of the past and present claim that you can then tap into the substrate, systematically accessing memories of previous lives that have been imprinted on this continuum of consciousness. These may include memories of your home, personal possessions, friends, livelihood, and the manner of your death.

The substrate consciousness can also be indirectly inferred on the basis of research done on children who report valid past-life memories and even show physical characteristics, birthmarks and the like, that trace back to their previous lives. Scientific investigations in this field have been done by the psychiatrist Ian Stevenson, who summed up forty years of research in his recent book, *Where Reincarnation and Biology Intersect*. So, apart from the reports of contemplatives, there seems to be indirect scientific grounds for asserting the existence of an individual substrate consciousness that carries on from one lifetime to the next.

The aspiration of the spirit of awakening begins to look feasible when we consider the possibility of our spiritual maturation continuing from one lifetime to the next. If our existence were confined to this life alone, *bodhichitta* would be a mere flight of fancy, because in this life alone we have no chance of alleviating the suffering of all beings. If each of us participates in a stream of consciousness that flows to a future without end, however, then there is plenty of time to heal others. The Dalai Lama often quotes this verse from *A Guide to the Bodhisattva Way of Life*: "For as long as space remains, for as long as sentient beings remain, so long may I remain for the alleviation of the suffering of the world."

Beyond the realm of the substrate consciousness, contemplatives from various traditions around the world and throughout history have discovered a third dimension of awareness, called in Buddhism *primordial consciousness*. This transcends the conceptual constructs of space and time, subject and object, mind and matter, and even existence and nonexistence. This dimension of consciousness is ineffable and inconceivable, but, as with the psyche and substrate consciousness, it can be experientially explored by means of meditation. Here meditative quiescence alone is not enough. This requires rigorous training in contemplative insight, or *vipashyana*, by which we break through all conceptual constructs and the "hardening of our categories," to the point that we can settle into the empty and luminous nature of awareness itself.

A couple of years ago, I asked my late friend and colleague Francisco Varela, a distinguished neuroscientist, whether this Buddhist view is compatible with modern scientific understanding of the brain. He jokingly responded that this was a "brutal question," for it is indeed compatible, but virtually all neuroscientific research is carried out with the assumption of the contrary view that the mind is nothing more than a function of the brain. And as long as cognitive scientists confine their research to the psyche and its correlations to the brain, their materialistic assumptions will remain unchallenged and untested.

Buddhists call this deepest level of primordial consciousness our *buddha-nature*, and three reasons are given why the buddha-nature is present in all beings. The first reason is that the *dharmakaya*, the consciousness of all the buddhas, pervades the whole of space of time. The second reason is that in the ultimate nature of reality there is no distinction between enlightened and unenlightened beings. Ultimately, we are of the same nature as the enlightened ones. The third reason is that all of us have the capacity to achieve the enlightenment of a buddha. The Mahayana

Buddhist tradition declares that it is this buddha-nature that is the source of our yearning to achieve genuine happiness, or nirvana. By nature, this dimension of consciousness is "brightly shining" and "originally pure," but it appears impure when it is obscured by attachment, hatred, delusion, and compulsive ideation. Replete with the qualities of Buddhahood, it is both primordially present since beginningless time and yet must also be perfected through proper cultivation. The buddha-nature is the immaculate true nature of awareness, to which nothing need be added and from which nothing need be taken, yet it has to be separated from its accompanying impurities, just as gold ore has to be refined so as to bring out and manifest the intrinsic purity of gold. In the *Lankavatara Sutra* the Buddha declares that the buddha-nature "holds within it the cause for both good and evil, and by it all forms of existence are produced. Like an actor it takes on a variety of forms."

If we can strive to realize our buddha-nature over multiple lifetimes, by first purifying our psyches, then by exploring our substrate consciousness, and finally plumbing the depths of primordial consciousness, then the great aspiration of *bodhichitta* appears viable.

On the Bodhisattva Path: Transforming Adversity and Felicity

In the Tibetan Buddhist tradition, two approaches are presented for exploring and manifesting the power of primordial consciousness. The first of these could be called a *developmental model*, in which the buddha-nature is characterized as something that we already *have*, a potential within each of us to achieve perfect spiritual awakening. In other words, the obscurations and afflictions of our minds are not intrinsic to our very existence. They can be irreversibly dispelled, allowing the innate purity of our minds to manifest. The second approach may be viewed as a *discovery model*, in which the buddha-nature is presented not as something we *have*, but rather as something we already *are*—not so much a potential, but a hidden actuality. According to this view, if we fathomed who we really are, if we could plumb the deepest dimension of our being, we would recognize that the essential nature of our own minds is primordial consciousness, which has never been contaminated by any mental affliction or obscuration.

As we venture onto the path of enlightenment, we are bound to encounter times of good and bad fortune. In order for us to flourish in our spiritual practice and not falter every time we encounter adversity, we must learn how to transform bad times into nourishment for our spiritual maturation. The sixth chapter of *A Guide to the Bodhisattva Way of Life* explains numerous methods useful for transforming adversity into grist for the mill, for deepening our compassion and other qualities that are innate to enlightenment itself. Shantideva cuts through a great deal of unnecessary frustration, depression, and despair when he poses these questions: "If there is something you can do about a problem, why get frustrated? If there is nothing you can do, why get upset?"

One method for transforming adversity so that it empowers us along the path is to use it as fuel for enhancing the spirit of emergence, the yearning to free ourselves from suffering and its inner causes. We wish to heal ourselves from delusion, craving, and hostility. Many of the difficulties we encounter stem in part from our own mental afflictions and harmful behavior in this lifetime. But on some occasions we suffer even when we are innocent of any wrongdoing. In such cases, if we are willing to accept as a working hypothesis the theory of reincarnation, in which each of our incarnations is conditioned by our behavior in the past, we can appreciate our present hardships as the consequences of our own mental afflictions and misconduct in previous lives. It is not that we are being punished for our sins. Rather, we are simply experiencing the natural repercussions of our earlier conduct. Viewing our lives in this way can lead to a deepening desire for freedom from the internal *sources* of suffering and not merely from the external *catalysts* for misery.

One of the primary obstacles to achieving enlightenment is arrogance—a sense of pride or self-importance. Adversity tends to deflate such pomposity, bringing a greater degree of humility to our practice. Tibetans often liken arrogance to the soil on top of a high mountain peak, so thin that nothing can grow in it. All the topsoil settles down into the valley, providing fertile ground for growth. So, likewise, it is in the valley of humility that the qualities of enlightenment grow, not on the barren peaks of arrogance.

Finally, the experience of adversity can provide a basis for empathy. As we come to know our own suffering, we can identify with others' problems. This can arouse first empathy and then compassion. Unfortunately, sometimes the experience of conflict can cause us to retaliate by inflicting similar misery upon others. So our challenge is to learn to transmute that pain into compassion rather than resentment or vengeance. In this way, our practice acts like an alchemical elixir to transform the adverse events of our lives into spiritual growth.

We are faced with the challenge of transforming not only bad times but also good times into spiritual practice, which can easily be neglected when everything seems to be going our way. In this regard, an eleventh-century Indian Buddhist contemplative named Padampa Sangye commented, "People can handle only a little felicity, but they can handle lot of adversity." As many of us have seen, great difficulties can bring out the best in people: self-sacrifice, compassion, altruism, service to others. But when people are nestling in the lap of luxury and comfort, this can easily breed arrogance and complacency.

Bodhichitta is the essence of the *bodhisattva* way of life and the elixir that transforms all our activities into spiritual practice. The practices of dream yoga and the Great Perfection that follow are central to the cultivation of insight, which is necessary to bring the *bodhisattva*'s aspiration to fruition. But the main course of this entire banquet of Dharma practices is the cultivation of *bodhichitta* itself.

Daytime Dream Yoga

WITH DAYTIME DREAM YOGA, we enter into the training of ultimate *bodhichitta*—the cultivation of contemplative insight into the
nature of reality, with special emphasis on primordial consciousness. Gyatrul Rinpoche, a senior lama of the Nyingma order and
one of my primary mentors, first instructed me in dream yoga in
1990.

Some people are born with a knack for recognizing the dream
state while dreaming. I'm not one of those people, but I have found
that this ability can be improved through practice. A key element
is to stay on the lookout, at all times, for situations that are exceptionally odd. Such was the catalyst for the following vivid lucid
dream: While driving with a friend, I noticed that the sun was
about to set. We decided to stop for a bite to eat, so we pulled into
a 1950s-style diner. As the two of us sat at a Formica table by the
window, waiting to be served, I glanced out the window and
noticed the sun high in the sky. It struck me; "That's impossible.
I *must* be dreaming!" At once, I was clearly aware that my whole
environment was a dreamscape. One of the oddest things about
my lucid dreams has been that I knew while dreaming that I had
another body lying in bed, even though I had no experiential evidence for it. All my perceptual awareness was confined to the
dream. In this particular dream, I enthusiastically stood up and
walked around the diner, asking the other people there, "Do you
know that this is a dream?" They looked back at me with blank
stares, so I concluded that I, the dreamed Alan in the diner, was

the only one who was awake to the fact that I, the Alan asleep in bed, was dreaming.

The practice of dream yoga begins during the daytime, where we examine the dreamlike nature of waking experience. Let's start with a meditation that can open up this avenue of exploration.

In preparation for the nighttime practice of dream yoga, as you are falling asleep each night, do so with a strong resolve. Think: "Tonight, I am going to pay attention to my dreams. I am going to remember them. May they be vivid. As I wake up, before I move, I am going to go back into the dream." As you wake up, you may emerge directly from a dream. Before you move your body, go back into the dream and maybe, if you are really delicate and can bring a butterfly wing touch to your dream, you may be able to slip right back into it and become lucid. That is the easiest way to attain lucidity. Barely emerge from the dream, then slip right back in with the recognition that you are dreaming. This is very subtle and might be difficult, but as you are emerging from the dream, try to be mindful of the contents of the dream. You may want to keep a dream log, a notebook containing some of the salient features so you can develop some recognition of your dream signs.

Practice

Begin, as you have done previously, by settling the body in an appropriate posture. Sit upright in a position that is comfortable, still, and vigilant. Take three deep breaths, and for just a few minutes attend to the breathing as you settle the mind.

Now, with a mind that is relatively calm and bright, examine introspectively how you conceive of yourself. When you think, I am, what appearances come to mind? As you investigate this, look at the array of images and ideas you associate yourself with. Then ask whether this is really you or simply mental content that you identify with. Is the real "you" anywhere to be found *within* this matrix of events within your body and mind that you looked at carefully in the earlier practice of the Four Applications of

Mindfulness? Or is there any evidence that you exist *outside* this matrix of experience, *separate* from all of appearances to the mind?

Open your eyes and look around, observing the shapes and colors that arise to your visual awareness. Note that these things you *perceive* are appearances to your mind; they are not purely objective things, independent of consciousness. Likewise for the sounds you hear, the odors you smell, and the bodily sensations you feel. All these consist of appearances to your physical senses.

Now close your eyes and attend to the things you *think* exist "out there" when you have your eyes closed. All these conceptual phenomena you envision also consist of images to your mind. Everything you experience is made up of such appearances, even your own sense of personal identity.

Look at your mind, noting what you actually observe. Watch what appears to you when you think, My mind, and see if there is any such entity, in and of itself.

Finally, examine whether your consciousness itself is a real, independent entity. See if you can simply be aware of being aware, attending closely to the sheer phenomenon of consciousness. Investigate whether it can be found under careful scrutiny, or whether it seems to elude such investigation.

In these ways, probe the nature of your own identity, the contents of your perceptual world and your conceptual world, your mind, and consciousness itself to see if there is anything in the world of your experience that can be found to exist independently. The realization that nothing exists in such a way is called insight into the *empty nature of phenomena*. But while all things are empty in this way, they still *appear* as if they had such independent existence, just as in a dream. In both the waking and the dream state, things actually exist in a way radically different from how they appear. In both, everything seems to exist from its own side, independent of our consciousness. But this manner of appearing is illusory, dreamlike. That doesn't mean that the world is not to be taken seriously, that our joys and sorrows are insignificant, or that everything is somehow meaningless. Rather, all of these phenomena are arising interdependently, just as the contents of a dream arise in relationship to the mind of the dreamer.

As you bring this meditation to a close, open your eyes, letting this awareness flow into your waking experience. Allow a seamless transition between your meditation and your active participation in the world.

For Further Contemplation

Shantideva explains that *bodhichitta* is of two types: a spirit *aspiring* to spiritual awakening, and a spirit of actively *venturing* to such awakening. The bridge between these two is a set of practices that structures the *bodhisattva*'s way of life: the Six Perfections.

The first of these perfections is *generosity*, the spirit of giving. This means giving in myriad ways: giving material goods, giving friendship and love, giving protection, giving spiritual counsel. The *bodhisattva*'s way of life is saturated with the spirit of generosity. The practice of *shamatha*, for example, can be an act of giving, altruistically making your own mind a useful instrument in the service of others. Generosity establishes the orientation of the whole path—one of service.

Second comes *ethical discipline*, epitomized in this principle: avoid inflicting injury to yourself or others, and when the opportunity arises, be of service. The theme of nonviolence, of *ahimsa*, is basic. When you get the chance, you actively try to alleviate others' suffering and bring them joy by way of your physical, verbal, and mental conduct. This is the ethical core of Buddhist practice.

The third perfection is often translated as *patience*, but it also means spiritual fortitude (*semshuk*), forbearance, or "true grit." It includes the willingness to apply ourselves to our inner spiritual practice and service to others, even when this means taking on hardships. There are plenty of difficulties in life as it is, but the path to enlightenment brings to the surface problems that might otherwise remain dormant. It's tough confronting our own vices, and that's what Dharma practice compels us to do.

Next comes *zeal*, or enthusiasm. This means delight in engaging in wholesome conduct, whether as a dedicated meditator, a devoted parent, a loving spouse, a kindhearted shopkeeper, a caring doctor, or simply as an altruistic member of society.

Upon the basis of the first four practices comes the perfection of *meditation*. This means balancing and refining the mind, especially in terms of meditative quiescence. In this way, we hone the mind into a fine tool for the exploration of reality and also for cultivating virtues such as loving-kindness and compassion.

Finally comes the sixth perfection of a *bodhisattva*'s way of life, and that is *wisdom*, which is the culmination of the Six Perfections. In short, the motivation behind the *bodhisattva*'s way of life is relative *bodhichitta*, and its fruition is the cultivation of ultimate *bodhichitta*, or insight into the nature of primordial consciousness.

The Tibetan lamas under whom I've studied have emphasized the importance of what they call *mi zö pey nyingjey*, or "unbearable compassion," declaring that it's a good thing not to be able to bear the suffering of others. When I first heard this, I wondered how the path to enlightenment could possibly be joyful, as we open ourselves increasingly to the misery of the world. When asked this question, His Holiness the Dalai Lama responded that this is possible by balancing compassion with insight into the nature of reality. Wisdom is the great medicine that radically and irreversibly heals the mind of its afflictions. Compassion is the motivation, but the immediate antidote to the ignorance that underlies all suffering is insight.

Daydreaming of Yourself

The aim of daytime dream yoga is to realize the dreamlike nature of waking reality, beginning with an examination of one's own personal identity. We start with this question: What does "I" refer to? You may have a concept of "I," but this is not the same as "I," just as the *concept* of hand isn't the hand. So it's important to distinguish between the ideas you have about yourself, and the "you" that those ideas are about.

Each of us has come into existence in dependence on causes and conditions, like having parents, for example. And we all have various attributes, such as our physical characteristics, gender, intelligence, memory, imagination, and language skills. Along with these qualities, each of us has a body, thoughts, emotions, memories, problems, and goals. And there are other things we have, such as relatives, friends, material possessions, and reputations. We can speak of "my country" and "my planet," or even identify the Milky Way we inhabit as "my galaxy."

All the things we identify as being "ours" are in a constant state of flux. Our moods shift, our bodies change, and our attention shifts. While we may generally have a sense that our bodies and minds are under our control, time and again this proves to be untrue. Our bodies age and become ill, whether we like it or not. Our emotions, thoughts, and attention often seem to have a mind of their own. And, of course, our control over our personal possessions, friends, colleagues, and general environment proves limited, sometimes to the extent that we seem to have lost control altogether. Each of us dreams at night—those dreams are ours and no one else's—but note how little control we have over them.

This implies there may be something arbitrary about the range of things we call ours. We regard some events and qualities as ours simply because we and no one else experience them, such as our thoughts, desires, and dreams. Other things are ours because we think they came from us and we can control them, like our thoughts, emotions, children, and accomplishments. Yet other things are ours simply because we identify with them as a result of some real or imaginary association, like our football team, nation, or race.

But the fact that we experience something doesn't make it inherently ours; the objects and people we think we can control often act contrary to our desires, and the fact that some things are ours is often a matter of social convention. If something were inherently ours, it would always be in our possession and under our control, but this isn't true even of our own consciousness, let alone anything else. In the meantime, since everything we identify with is impermanent and subject to change, eventually it will no longer be ours, either because it or we will have disappeared altogether. In short, our sense of really *having* anything at all is an illusion. Our attributes and possessions are no more inherently ours than those we identify with in a dream.

Now let's examine the nature of the self that ostensibly has all these attributes and possessions. Think of who you *are*, not what you *have*. Most likely, what comes to mind are mental images with which you have identified. But none of them are intrinsically yours, and because you are experiencing them as objects of your mind, it doesn't seem plausible that they are really you. They are just things you experience and cling to as "I" or "mine."

Recall an instance when you have been either praised or abused. In the former case, you may have felt elated, for you were the person being commended. But upon reviewing the words used, you will see that what the other person was extolling wasn't *you*, but some quality, possession, or accomplishment that was attributed to you. But none of those things is really you, so your elated response to the praise was based on an illusion. The same is true when you're insulted. No one's ever really insulted you, they've just addressed appearances to their own minds, none of which are inherently you. Thus, there's no need to take personal offense, any more than if you are ridiculed in a dream.

When we carefully scrutinize that which we regard as "I" and "mine," we find nothing that is intrinsically "I" or "mine." In Buddhism, we say that they are "empty" of such an inherent existence. But this is not to say that we don't exist or that we don't have any qualities or possessions.

We do exist, as do other people and our natural environment, but *how* do we exist? In accordance with the Middle Way (Madhyamaka) view, everything consists of patterns of events, arising in a perpetual state of flux in interrelationship with the environment—never separate, never isolated, and never independent. So any sense of yourself or anything else as existing independently is illusory.

All conditioned phenomena arise as dependently related events because they depend on:

1. Prior causes and conditions
2. The components and attributes of the phenomenon itself
3. The conceptual designation that identifies the phenomenon *possessing* these components and attributes

We could analyze any natural phenomenon in terms of these three modes of dependence, but let's continue to focus on the nature of the self. After all, each of us lives and acts within the center of our own world, so it's reasonable to start from the center and then move outward.

As for the first mode of dependence, everyone comes into existence in dependence on prior causes and conditions, such as our parents. Second, each of us exists in dependence on our bodies, minds, and other personal characteristics. But those two factors—prior causes and present qualities—are not enough to make a person. For *you* to come into existence, somebody has to think "you." This is the power of conceptual designation. By identifying you as the bearer of your attributes and the possessor of your body and mind, you are brought into existence. You and others think you are, therefore you are. But if that conceptual designation is withdrawn, you vanish, leaving only your components and possessions behind, which are no longer yours. By the very fact that you exist as a sequence of dependently related events, you are empty of inherent existence. The significance of this is that we live in a participatory world, in which our own thoughts play a key role in determining what we experience as reality. Wake up to that fact, and you enter the world of lucid daydreaming. This is the first step in the daytime practice of dream yoga.

Geshe Rabten once commented that if you have first developed relative *bodhichitta* and then gain insight into the empty nature of your self, you will joyfully experience that as if you have *found* the most precious of all treasures. But if you gain such insight without having first cultivated a selfless attitude of altruism, you will feel as if you have *lost* the most precious of treasures. You have realized not that you don't exist at all, but that you don't exist independently from everyone else and your environment. So if you have been living as if your welfare were separate from those around you, it will come as an unpleasant shock to discover that this self you have been cherishing above all others doesn't even exist.

Daydreaming the World

It is not only the self that is illusory, that emerges by the power of conceptual designation. The same is true for the entire world of experience. Everything we experience exists in relation to our perceptions and conceptions. Everything perceived by our five physical senses and our sixth mental sense—sights, sounds, smells, tastes, touch, thoughts, mental images, and emotions—all of these are like reflections in a mirror, like an apparition, or a dream. And yet, from among these appearances, the conceptual mind isolates and designates objects that it conceives of as possessing certain attributes. In this way we construct the objects that make up our world—from both the subjective and objective sides—and these objects all bear certain attributes, such as spatial and temporal components. We bring our world into existence by focusing on certain appearances and ignoring others, then making sense of those appearances through our conceptual demarcations and interpretations. Out of ignorance, like a non-lucid dreamer, we take this conjured-up world to be substantial and independent. Wake up to the reality of yourself and the rest of the world as a matrix of dependently related events, each one empty of inherent existence, and you fully venture into the daytime practice of dream yoga.

This way of viewing the world is perfectly compatible with modern neuroscientific understanding of experience. According to recent research, the principal difference between dreaming and imagination on the one hand, and waking perception on the other, is that waking experiences are directly aroused by stimuli from the external world.

In contrast, when we are dreaming, many similar reflections of the outside world arise—of sights, sounds, smells, tastes, thoughts, and emotions. These are not directly aroused by stimuli from our intersubjective world. Likewise, in imagination while we are wide awake, we may bring something to mind that no one else experiences. But neuroscientists have recently discovered a great deal of overlap between the types of brain functions that correspond to dreaming, imagination, and waking perception. Even waking experience entails a kind of active imagination, fashioning a world under the influence of the external physical stimulation of brain, as opposed to internal stimulation alone.

The colors you perceive as you scan your visual surroundings are not intrinsic qualities of objects out there. As the neurologist

Antonio Damasio points out, "There is no picture of the object being transferred from the object to the retina and from the retina to the brain." Rather, these images are catalyzed by photons striking your retina and producing electrochemical events along the optic nerve leading back to your visual cortex, even though the shapes and colors you perceive *appear* to be inherent qualities of objects existing in the real outer world. Some brain scientists have concluded that these perceived shapes and colors exist only inside the brain. But no one has actually seen the redness of a rose or the blue of the sky among the neural configurations of the brain. This is just a speculative conclusion based on the assumption that, because visual images don't exist in the physical world outside the brain, they must exist inside the brain. Dream on!

This illusory nature is also true of the sounds we hear, the odors we smell, the tastes we experience, and the tactile sensations we feel. All of these consist of appearances to the mind, which do not inherently exist in the world outside the brain or inside the brain. But they appear to be attributes of inherently existent objects in a real objective world, and by grasping onto them as such, we persist in our present state of nonlucid daydreaming.

At least since the time of Descartes, scientists have recognized the subjective nature of the world of our senses and have sought to understand the real, physical world, as it exists independently of our senses. What comes to mind as you try to conceive of the universe as it really exists "out there"? For example, think of an atom. You will probably picture a very small nucleus with electrons circling around it within a much larger domain of empty space. If you probe into the nucleus you might imagine protons and neutrons. If you know a little bit more about physics, you might imagine even smaller particles like quarks. You have acquired these mental images from physicists who present them as models of the fundamental constituents of the physical world, which are really out there, whether anyone is looking. But the images that come to mind when we think of elementary particles, atoms, fields, and energy are free creations of the human mind. They are not snapshots of the real constituents of the physical world as they exist independently of consciousness. They are useful models, to be sure, but they exist only in relation to the mind that conceives them, just as sensory experiences exist only in relation to our modes of perception.

This Middle Way view, which avoids the philosophical extremes of substantialism and nihilism, is summed up in *The Perfection of Wisdom Sutra in 20,000 Verses*. In this text, Subhuti, one of the disciples of the Buddha, declares, "A Bodhisattva reviews all phenomena as . . . similar to an apparition, a dream, a mirage, an echo, an image, a reflection of the moon in the water, a magical creation, a village of sprites. . . . Even *nirvana*, I say, is like a dream, like an illusion. If I could apprehend any phenomenon more exalted than *nirvana*, of that also I should say that it is like a dream, like an illusion."

Daytime Dream Yoga

The daytime practice of dream yoga is of great value in itself, and it is also a vital preparation for the nighttime practice of dream yoga. In order to recognize dreams for what they are, it can be useful to get into the habit of testing the nature of our experience throughout the course of the day. Stephen LaBerge, a prominent Stanford University dream researcher and coauthor of *Exploring the World of Lucid Dreaming*, has devised a technique for doing just this. Phenomena in a dream, especially written material, tend to be unstable. If you read something in a dream, turn your eyes away from the writing and then look again; the chances are very high that it will be different the second time you read it. Turn your eyes away and look for a third time, and it is even more likely that it will have changed. To test whether you are dreaming right now, read this sentence, turn your eyes away, and then look at it again. If it reads the same way a second time, chances are you are not dreaming. Turn your eyes away and look a third time, and if it still reads the same, it is even more likely that you are not dreaming. This is called a state check of the nature of your present experience.

In daily life, when something very unusual happens, people commonly exclaim, "It was unbelievable! Unreal! I felt as if I were dreaming." We sometimes say to ourselves, "I had to pinch myself to see whether it was real or I was dreaming." LaBerge comments that pinching yourself isn't a dependable way to conduct a state check, and my own experience corroborates that. Very recently I was surprised and delighted to find that I could hover at will in midair. This felt so real that I was confident I wasn't dreaming, but I pinched myself just to test my assumption. Sure enough, I felt the pinch on my leg, which reinforced my conviction that I really could levitate. I later woke up, though, and since then I haven't been able to become airborne again. So either I was dreaming I could levitate, or I'm now in the midst of a prolonged dream in which I seem to be grounded for life. The moral of this story is that just because we can touch something doesn't necessary mean it exists independently of our experience. The state check proposed by LaBerge is a lot more reliable than the pinch test.

On the basis of his test, you may come to the conclusion that right now you are awake, not dreaming. This is true: relative to your ordinary dream state, you are now awake. But relative to primordial consciousness, the awakened state of awareness of a buddha, you *are* presently dreaming, experiencing an illusory self in an illusory world fabricated by the power of thought. In an ancient text called *Natural Liberation*, taught to me by Gyatrul Rinpoche, the eighth-century Indian contemplative Padmasambhava gives this advice regarding the daytime practice of dream yoga: continuously imagine that you are dreaming your environment and everyone in it, even though, relatively speaking, you know you are awake.

Conversely, in a nighttime dream, the dreamer is not identical to the dreamed persona, since the dreamer is fast asleep in bed and the dreamed persona is moving around in the dream. As the dreamer, you dream yourself as a particular character. You might even dream of yourself as being of a different species or gender, or as being older or younger than you are in the waking state. Or you might take on qualities, behavioral patterns, or characteristics in the dream that you do not normally exhibit in the waking state. In one workshop that LaBerge and I led, one of the participants, adept at this practice, reported during our workshop a lucid dream in which she transformed herself into a revolving phonograph

record. After viewing the dream world from that dizzying perspective for a while, she then transformed herself into a butterfly
and flew out the window. The dreamed persona is an emanation,
a creation, an artifact of the dreamer.

Let's place this same idea in the context of the waking state.
Right now, think of yourself as a dreamed persona. Who is the
dreamer dreaming you? A likely candidate is your own primordial consciousness, the deepest dimension of your being. Those
of us wandering through life in a nonlucid daydream have lost
touch with our actual identity, our true nature, and are caught up
in grasping onto things that are not "I" or "mine" as if they are
our true identities and possessions. Similarly, we grasp onto the
world around us as inherently real and objective, just as in a nonlucid dream. The central aim of daytime dream yoga is to become
lucid during the waking state as a preparation for becoming lucid
when we are asleep, opening the way to the nighttime practice of
dream yoga.

13

Nighttime Dream Yoga

ON THE DAY OF his enlightenment the Buddha sat under the *bodhi* tree firmly resolved not to move until he attained spiritual awakening. The night was dramatic, with Shakyamuni's various realizations bursting forth, and finally, at daybreak, came his final realization—his *bodhi*, his awakening. Buddha's enlightenment provides a good introduction for the current topic, nighttime dream yoga. There is a fantastic parallel. The whole idea of dream yoga is that in the midst of dreaming, you awaken. In modern scientific terminology this is called "paradoxical sleep," because you are asleep and yet you are wide awake simultaneously. If you become adept at lucid dreaming or dream yoga, you are fully cognizant of the fact that you are dreaming while right in the midst of it.

What happens when you fall asleep? In the beginning people commonly enter a dreamless state where there is no form, no content, no narrative. It is like the "formless realm" in Buddhism, a dimension of existence where beings are present and conscious, yet there is no tangible content to awareness, and the beings dwelling there are disembodied. So the dreamless state is analogous to dying from the human realm and being reborn in a formless state. This is one type of sleep in which there is no rapid eye movement (REM), which is characteristic of dreaming. Another kind of sleep that lacks REM occurs when you are not dreaming, but neither is the mind devoid of content. Here there is no clear, coherent story line going on, just images coming up without emotional charge behind them. This is analogous to being born into a form realm; they may be abstract or archetypal forms, but still just forms. According to Buddhist cosmology, beings dwelling in this dimension are embodied in a subtle, ethereal way, and they do experience various types of appearances, but their minds remain in such a refined mode that they don't engage in any type of unwholesome conduct. There's no "negative karma" being accumulated in either the form or formless realm.

Then after about ninety minutes from the time you fall asleep, the chances are you will start to have your first dream. You enter into REM sleep and a specific configuration of EEG activity takes place in the brain. There are other responses too that allow researchers to recognize on the basis of various scientific, objective measures that one is dreaming. Characteristically in a dream there is a story line. Usually you are embodied; you take on a "physical" form, in the sense that you can touch, see, and hear your physical presence in the dream, but that form is not "material" because it's not a configuration of mass-energy. In some dreams you are more like an abstract awareness in space, but often, as we all know, we acquire a certain persona in a dream. Then we maneuver through the dream.

This is similar to being reborn into what Buddhists call the "desire realm," and we know that dreams often express desires. Sensual desires underlie and drive many dreams. Another common dream feature is bewilderment—delusion, dullness, a state of confusion. For example, I find that in nonlucid dreams I often get lost. I remember one dream where I was in a big hotel, wandering through a maze of corridors wondering, "Where's my room? Where's my room?" Both Buddhism and Freudian psychology consider nonlucid dreams to be states of delusion: we think we are dealing with an objective reality independent of our minds, but we are not.

Then finally the dream comes to an end and you "die" from that desire realm, after which you might spend some time in a formless realm between dreams. Then another dream comes along. The last two hours of a full night's sleep contain the highest density of dreams. One single dream, with its own continuous narrative, can go on for as long as forty-five minutes.

Researchers have found, by the way, that dream time is more or less the same as waking time. That is, if it felt like forty-five minutes in the dream, it was probably about forty-five minutes in the waking state. So that is the basic format for dreaming. Using the Buddhist death and rebirth analogy, in one night you "die," and then are metaphorically reborn into different realms. You die and you're reborn, you die and you're reborn, and you keep on going, propelled each time by what? In the modern West we would say you are propelled by your subconscious, and based on that we analyze dreams in order to shed light on the unconscious. In Buddhism, however, it is said that dreams emerge from the substrate consciousness, or the basis of death and rebirth that is the cycle of life.

In this way you experience the quintessence of *samsara* in a single night. Recalling your dream from the perspective of having just awakened, you may feel, "Oh, why did I grasp onto that dream persona? I wasn't really that person." You ask, "Why did I go through all that turmoil? Why did I grasp onto everything being real in those dreams, becoming so upset and so saddened, so topsy-turvy from all the emotions arising? How could I be so deluded?" The reason is simple: you forgot who you are and identified with that which you are not. That happens, of course, because when you fall asleep, you become an amnesiac, even from dream to dream. Rarely when we are dreaming do we remember who we were in preceding dreams. It is very difficult to remember even the last dream of the night, let alone all those that came before it. As you awaken, the dream may slip away so quickly that trying to remember it is like trying to clutch water. Of course, according to the Buddhist worldview, such amnesia saturates the whole of samsaric experience as our streams of consciousness transmigrate from one embodiment to the next.

On the one hand, when we are dreaming we forget who we are. On the other, it is more than merely a matter of forgetting, because if we really had forgotten, we might be concerned about "Who am I?" Questioning that would be a step in the direction of wisdom— recognizing that I don't know who I am. And it would be a further step in that direction to recognize, "I don't know who I am, and I am not even sure whether this is real or not." If we can ask that, we are halfway to lucidity.

The Buddha claimed that he had *awakened*, and from his perspective we are all asleep. All our states, including waking and sleeping, are a dream. We have the capacity to awaken, but it is as if we have forgotten our true nature, which is none other than our buddha-nature. And, in the midst of such ignorance, we take that which is not "I" and is not "mine" for that which we perceive as "I" and "mine." We grasp onto our personal history, body, gender, talents, skills, and defects. Fixating on our desires, our hopes, and our fears, we further cement our reified sense of personal identity. And while identifying with myriad things that are neither "I" nor "mine," we ignore who we actually are. That question isn't even raised. Notice the remarkable parallel between awakening within a dream and the Buddha's awakening to reality as a whole. When we become thoroughly lucid within a dream, we fathom the nature of our true identity and the dream world around us, and this insight yields great joy and freedom. So was this true, on an infinitely vaster scale, of the Buddha's enlightenment.

Tibetan Buddhist contemplatives report that there are important parallels between falling asleep and dying, between the dreaming state and the *bardo*, and between waking up and being reincarnated. There is also a correlation between becoming lucid in a dream and realizing the illusory nature of phenomena in the waking state. In both cases, you "wake up" in the midst of a dream-like reality and see things as they truly are.

"False awakening" is another common experience studied by lucid dream researchers. Stephen LaBerge comments:

> Sometimes false awakenings occur repeatedly, with the lucid dreamer seeming to awake again and again only to discover each time that he or she is still dreaming. In some cases, lucid dreamers have reported enduring literally dozens of false awakenings before finally waking up "for real." . . . Very occasionally, a dreamer may recognize a false awakening as a dream. However, this is often difficult because the dreamer already believes himself to be awake and never thinks to question the assumption.

Someone who has thoroughly fathomed the nature of reality as a whole is called a Buddha, an Awakened One, or an Enlightened Being. But just as false awakenings occur in the apparent transition from the sleeping state to the waking state, spiritual false awakenings can also occur. Having experienced some exceptional shift in their consciousness, some people conclude that they are enlightened and swiftly proclaim this to the world. But in many cases, the mystical states of consciousness they experienced prove transient, and they fall back into their accustomed attitudes and behavior. It is important to recognize such false awakenings for what they are, without coming to the premature conclusion that because one's own awakenings have been transient, no one else has found anything more enduring.

No spiritual tradition has a monopoly on defining "enlightenment," but in the Buddhist tradition this realization implies that one is forever free of all mental afflictions and obscurations, such as egotism, craving, hostility, envy, and arrogance, as well as the symptoms of such afflictions, including anxiety, depression, and frustration. The heart and mind have been thoroughly, irreversibly healed of their afflictive tendencies, and this is reflected in one's behavior. But reports of false awakenings occur even in traditional Buddhist literature. There is one such account involving an elder monk and his novice disciple. While the teacher mistakenly thought he was already enlightened, his young disciple had actually achieved such liberation but continued in his training to acquire further knowledge and virtues. Intuitively recognizing that his teacher had misappraised his own degree of spiritual maturation, the disciple devised a strategy for bringing the old monk to his senses. Mentally conjuring up an apparition of a raging elephant, he projected this illusion so his teacher could see it. The teacher mistook it for a real elephant, and panic-stricken, took to his heels. When the disciple caught up with him, after dissolving the apparition, he quietly asked, "Master, is it possible for an enlightened being to experience such panic in the face of an illusion?" This was the wake-up call his teacher needed, and he returned to his own practice with a clearer understanding of what still needed to be accomplished.

Practice

Let your awareness come to rest in the body, in the field of tactile sensations, including your feet, calves, thighs, buttocks, torso, neck, and head. Sense the rhythm, the ebb and flow, of the in- and out-breaths. Note these tactile sensations and observe how they shift during the course of respiration.

Give your mind a rest, this mind that is always scurrying from one stimulus to another, seeking sources of excitement. Opt out of excitation and choose instead serenity. From sheer habit, involuntary discursive thoughts and mental images are bound to arise, popping into the space of awareness. With each out-breath like a gentle gust of wind, let the contents of the mind be released and swept away.

Even while the body is sitting upright, with each out-breath allow the body as a whole to settle into a deeper and deeper state of repose, a profound relaxation. Let your mind abandon all the cares of the day, the cares of the night, and the cares of the future. Let it come to rest in the quiescence of the in- and out-breaths. Relax so deeply in body and mind that you feel as if you are in the process of consciously falling asleep. It's as if you are closing down the house for the night, as the lights of each of the physical senses are turned off. But leave one light on—the light of the mind. Leave on the light of mental perception.

The practice in this session can be done during the day, when you're wide awake, and also at night, as you are in the process of falling asleep. This is a practical method for falling asleep consciously, for observing the transitions through which the mind passes as it moves from the waking state to the nondreaming, sleeping state. Keep one light on as your senses shut down. Fall asleep and sustain mental awareness in the process. As your awareness withdraws from the external world of vision and sound and tactile sensations, and as it withdraws from the internal world of concepts, memories, desires, hopes, and fears, recede into an inner, formless quiescence in which you are wide awake.

Now redirect your focus, as if you were asleep. Turn the bright beam of your attention to the domain of experience of the mind, that realm in which mental images, thoughts, emotions, and dreams occur. And without getting caught up in the events of the mind, observe them. Observe them clearly and lucidly, without intervention. Notice even the tiniest impulses, the subtlest surges in consciousness, the fleeting images. As if you were lucidly dreaming, be aware that all of these phenomena are nothing other than expressions of consciousness, which is itself formless. None of them are you, and none of them exist independently of your own awareness.

You initially withdrew the attention from the outside environment to the body, the field of tactile sensations, then you withdrew once again, more deeply, into the field of the mind. Now withdraw to the center, the center for which there is no periphery, the center without boundaries. Allow your awareness to rest in your most intimate knowledge, the knowledge of being aware. Rest in this utter simplicity—aware of being aware, without an object. When you do so, you repose in luminosity itself, the clear and knowing nature of awareness.

What do you see? In the midst of the many stimuli to the mind, the flux of the environment of the body and the mind, can you discern an ongoing stillness? If so, this is called the innate state of meditative quiescence itself, not to be achieved, already present. When resting in awareness, can you see that there is no object that is awareness? It is not a real entity. It has no inherent identity of its own. It is as empty and open as space itself. But apart from that spacious quality, can you discern the innate luminosity, the brightness of innate awareness that is always present? This is said to be the nature of awareness. This is coming home to awareness.

Dedicate merit and bring the session to a close.

For Further Contemplation

There are many different techniques for recognizing the dream state and thereby opening the doors to the practice of dream yoga. Some of those in the Tibetan tradition involve visualization. As one falls asleep, something is visualized at the heart or throat *chakra*. Some people, I believe, are able to fall asleep maintaining such a visualization. When successful, they pass directly from the waking state into the dream state, maintaining the visualization all the way through. This requires a mind that is so calm that hardly any effort is required to create and sustain the visualization. If you have such a calm mind this could be a very useful technique. But judging from my experience, and that of some of my teachers, these visualization techniques are a bit too demanding for most of us. The effort they require can keep us awake. In my own case, when I am visualizing, I am not falling asleep. And when I finally release the visualization, I lose consciousness immediately, which prevents me from carrying the visualization over into the dream state.

Here are some techniques you might try that can facilitate lucid dreaming. As you fall asleep, the "sleeping lion posture," that in which the Buddha passed away, can be conducive to this practice. This entails lying down on your right side, resting your right cheek in your right hand, with your left arm along your left leg. Buddhist contemplatives recommend this pose not only for dream yoga but also for falling asleep in general. You might assume this position, then bring your awareness into your body. You are like a submarine running smoothly beneath the turbulence of all the waves and froth on the sea's surface. From down in the quiet of the body you simply don't attend to all the cares, emotions, thoughts, memories, and so on. Finally you will fall asleep with clear mindfulness. It is, I think, is a very practical method.

Alternatively, you may try resting your awareness in the domain of the mind, in the manner taught by the Tibetan lama Namkhai Norbu. Here, instead of the field of tactile sensations being the mind's object, you focus on the theater of the mind itself. The goal is to rest clearly and not be carried away by thoughts and other mental phenomena. You settle, attending to the mind without losing the continuity of awareness. This is an excellent preparation for lucid dreaming. Those of you who have experienced lucid dreams know that often, soon after recognizing that you are dreaming—perhaps after no more than a few seconds—you lose it, either falling back into nonlucidity or becoming so excited that you wake up. So it is important to learn how to sustain lucidity. The practice is analogous to cultivating *shamatha* as a support for *vipashyana* so that you can *sustain* your experiential insights into the nature of reality. One way to achieve this is to develop the imperturbability of your resting awareness. Learn to settle in awareness without being carried away by the actors in the theater of the mind. Recall the metaphor: become the gracious host in the midst of unruly guests, the unruly guests being whatever comes up, rising and passing in your mental field. Be able to sustain that continuity even when there is no continuity or coherence to the contents of the mind. Your awareness remains coherent—still and continuous in the midst of it all. When you can do this, when you can sustain your lucidity for minutes on end, you have laid a foundation for doing likewise in the dream state. As Lerab Lingpa stated earlier, settling the mind in its natural state is a foundation for all more advanced states of *samadhi*.

Another option is to disengage your awareness from both body and mind. Here you choose not to be concerned, even with the contents of your mind. You simply let your awareness settle in its own space, without reference to any object. There is now no subject/object relationship, just primordial knowing, the knowledge before knowledge of anything else, the knowledge of simply being aware.

If you are intent on exploring the world of lucid dreaming and the dimensions of consciousness that can be accessed by way of dream yoga, then remember that the highest dream frequency period occurs during the last two hours before you wake up. Those dreams often tend to be the clearest, most frequent, and longest in duration. Therefore, you should plan on waking up about two and a half hours before you normally do. Set your alarm, wake up, and stay awake for thirty to forty-five minutes. During this time engage your mind with the theory and practice of lucid dreaming. Read and contemplate one of the excellent books on lucid dreaming or dream yoga. Let your mind be saturated with these thoughts; let this be the reality you attend to. Then put the book away and go right back to sleep with this strong resolve: "Now, in this prime time for dreaming, I am going to recognize the dream as such." Stephen LaBerge has found that by doing this, your chances of having a lucid dream are increased twenty-fold. This is an enormous dividend for making the sacrifice of waking up early and staying awake for a short while.

People bring various motivations to the practice of lucid dreaming and dream yoga. Some enter the practice primarily to enjoy their most enticing fantasies—making their practice yet another temporary escape, or diversion, from their normal waking reality. The Buddhist practice of dream yoga goes way beyond the achievement of knowing that you are dreaming while you are dreaming. This Buddhist training can be divided into several stages:

- Recognizing the dream state
- Transforming the dream
- Seeing through the dream

Recognizing the Dream State

The first step is to ascertain the dream state as such, to become lucid while dreaming. Along with the other techniques mentioned, this first stage can be achieved by recognizing one of your dream signs. Having trained to recognize these signs in the waking state, you may be able to carry this over to the dream state and recognize it for what it is. Or you may notice something extraordinarily weird in a dream and reflect, "How could that be real?" At any time, day or night, when something improbable or odd happens, do a state check as described by Stephen LaBerge and see if you are dreaming. The fact that events *seem* perfectly real is no guarantee that you're awake.

Once you are able to become lucid in dreams, learn to sustain that lucidity. If the dream starts to fade—as sometimes happens when you become so thrilled you start to wake up or the dream gets fuzzy and you start to lose it—fill your awareness with stimuli. Start spinning, twirl your body round and round. That floods your awareness and the dream is restored. Another solution is to rub your hands together or give your whole body a rubdown. The trick is to get engaged with the dream so that the dreamscape becomes your reality.

Transforming the Dream

Imagine that you can sustain lucidity for five, ten, fifteen, or even twenty minutes in a dream. Now begin to deliberately do novel things in the dream, such as flying. You are now in a position to take off on your own expedition, exploring the frontiers of your mind. Still, at this stage, things in the dream seem to be solid and real, independent of consciousness. The second stage of traditional dream yoga, a practice going back at least twelve hundred years, is to exercise your skill in transformation. Apply your will and imagination to the contents and the events of the dream, including your own form. You can be a shape-shifter. If you are a man, turn into a woman. If you are old, become young. If you are with a crowd of people, turn them into one or two people. If you are with one or two people, transform them into many. Transform the small into the large and the large into the small. In other words, be an artist recreating the canvas of your dreams. Then see if there is anything "out there" objectively, or anything "over here" subjectively, of your own identity, your own embodiment in the dream—anything that is too real and tangible to be changed. Is there anything in the dream that resists your imagination? If so, investigate it more deeply until you clearly recognize its illusive nature. This insight will break down the barriers of objectification that dominate nonlucid dreams.

Seeing through the Dream

As you explore shape-changing, this is bound to arouse elements from the substrate consciousness, because you are plumbing the depths of consciousness. The chances are very likely, in the course of this training, that you will trigger nightmares. Some of the more negative habitual propensities in the substrate consciousness are bound to be stirred up, and they can manifest as some troubling, perhaps terrifying dreams. They may even be repetitive. When you first start having these nightmares, if you become more and more adept at transforming them, then you can do the obvious thing: make them go away. If some terrifying monster is threatening you, you can turn it into a puppy, an ice cream cone, or a bouquet of flowers. Recall that during his enlightenment, when hordes of demons converged on the Buddha, brandishing their weapons, he turned them into flowers.

You can also take this a step further. When another nightmare comes up, you can go into the third phase of dream yoga practice. Knowing that your embodiment in the dream cannot be harmed by any of the apparitions in the dream, relax and allow it to be attacked. If a crocodile is moving in on you with its beady eyes bulging just above the water, as it opens its jaws to devour you, relax and greet it graciously, "Lunch is served. Enjoy!" Relax and release your identification with your dream body, knowing there is no possible harm that can be inflicted on it or you, certainly not by a dreamed crocodile. Let it munch and crunch, and when it is all over you can simply reform yourself, and if you're in an especially generous mood, you may ask the crocodile if it would like a second course—with no fear and no need to transform anything. This is phase three, and it indicates the depth of your insight into the true nature of dreams.

At some point in your practice of dream yoga, you may become curious to know what it would be like to experience lucidity with no content whatsoever: to experience deep, dreamless sleep lucidly. To explore this, you may release the dream and simply be aware of being aware. You don't have to worry about your aching knees and your posture and little itches are here and there, or any other distractions to meditation. Now you are asleep, so your mind is naturally withdrawn from your physical senses and your body. You are already in a meditative arena; all you need do is meditate. So, perhaps, after the crocodile has eaten you as a three-course dinner, you may decide, "That's enough of that," and dissolve it. Then rest your awareness in awareness itself.

When you awaken from dream yoga practice, Padmasambhava advises:

In the morning when you wake up, forcefully and distinctively consider that not a single one of any of the dreams I had last night remains when I awaken. Likewise, not a single one of all these daytime appearances today will appear tonight in my dreams.

The dreams of the day are not fundamentally more real than the dreams of the night. They are equally illusory. From the perspective of the Awakened One we are dreaming right now. Ontologically speaking, this waking realm is no more real than the dreams we will experience tonight. What then would it be like to be lucid during the waking state? What kind of freedom, what kind of exhilaration, what kind of choices could be made were we to fathom the nature of this waking dream? What could be more fascinating? I cannot imagine a greater adventure.

14

The Great Perfection

DURING THE FIRST TWENTY YEARS of my training in Buddhism, studying and practicing under the guidance of such teachers as Geshe Ngawang Dhargyey, Geshe Rabten, Gen Lamrimpa, Sakya Dagmola, Balangoda Anandamaitreya, and His Holiness the Dalai Lama, I was exposed primarily to the developmental approach to spiritual maturation and awakening. Then since the beginning of the 1990s, I have been under the guidance of the Nyingmapa lama Gyatrul Rinpoche, who has been training me in the discovery approach of the Great Perfection, or Dzogchen. During this time, I have also had the good fortune to receive further instruction on this contemplative tradition from other Nyingmapa lamas and from His Holiness the Dalai Lama.

Lamas of the Nyingmapa order view Dzogchen as the pinnacle of Buddhist theory and practice, and they declare that it is especially relevant and effective in morally degenerate times, such as the current era. So there's an intriguing paradox here: Dzogchen is presented as the most subtle and profound of all Buddhist theories and practices, yet it is also said to be especially suitable for people whose minds are coarse and unrefined.

Many Buddhist teachings, presenting the developmental approach, emphasize the importance of strenuously purifying and transforming the mind, which is heavily burdened with afflictions and obscurations. This view sees the buddha-nature as our *capacity* for achieving enlightenment, but warns that unless we diligently apply ourselves to disciplined practice for a very long time, that capacity will remain only a promise. From this per-spective, the path to enlightenment looks like a long and arduous road. In contrast, according to the discovery approach taught in Dzogchen, our buddha-nature is the essential nature of our minds. It is primordially pure and replete with all the qualities of a bud-dha right now. All we have to do is unveil it. And the way to do that is not by assiduously developing virtues and counteracting vices, but by effortlessly letting awareness rest in its own natural state. In this way, the qualities of enlightenment emerge sponta-neously. One classic text on Dzogchen by the nineteenth-century master Düdjom Lingpa is even called *Buddhahood without Meditation*. This sounds awfully good, almost too good to be true. But many people in the West are flocking to such teachings and meditation retreats, responding to this approach with a sense of relief, in contrast to the dismay they feel when they confront the arduous disciplines taught in many contemplative traditions, including Buddhism. However, as alluring as the teachings of the Great Perfection are for people caught up in the busyness of the modern world and who just can't find time to meditate, they do not provide a quick fix to enlightenment.

The great danger here is that Dzogchen, like Zen and Vipassana, is being taken out of context in the modern world. The rich and textured teachings of Zen can be simplistically reduced to "just sitting," and the profound practices the Buddha taught in the Four Applications of Mindfulness can likewise be reduced to just being mindful. In the same way, the theory, meditation, and way of life taught in Dzogchen can be dumbed down to just being present and spontaneous, rejecting nothing and practicing nothing.

When the teachings of the Great Perfection are studied thor-oughly, it becomes clear that this path is not simply a passive dis-covery of one's buddha-nature, but also involves a demanding sequence of practices imbedded in a sophisticated way of view-ing both relative and ultimate reality. The authentic practice of Dzogchen results in the perfect spiritual awakening of a buddha, but this requires a great degree of preparation. Without achieving *shamatha*, without realization of the Four Immeasurables, *bodhi-chitta*, and direct insight into the absence of inherent nature of all phenomena, Dzogchen will not be *fully* effective. Yet this is not to say that Dzogchen has to be postponed until we have thoroughly fathomed these more elementary stages of practices. Many people find Dzogchen helpful even in early stages of practice. But it is important not to reduce this profound system of theory and practice to "just being aware." This type of reductionism is common in the modern practice of Zen and Vipassana, but people who do this shouldn't expect such practice to yield the same benefits they have provided for the generations of Buddhist contemplatives who preceded us.

The question is one of balance. On the one hand, classics of the Great Perfection declare that *shamatha, bodhichitta,* and realization of emptiness can all arise from the simple practice of resting in the natural state of pristine awareness, *rigpa*. But it is very easy to mistake the substrate consciousness or simply a state of mental vacuity for this primordial dimension of empty, luminous, pure consciousness. Especially when we experience a sense of bliss, clarity, and nonconceptuality in our meditation, we may cling to these experiences and mistake them for the actual state of *rigpa*. But as the great nineteenth-century Dzogchen master Patrul Rinpoche warns:

> A beginner may be able to let the mind rest naturally in itself, and try to maintain it. However, it is impossible for them to be free of fixation on the many experiences such as "bliss," "clarity," and "non-conceptuality" that come in the state of calm and stillness.

To elaborate, it is possible to experience the substrate consciousness without insight into the nature of any other phenomena. Access to the substrate consciousness is a direct outcome of *shamatha*, with no need for *vipashyana*. In contrast, to realize pristine awareness one must recognize the empty nature of the whole of *samsara* and nirvana, and perceive all appearances as displays of primordial consciousness. To gain access to the substrate consciousness, you withdraw the mind into its own individual ground. In contrast, to realize pristine awareness, you open your awareness to the "one taste" of all phenomena as displays of primordial consciousness.

So how are we to avoid the pitfalls of mistaking mundane meditative experiences for pristine awareness? By bringing the profound and simple, yet very challenging practices of Dzogchen into context, appreciating the subtle blend of effort and relaxation, control and release, development and discovery that this path entails, we may succeed.

Practice

In his book *A Spacious Path to Freedom*, Karma Chagmé cites the fourfold instructions on the union of Dzogchen and Mahamudra by the Tibetan contemplative Siddha Orgyen:

1. Rest in unstructured awareness.
2. Let go of memories and thoughts.
3. Transform adversity into an aid.
4. Let go of appearances.

Mahamudra is a system of meditative practice closely related to Dzogchen, and in the following passages it refers to the ultimate nature of awareness, *dharmakaya*. His instructions are so profound and lucid that I offer them here with no commentary of my own.

1. Rest in Unstructured Awareness
Be at ease, like a brahmin spinning yarn. Be loose, like a sheaf of straw on which the cord has been cut. Be gentle, like stepping on a soft cushion. Otherwise, you will trap yourself as if you were caught in a spider's web. Even if you tighten up your whole body and mind like a woodcutter clinging to the side of a cliff, the mind resists stillness. In a state free of an object of meditation and a meditator, post a sentry simply by withdrawing the mind without distraction, then evenly let it be. Thus awareness circles back to its own resting place, like a mother camel who has been sent away from her calf.
Therefore, the critical point of sustaining the mind is simply knowing how to relax in a state of nondistraction

without meditating. This is profound. Again, it is said that relaxed consciousness is not something easy.

2. Let Go of Memories and Thoughts

This mind primordially, originally exists as the dharmakaya. The six fields of experience arising as various memories and thoughts are forms of the dharmakaya, and the mind moves after each of those objects. Once there arises in the mind-stream the experience of all of them, recognizing their own nature in their own state, the essence of Mahamudra is seen. In such realization there is no expulsion of bad things that are not of the meditation and there is nothing to be affirmed. Whatever thoughts arise, do not be distracted by them but practice like the flow of a stream.

3. Transform Adversity into an Aid

Whatever appearances of the eight mundane concerns arise, do not regard them as a problem, but relate to them as aids. If you know that point there is no need to intentionally seek non-conceptuality, there is no need to regard thoughts as a problem. Your awareness is then bountifully sustained, without the onset of a famine of spiritual practice. So, without seeking mental stillness, vividness, or bliss, practice without rejecting or accepting anything that appears. Such ordinary consciousness is without fabrication or structure. This very self-illumination is the encounter with all phenomena.

4. Let Go of Appearances

Then all memories and thoughts that arise, all appearances, and all experiences of activities, arise in the nature of Mahamudra. Just as no ordinary rocks are found on a golden island, various phenomena of samsara and nirvana naturally do not lose their freshness; their countenance does not change; and they arise as self-originated, innate, primordial consciousness, in the nature of unfabricated, uncreated, primordial Mahamudra.

For Further Contemplation

We will begin by contextualizing this profoundly simple practice within the larger framework of Buddhist teachings. This may enable you to gain a deeper appreciation for the simplicity of this practice—a simplicity that is by no means easy to master. Theravada, which emphasize the foundations of the Buddhist Dharma, is aimed at one's own individual liberation (*pratimoksha*). This is the pursuit of *nirvana*, the pursuit of freedom from *samsara*—suffering and the sources of suffering. The general theme that runs through these foundational teachings and practices is recognizing the afflictions, or distortions, of the mind: attachment, hostility, delusion, and so on. As these arise, you recognize them and learn how to counteract them. You are your own healer, applying antidotes. It is a profoundly sensible approach.

One very inspiring report from the Buddha, and from many other contemplative adepts after him, is that the mind is not irreversibly prone to these mental afflictions. It can be healed permanently. The focus is on one's own existence, a reasonable place to start, and the practice requires a lot of effort. In these early teachings of the Buddha one often encounters exhortations to strive diligently, to resist when you are about to fall into anger, into abuse, into any type of unwholesome behavior, be it of body, speech, or mind. The practice involves *conceptual elaborations* (*prapañcha*), that is to say, there is much to be understood and to be done in terms of purifying and transforming the mind.

A second school of Buddhism is known as the Mahayana, the Great Vehicle. Here the motivation for spiritual practice is not just one's own liberation, but freedom for all sentient beings. And the goal is not simply freedom from suffering and its inner causes—mental afflictions—but the elimination of all mental obscurations so that our full capacity for wisdom, compassion, and the power of consciousness can manifest. This path does not negate the pursuit of individual liberation, but extends it to embrace all beings. Every aspect of our existence, ever since we were conceived (let alone the question of our previous incarnations), has occurred in dependence upon others—upon the kindness of our parents,

teachers, school friends, everyone around us. Geshe Rabten
shared his own experience with me many years ago:

> While reflecting on the development of a spirit of awaken-
> ing, in which concern for oneself is changed to concern for
> others, I realized that we are dependent upon the kindness
> of others for all our activities, through all stages of spiritual
> development, just as an infant must rely on others for all its
> needs. Apart from this dependence on living beings, one has
> no power whatsoever.

When we recognize this, it goes without saying that our individual pursuit of happiness must take into account and embrace all
of those who have enabled us to live and to pursue our own happiness. So we expand the field of our caring concern and aspire
for the highest, most perfect state of spiritual awakening, that of
a buddha, in order to be of greater service to others.

Like the pursuit of individual liberation, the Mahayana path
also entails counteracting, sometimes strenuously, the afflictions
of the mind. It also includes diligently cultivating wholesome
qualities—of balanced attention, loving-kindness, compassion,
insight, and the like. It too is a practice with conceptual elaborations, requiring striving for transformation. But now the breadth
is greatly expanded because this is done for the sake of all beings
without exception.

The third vehicle of the Buddhist Dharma, the highest echelon
of theory and practice, is called the Vajrayana, or Diamond Vehicle.
Just as the Mahayana incorporates the practices for individual liberation, so does the Vajrayana encompass the Mahayana. It is like
fuel-injected Mahayana—there is a sense of urgency in Vajrayana
practice, motivated not by impatience but by deep compassion.
The problems that beset sentient beings are so terribly dire. And
if there are remedies out there then, as the Vajrayanists might say,
"Get to it!" Vajrayana entails taking all the energy that we have
available to us, including the energy of the mental afflictions, and
transmuting it by way of a kind of spiritual alchemy. That energy
is transmuted into the spiritual path using techniques where conceptual elaborations transform negativity into fuel for spiritual

maturation. The late Lama Thubten Yeshe, a disciple of Geshe Rabten, wrote a clear and accessible book on this topic called *Introduction to Tantra*.

Finally we arrive at Dzogchen, regarded by many Tibetans as the culmination of the Vajrayana. Here there is no longer the same sense of diligent striving, of development, of transformation—no longer the conceptual elaborations of complex philosophical and psychological systems and theories. Instead there is simplicity. The primary emphasis is on releasing the mind and settling deeply in the nature of pure awareness, which needs no modification and which cannot be developed. So the development approach gives way to discovery. Dzogchen is a practice without conceptual elaborations, a practice of nonmeditation. In a very profound way there is nothing to be done. But Dzogchen doesn't turn its back on everything that has been said thus far; it incorporates all of it in a very special way.

The goal of Dzogchen practice is the realization of *rigpa*—pristine awareness, which is the fundamental nature of our own minds and, in the final analysis, nothing other than the buddha-nature. The realizations of emptiness and of rigpa are strongly emphasized in the Tibetan Buddhist tradition. So what is the relationship between them? It is said by many of the great adepts, including the present Dalai Lama, that in order to fathom *rigpa* you must realize emptiness. What does this mean?

In the Madhyamaka, or Middle Way, teachings on emptiness, which are fundamental to and thoroughly compatible with Dzogchen, the world that we experience, right here and now, is said to be dreamlike. But the notion that the phenomena we experience in the waking state have no more an inherent, objective, real existence than a dream seems to fly in the face of experience. Indeed, Madhyamaka masters say there is a profound incongruity, or incompatibility, between the way phenomena *appear* to us and the way they *are*. If you were at a restaurant table eating with friends, as you observed the person next to you, he would appear to exist objectively, independently of your own or anyone else's awareness. To confirm this, you could reach over and poke him, and to make this more "scientific," you could ask other people at the table to poke him, too. With this first-person physical contact and third-person corroboration of your own experience, you could conclude that this person is objectively real, independent of anyone's perceptions or conceptions. But recall that you can do the same thing when you are dreaming. Appearances, including tactile sensations, can be misleading. So the Buddhist Middle Way philosophy teaches that phenomena appearing to exist independently do not exist in that fashion. For them to come into existence they must be conceptually designated. The phenomena we experience do not exist independently of our modes of perception or conception, so they are said to be empty of inherent, objective existence, like events in a dream.

This realization could be characterized as "being in a lucid waking state." To probe the relationship between the realization of emptiness and of pristine awareness, imagine you are dreaming. In this dream you decide that mundane concerns are not bringing you the fulfillment you seek, so you decide to look for something else. You scan through the yellow pages, check with friends, and eventually find a qualified Buddhist teacher, say, a Tibetan lama. In your dream, you meet with the lama and request guidance. After giving you many of the basic teachings of Buddhism, the lama feels it's time to instruct you in the meditation on emptiness, Explaining how nothing exists from its own side, independent of conceptual designation, he reveals to you the dreamlike nature of all phenomena. As you probe the nature of phenomena for yourself, the more you examine the nature of your own identity, your mind, and everything around you, the more you realize there isn't inherent nature in anything. You then come to recognize: "This is really like a dream, and all of these phenomena are merely objects coming into existence by the power of conceptual designation, by means of which I then reify my world. I compartmentalize my world, I separate subject and object . . . yes, I see it is really dreamlike." Remember, in this scenario, you are *actually* dreaming.

And now the lama, observing your progress, says, "Now that you've gained insight into emptiness, I think you're ready for Dzogchen. So, I've got some news for you. You're not at all the person you think you are. You're not this dreamed persona you're identifying with. In fact, all that you think you are is just an appearance. I am just an appearance, and all that we are experiencing here is a manifestation, a display, of pristine awareness. You are not *in* this dream. You are, in reality, the dreamer—the dreamer of me, the dreamer of you, you are the dreamer of the entire environment. This is not *like* a dream, it *is* a dream! Now, awaken!" Therefore, while dreaming, you have recognized the nonobjective nature of the contents of the dream. In addition to that, you have recognized that you are the dreamer and not the dreamed. So by awakening, becoming lucid in your dream, you experience a facsimile of *rigpa*.

Now let's apply this to the waking state. The Buddha and later Madhyamaka masters such as Nagarjuna, Shantideva, Tsongkhapa, and the Dalai Lama all declare that the waking state is like a dream. And they offer methods of contemplative inquiry to realize the noninherent nature of these phenomena right here and now. On this basis Dzogchen masters declare: this is not *like* a dream, this *is* a dream, and we are just dreaming that we are sentient beings, but really we are buddhas. We have never been anything other than awakened beings. All we really need to do is recognize who we already are.

If the Madkyamaka view of emptiness states that all phenomena without exception are devoid of inherent existence, existing by the power of conceptual designation, what about *rigpa* itself? In Dzogchen, *rigpa* is described as the ground of being, as the basis and the all-encompassing "one taste" of the whole of *samsara* and nirvana. In other words, *rigpa* sounds like something ultimately "real." Moreover, it is said that *rigpa* transcends all conceptual elaboration, all categorizing—of arising and passing, suffering and joy, self and no-self, good and bad, subject and object, mind and matter, even existence and nonexistence. *Rigpa* is beyond all of them. As Patrul Rinpoche declares:

This all-penetrating, unimpeded awareness is the key point of inexpressible and naturally inherent wisdom, being beyond all philosophical extremes such as rising and ceasing, existing and non-existing, so beyond words and concepts.

In this case, is *rigpa* something that comes into existence by the power of conceptual designation? No, clearly not. How could it, when it transcends the very modality of conceptual designation, of conceptual constructs? It is beyond all of that so it couldn't possibly come into existence as a result of thinking. But it is said in the Madhyamaka teachings on emptiness that if you assert the existence of something independent of conceptual designation, that implies that it *exists by its own inherent nature*. How do we solve this dilemma?

The answer becomes readily apparent if we backtrack a bit. Recall that the status of *rigpa*, of pristine awareness, defies the very categories of existence and nonexistence. *Rigpa* is not inherently real, nor is it inherently unreal. It is not "this," it is not "that," it does not fall into any of our conceptual categories. So, being beyond existence and nonexistence, it is neither truly existent, nor is it brought into existence by the power of conceptual designation.

Now imagine that you hear teachings and read books on Dzogchen, and eventually you get some kind of an idea or notion of *rigpa*. You hear the familiar refrain that *rigpa* is conceptually unstructured consciousness, pristine awareness, the ground of *samsara* and nirvana, spontaneously manifesting as displays of the entire world, and yet defying all conceptual constructs. But as you ponder those statements, you are generating conceptual constructs of *rigpa*. What you are calling *rigpa* is now appearing to your mind as an object. When you truly rest your awareness in *rigpa*, however, the very dichotomy of subject and object dissolves; there are no reified objects of the mind because there is no reified division of subject and object. This is the first of two major phases of Dzogchen practice, known as the Breakthrough. When the mind is resting in its primordially awakened state that permeates all of existence, that's *rigpa*. But at that point *rigpa* is not an object of the mind at all. And the question of whether it is inherently existent doesn't even arise.

The Clear Light of Death

Is it possible for people like us to achieve such exalted states of spiritual realization, defying even death itself? In a very practical way the answer is yes, even if we do leave a corpse behind at the end of this lifetime. This has everything to do with who we think we are, what are we grasping onto as "I" and "mine." As long as I grasp onto this body, I am going to die; my body is destined to vanish, one way or the other. Insofar as I grasp onto my mind, my psyche, my personality, my personal history, my knowledge, my interests, and other things that I have acquired, I will die. In the dying process the body, the brain, and the nervous system lose their capacity for supporting the psyche, which finally disappears. But, according to Buddhist contemplatives, it doesn't vanish without a trace. Just as in the cultivation of *shamatha*, the psyche withdraws into the substrate consciousness that carries on from lifetime to lifetime. Then, in the culminating phase of the dying process, even the substrate consciousness becomes dormant and all dimensions of consciousness are reduced to the utter simplicity of *rigpa*, which manifests at that moment as the *clear light of death*.

The clear light of death, which is none other than your own buddha-nature, is unborn. It doesn't arise in dependence upon causes and conditions, nor is it conditioned by your brain or the environment. As such, it is not subject to death and decay. You can learn while alive to let go of more and more subtle levels of grasping—releasing your mind, your speech, your body, personal history. By coming to rest deeply in this pristine awareness—knowing that the remaining primordial, unborn consciousness is who you are—you don't die. This is a practical approach to immortality, even if your body dies and your psyche vanishes.

Those who are able to recognize the nature of awareness when they are in their final sequence of experiences in the dying process commonly remain in the clear light of death for a matter of days or weeks and rarely even months, during which the heartbeat, breathing, and all metabolic signs stop. But they are still meditating. Warmth lingers at the heart, and the body does not decompose. There can be little debate now that this actually happens. It has been seen by many people—Buddhists and non-Buddhists, including medical doctors in the recent past.

I first saw evidence for this in 1992, when I was in Dharamsala, India, with a group of neuroscientists studying advanced Tibetan yogis. As soon as we arrived in town, we received a message from the Private Office of His Holiness the Dalai Lama, encouraging us to make haste to the home of Ratö Rinpoche, a senior Tibetan lama who lived near the headquarters of the Tibetan government in exile. His breathing and heartbeat had ceased six days earlier, and his attendants observed that his body had not deteriorated and that warmth remained at his heart. The neuroscientists and I arrived just hours after he finished this final meditation in the clear light of death, which was indicated by the first signs of physical decomposition. His body had barely begun to fade, and there was no unpleasant odor in the room.

Ratö Rinpoche was recognized when he was a small child as a *tulku*, a reincarnation of a highly realized master. So he was born, so to speak, as a spiritual aristocrat, receiving training from accomplished teachers from the time he was a child. But not everyone who displays such realization of the clear light of death is an incarnated lama. One of my principal teachers, the Tibetan contemplative Gen Lamrimpa, was simply a Tibetan monk who was ordained as a child in Tibet, studied in India, and spent the final decades of his life in intensive meditation. He passed away in the fall of 2003, and following the cessation of his respiration and heartbeat, for five days he remained in this clear light of death. His life and death were an inspiration to all his students, in the East and the West.

I first met Gen Lamrimpa in 1980 when I engaged in a five-month solitary retreat in the mountains above Dharamsala, practicing under the guidance of His Holiness the Dalai Lama. An old friend of mine, Jhampa Shaneman, let me move into his retreat hut that he wasn't using at the time. It was nestled among a cluster of meditation cabins occupied by seasoned Tibetan yogis, and Gen Lamrimpa was my nearest neighbor. I visited him about once a week to consult with him about my practice, and I was struck by his deep insight and warm compassion. Years later, he accepted my invitation to lead a one-year *shamatha* retreat in the Pacific Northwest, during which he and I shared a cabin, and I continued training with him. In my mind, he was a yogi's yogi, meditating at times from five o'clock in the morning until one o'clock the next morning. No one who knew him was surprised that he died with such equanimity and good cheer, and that his final days were spent dwelling in the deepest state of consciousness.

Not everyone who realizes the clear light of death is known in life as an accomplished yogi like Gen Lamrimpa. Lama Putse, the Chanting Leader of Ka-Nying Shedrub Ling Monastery in Boudhanath, Nepal, was respected by his fellow monks as an expert in all aspects of ritual and a skilled proofreader of Buddhist scriptural treatises. But little did they know of the depth of his meditative realization. The following is an excerpt from their newsletter published shortly after his death on March, 31, 1998:

> To our amazement, Lama Putse remained for 11 days in the after-death meditative state of "tuk-dam." During that time, there were none of the usual signs of the decay after death. His body remained fresh and completely odor-free, the flesh soft and supple with no sign of rigor mortis. His face was composed and life-like. On the evening of 8th April, at our request, Dr. David R. Shlim, respected chief physician of CIWEC Clinic, came to the monastery to view Lama Putse. Dr. Shlim was astonished at the extraordinary condition of the body and remarked that he could think of no explanation, from either a medical or scientific standpoint, for such an occurrence. . . . During the 11 days of "tuk-dam," several monks remained in Lama Putse's room to perform puja 24-hours a day. The room had a very mild pleasant fragrance and a noticeable freshness. . . . Lama Putse concluded his "tuk-dam" meditation on Saturday, 11th April. When "tuk-dam" is finished, the person's mind deliberately separates from the physical body and the body begins to decompose rapidly.

All the contemplatives in these accounts were apparently able to recognize primordial consciousness when they were dying, which is why that experience is known as the clear light of death. It was their recognition of this state that enabled them to sustain it, delaying the deterioration of the body. If your awareness "sees its own face" at death, this will be like recognizing an old friend.

Tibetans call this the meeting of the mother and child clear light of awareness, for the experience is like a child crawling up onto its mother's lap. It's a homecoming. This is the ultimate ground state of your awareness, not some alien territory. If you have become familiar with this state of consciousness through your meditative practice, at death this experience will not be disorienting. You will recognize the ultimate ground of your existence.

Rainbow Body

Some meditation masters who are far advanced along the Vajrayana path reveal something even more startling at death called the "rainbow body." Dzogchen, like other Vajrayana practices, includes the theme of alchemy, of transmuting the mental afflictions into the elixir of primordial wisdom. But there is also a process for transmuting the body itself. The *Kalachakra Tantra*, another of the most profound systems of theory and practice within Vajrayana Buddhism, gives detailed explanations of how to achieve the alchemical transmutation of the body through advanced meditative practice involving complex visualizations and deep realization. With the culmination of such practice, the material elements of the body are extinguished, leaving only a body of "empty form."

Over the past decade, I've heard of two Tibetan contemplatives who displayed a partial realization of the rainbow body at death. One was a Gelukpa Geshe, who lived in Lhasa, and the other was a lama of the Jonangpa order who lived in Dzamthang Monastery in Eastern Tibet. In these two cases, witnesses reported that at death, the lama's body shrank down to the size of a small child, but retained the proportions and features of the adult lama. The Tibetan Buddhist belief is that in such cases the material constituents of the body largely dissolve into the pure energy of primordial consciousness, but in these cases this alchemical transmutation was not quite complete.

Penor Rinpoche, the former head of the Nyingma order, for whom I translated in June 2000 in Los Angeles, maintained at that time (he was then in his sixties) that he personally knew of six cases of Tibetan contemplatives completely achieving the rainbow body during his lifetime. This occurs when a person goes through the dying process, enters the clear light of death, releases it, and in doing so the body simply vanishes, commonly leaving only those parts that are no longer alive: the hair and the nails. What's implied here is a profound transmutation and exhaustion of material components of the body. So according to Tibetan accounts, manifesting the rainbow body is a rare event—it has occurred in the recent past about once every decade—which is remarkable, considering that over the last fifty years Tibetan civilization has undergone a full-scale genocide at the hands of the Chinese communists, who also destroyed virtually all Tibetan monasteries and contemplative retreat centers.

David Steindl-Rast, a Benedictine monk, became curious about the rainbow body after he heard reports of several Tibetan masters, known for their wisdom and compassion, who had shown signs of this accomplishment at death. According to the accounts he heard, at their death, rainbows suddenly appeared in the sky, and after several days their bodies disappeared. Sometimes fingernails and hair were left. Sometimes nothing was left. This made him reflect upon the resurrection of Jesus Christ, central to his own faith. He commented, "If we can establish as an anthropological fact that what is described in the resurrection of Jesus has not only happened to others, but is happening today, it would put our view of human potential in a completely different light." Father Steindl-Rast contacted Father Francis Tiso, an ordained Roman Catholic priest who had studied the Tibetan language and culture, asking him to investigate this matter. Father Tiso learned of Khenpo Achö, a Gelukpa monk who had lived in eastern Tibet and whose body had vanished after his death in 1998. He was then able to locate the village in Tibet where Khenpo Achö had died, and he conducted taped interviews with eyewitnesses to Khempo Achö's death. Father Tiso reported, "Everyone mentioned his faithfulness to his vows, his purity of life, and how he often spoke of the importance of cultivating compassion. He had the ability to teach even the roughest and toughest of types how to be a little gentler, a little more mindful. To be in the man's presence changed people."

According to the eyewitnesses he interviewed, when Khenpo Achö was dying, his breath stopped and his flesh became somewhat pinkish. One person said it turned brilliant white, and everyone there said it started to shine. At the suggestion of a friend of his bearing the same name, Lama Achö, Khenpo Achö's body was wrapped in a yellow robe, and as the days went by, eyewitnesses maintained that they could see, through the robe, that his bones and his body were shrinking. After seven days, they removed the yellow cloth, and no body remained.

In Dzogchen literature, this achievement is known as the *small rainbow body*. Far more rare than even this is the achievement of the *great transference rainbow body*. With this realization, the full alchemical transmutation of the material constituents of the body into the energy of primordial consciousness may take place while you are still alive and in good health. I have come across only a few reports of this happening over the past twelve hundred years in Tibet, though there may be more of which I'm unaware. One was Padmasambhava, who lived in the eighth century. Another was his contemporary Vimalamitra, and a third was Chetsün Senge Wangchuk, who lived in the eleventh to twelfth centuries. In addition, I have heard that two other Tibetan masters, Nyenwen Tingdzin Zangpo and Chetsün Senge Shora achieved this state. It is an open question whether this is what Jesus manifested following his death.

Padmasambhava's transmutation was completed before he would have died—there was no more matter to his body, nothing to die even physically. So it is said he didn't die at all. Apparently he just dissolved his body into light, and left Tibet for another realm where he was more urgently needed. But the deeper reality is that his very being extended infinitely into the all-pervasive space of the *dharmakaya*, or buddha-mind. Düdjom Lingpa presents this overview of the different levels of achievement of the rainbow body:

Those having the most superior of faculties are liberated as a great transference embodiment, extending infinitely into the all-pervasive dharmakaya, like water merging with water, or space merging with space. Those having average faculties attain enlightenment as a great rainbow body, like a rainbow vanishing into the sky. For those with inferior faculties, when the clear light of the ground arises, the colors of the rainbow spread forth from absolute space, and their material bodies decrease in size until finally they vanish as rainbow bodies, leaving not even a trace of their aggregates behind. That is called the *small rainbow body*. When the clear light of the ground arises, the material bodies of some people decrease in size for as long as seven days, then finally they leave only the residue of their hair and nails behind. The dissolution of the body into minute particles is called the *small transference*. For those of superior faculties this dissolution of the body into minute particles may occur even during the Breakthrough.

A Contemplative Science of Consciousness

In our modern, materialistic world, all such accounts sound like pure fantasy. The great science fiction writer Arthur C. Clarke once commented, however, that any sufficiently advanced technology is indistinguishable from magic for those who don't understand it. And John Searle, a contemporary philosopher of mind, recently said, "In spite of our modern arrogance about how much we know, in spite of the assurance and universality of our science, where the mind is concerned we are characteristically confused and in disagreement." Which is not to say that he, as a proponent of scientific materialism, would find the previously stated claims in any way plausible. But perhaps this remark should be taken as a cautionary note about mistaking mere assumptions for knowledge.

Tibetan Buddhists, relying on the discoveries of the Buddha and fifteen hundred years of Indian Buddhist contemplative experience, have over the past twelve hundred years preserved and developed a highly advanced science of consciousness. We in the modern West are only now in the very infancy of developing this science. While we are highly advanced in terms of the physical sciences, when it comes to understanding the nature and potentials of consciousness, we are still in the Dark Ages. It is a task requiring rigorous, empirical investigation, not blind faith or metaphysical rationalization. In light of Arthur C. Clarke's comment, the contemplative technologies of the Tibetans may be so advanced that they are indistinguishable to us from magic.

Overall, there is nothing that strikes me as being so profoundly universal, perennial, and primordial as Dzogchen. Many aspects of Buddhism are unique, such as the Four Applications of Mindfulness and the Madhyamaka teachings on emptiness. But we find teachings profoundly similar to Dzogchen in diverse contemplative traditions throughout history, in the East and the West. Ultimately, I am prone to think that Dzogchen is too primordial, too universal, to be confined to any one particular spiritual tradition.

Concluding Reflections

It is said, especially in the Nyingma order of Tibetan Buddhism, that Dzogchen is the crown jewel of all of the levels and modes of Buddhist practice. For many centuries Dzogchen was taught only to people who had gone through a series of initiations, and who had already engaged in extensive preliminary practices. In general, that is still good counsel. At the same time it is also true that the Nyingma tradition has preserved a number of prophesies that allegedly relate to our era, when Tibet would be crushed and Tibetans' freedom to preserve their spiritual heritage would be denied them. It was foretold that there would be a flowering of Buddhism outside Tibet. This is beginning to happen. Our era is said to be degenerate in many ways, which is obvious to many of us. Paradoxically, it was predicted that in this degenerate era, Dzogchen would blossom. One would think that when things are degenerate and people are crude, materialistic, and full of aggression and egotism, Dzogchen would be too subtle to be of use. But the prophesies say that on the contrary, Dzogchen is now ripe.

More and more teachers, including very traditional ones like my own revered Lamas Gyatrul Rinpoche and His Holiness the Dalai Lama, are making these teachings available to the public—not just to those who have been initiated into Vajrayana. Dzogchen is being presented to people who are not even Buddhist practitioners. So Dzogchen is something that seems to be very contemporary, while remaining utterly primordial.

One of the most intriguing and promising aspects of Dzogchen theory and practice is the idea that by releasing the mind, letting go of grasping, the innate qualities of Buddhahood itself rise to the surface. It is commonly said in Dzogchen literature that if you fathom *rigpa*, you don't need to do any other practice to cultivate *bodhichitta*. Great compassion, loving-kindness, and empathy—all of these virtues will arise spontaneously from your own primordial consciousness. These qualities of awareness emerge naturally when we just stop impeding, constricting, and strangling awareness—if we will just not-do and do that not-doing *luminously*. If we are not-doing in a state of luminosity, the mind untangles itself and a wellspring of joy and all the qualities of enlightenment emerge.

Gyatrul Rinpoche has chided his students time and time again when giving us Dzogchen teachings, saying, "You know why you have not fulfilled your spiritual aspirations? You don't believe in yourselves. It is not that you don't believe in Buddhism or the Nyingma tradition; it is that you don't believe in yourselves." So it is. The challenge before us is a primordial one: to discover who we really are, to know ourselves. This will set us free.

The Santa Barbara Institute for Consciousness Studies

THE MISSION OF THE Santa Barbara Institute for Consciousness Studies is to promote research and offer education for advancing understanding of the nature and potentials of consciousness. The institute has been established by a group of cognitive scientists, contemplatives, scholars, and educators, led by Alan Wallace, who serves as its president. The institute's activities are focused primarily on three areas:

1. Basic research
2. Applied research
3. Education

Basic Research

Basic research entails the investigation of the nature, origins, and role of consciousness in human existence and the natural world. Following the suggestion of America's pioneering psychologist William James, this study has three branches:

1. First-person observation of mental states
2. Third-person exploration of mind/brain correlates
3. Third-person study of mind/behavior correlates

The second and third approaches are already well established in the fields of psychology, neuroscience, and behavioral science. In particular, recent technological advances in cognitive neuroscience are shedding fresh light on mind/brain interactions and the neural bases of specific conscious states. However, while the scientific study of the brain and behavior can reveal much information about the brain side of the interaction, such research cannot, by itself, produce data about the nature of conscious mental phenomena themselves. In order to obtain this kind of data, third-person objective studies of consciousness are inherently and fundamentally reliant on first-person subjective reports of mental processes.

While there is a high degree of rigor in the third-person study of neural and behavioral correlates of consciousness, there is presently no comparable degree of precision or reliability in the domain of first-person observations and descriptions of mental events. The development of such rigor is obviously necessary if the exploration of the interactions and the possible correlates between mental processes and neural and behavioral events is to achieve its fullest potential. Thus, the possibility of enhancing and refining the first-person observation of the mind is one of the central fields of inquiry at the Santa Barbara Institute.

By embracing neural, behavioral, and introspective approaches to the study of consciousness, the Santa Barbara Institute provides a forum for interdisciplinary classes and research among the disciplines of psychology, neuroscience, philosophy, religion, the health sciences, and other fields.

Applied Research

The Santa Barbara Institute's integrative program of research is focused on the pragmatic study of human flourishing, or well-being, a topic that is rapidly gaining attention in the new field of "positive psychology." The roots of this concept can be traced back to the ancient Greek notion of *eudaimonia*, commonly translated as "genuine happiness." This term was later adopted into the Christian tradition by Augustine, who called it a "truth-given joy." Understood in this way, it is closely analogous to the classical

Indian term *ananda*, referring to the bliss that is innate to the deepest dimension of consciousness.

In the modern context, it may be understood as a state of well-being, or human flourishing, that stems from one's own mind when the mind is in a state of healthy balance. Thus, such happiness is quite distinct from the transient pleasures that are directly aroused by pleasurable sensory and intellectual stimuli or drugs. Most notably, this state of contentment is not the result of finding distraction from misery through some kind of self-indulgence. Rather, it is the fundamental bliss that arises in experiencing things as they are.

The mental balance that gives rise to such bliss may be understood to have four components: motivational balance, attentional balance, cognitive balance, and emotional balance.

Motivational balance pertains to the cultivation of healthy desires and motivations that are centered on the pursuit of genuine happiness, as opposed to superficial, transient pleasures. Three types of imbalances may be identified and remedied: motivational deficit, hyperactivity, and dysfunction. When the mind succumbs to a motivational deficit imbalance, the person falls into an apathetic loss of desire for happiness and its causes. In cases of motivational hyperactivity, the mind is dominated by obsessive desires that obscure the reality of the present moment. And motivational dysfunction refers to the arousal of desires for things that are not conducive to one's own or others' well-being.

Attentional balance is a state in which the mind is free of the extremes of agitation and dullness. Scientific study in this area is especially urgent in today's world, where there is a growing epidemic of attention deficit and hyperactivity disorders (ADHD). While drug therapy is often necessary in the treatment of such disorders, few people regard it as an optimal, or totally satisfactory, form of therapy. We clearly need to develop other forms of intervention, not only to counteract the disorders, but also to prevent them from arising in the first place.

In speaking of the importance of healthy, balanced attention, the philosopher William James commented, "The power of voluntarily attending is the point of the whole procedure. Just as a balance turns on its knife-edges, so upon it our moral destiny turns." The faculty of sustained, voluntary attention plays a particularly crucial role in education. More than a century ago, James presented us with the following challenge: "The faculty of voluntarily bringing back a wandering attention, over and over again, is the very root of judgment, character, and will. . . . An education which should improve this faculty would be the education par excellence. But it is easier to define this ideal than to give practical directions for bringing it about." The development of tangible techniques to "bring it about" is one of the areas to which the Santa Barbara Institute is most deeply committed.

Cognitive balance refers to apprehending reality as it is. A common characteristic of a cognitive hyperactivity disorder is the inability to distinguish between one's own conceptual projections and the perceivable world of direct experience. In cases of such cognitive imbalance, projection and perception are commonly conflated. While this is most conspicuous in the mentally ill, it is to a lesser degree all too prevalent among people who are considered healthy—people who, in Freud's terms, suffer only from "normal neuroses." A cognitive deficit disorder entails the denial of, or simply an inability to note, internal or external phenomena that are presented to one's senses. At the Santa Barbara Institute studies will be conducted and classes will be held on methods and disciplines for enhancing cognitive balance, especially through training in discerning mindfulness. Such training may be instrumental in treating the mentally ill as well as in training "normal" individuals to achieve exceptional degrees of mental health and well-being.

Emotional balance is crucial to any understanding of mental health. Emotional imbalances fall into three categories: emotional deficit, hyperactivity, and dysfunction. At the Santa Barbara Institute research will be conducted and classes will be taught that examine the nature of destructive and constructive emotions. How do they arise, and what are their distinguishing characteristics? What impact do they have on our overall well-being as individuals and as members of society? On a thoroughly pragmatic note, research will be done to explore ways in which destructive emotions can be attenuated and constructive emotions can be cultivated.

Together with the University of California, San Francisco, and the Mind and Life Institute, the Santa Barbara Institute is presently cosponsoring a clinical study called "Cultivating Emotional

Balance." This project was initially conceived by UCSF psychologist Paul Ekman at a recent "Mind and Life" conference with His Holiness the Dalai Lama. The proceedings of this cross-cultural meeting have been published by Daniel Goleman under the title *Destructive Emotions: A Scientific Dialogue with the Dalai Lama.*

Alan Wallace, who served as interpreter for the Dalai Lama during that meeting, has collaborated in the overall design of this clinical study and is serving as one of its two trainers. A pilot study was completed in the winter of 2003, in which fifteen schoolteachers were taught methods for cultivating emotional balance, drawing from modern psychology and the Buddhist meditative tradition. The results from this study have been very encouraging, and the full clinical trial is scheduled for the winter of 2005.

The Santa Barbara Institute is now developing the "Shamatha Project," a scientific study of contemplative means of enhancing attention skills, in collaboration with the Center for Mind and Brain and the Department of Psychology of the University of California, Davis. This project will include three to twelve months of residential training with Alan Wallace as instructor. Longitudinal scientific studies of the participants will be conducted before, during, and after this period to assess the impact of training on attentional and emotional balance. This research project is tentatively scheduled to begin in 2006.

Education

In 2005, the Santa Barbara Institute will begin to offer courses for the general public on the themes of motivational balance, attentional balance, cognitive balance, and emotional balance. Residential workshops on these themes will be held, ranging in duration from three to ten days. Eventually, other courses will be offered on the nature of consciousness explored from interdisciplinary and cross-cultural perspectives. The Santa Barbara Institute will also invite guest lecturers from the fields of psychology, neuroscience, mental health, philosophy, and contemplative traditions to give public lectures and to lead workshops on various themes pertaining to the study of consciousness.

As the Santa Barbara Institute develops, we hope to acquire a suitable facility for an ongoing, one-year contemplative training program involving four three-month residential courses devoted to the cultivation of motivational, attentional, cognitive, and emotional balance, and the exploration of the nature and potentials of consciousness from a first-person, experiential perspective. This one-year training will provide students with basic contemplative skills for the cultivation of genuine well-being for the rest of their lives.

Graduates of this introductory course who wish to proceed to the level of professional contemplative training will be provided with a four-year graduate course in the three aspects of mental balance and the first-person investigation of consciousness. Individuals who have developed such skills to a high degree will then be an invaluable resource for psychologists, neuroscientists, and other cognitive scientists who wish to combine their professional skills in the third-person study of the mind with the professional first-person skills of these contemplatives.

Such high-level collaboration among experts in the behavioral, neural, and introspective exploration of the mind may open up unprecedented opportunities for fathoming the nature and full potentials of consciousness.

Eventually, a graduate program in the interdisciplinary theoretical study of consciousness may be developed in affiliation with one or more universities. This program will be offered as a series of courses on the Santa Barbara Institute campus, online, or using a combination of both. Materials will be drawn from philosophy, cognitive psychology, psychiatry, cognitive neurophysiology, and the contemplative traditions of the world.

Summary

The Santa Barbara Institute for Consciousness Studies draws on a wealth of interdisciplinary and cross-cultural experience, research methodologies, and insights into the nature and potentials of consciousness, bridging the sciences and humanities, the ancient and the modern, and the fruits of exploration from the East and the West.

Notes

Introduction

3   *"I am still unable"* Plato, *Phaedo*, trans. Robin Waterfield (Oxford University Press, 2002) p. 230A.

4   *"Genuine happiness, on the other hand"* Augustine, *The Confessions*. Trans. Maria Boulding. (Hyde Park, N.Y.: New City Press, 1997), p. 33.

I Mindfulness of Breathing

16   *"Just as in the last month"* Trans. Bhikkhu Bodhi. *The Connected Discourses of the Buddha*, vol. 2. (Boston: Wisdom Publications, 2000); *Samyutta Nikāya* V, 321–22; p. 1774.

18   *Here are some guidelines* Tsong-kha-pa, *The Great Treatise on the Stages of the Path to Enlightenment*. Trans. Lamrim Chenmo Translation Committee. (Ithaca, N.Y.: Snow Lion Publications, 1402/2000); I, pp. 100–108.

2 Settling the Mind in Its Natural State

27   *"Whatever kinds of mental imagery occur"* Lerab Lingpa (gTer ston las rab gling pa), *rDzogs pa chen po man ngag sde'i bcud phur man ngag thams cad kyi rgyal po klong lnga'i yi ge dum bu gsum pa lce btsun chen po'i výma la'i zab tig gi bshad khrid chu 'babs su bkod pa snying po'i bcud dril ye shes thig le.* Ed. Ven. Taklung Tsetrul Pema Wangyal. (Darjeeling: Orgyan Kunsang Chokhor Ling, n.d.), p. 640.

28   *"By applying yourself to this practice"* Düdjom Lingpa (bDud 'joms gling pa). *The Vajra Essence, Dag snang ye shes drva pa las gnas lugs rang byung gi rgyud rdo rje'I snying po.* Sanskrit title: *Vajrahṛdayaśud-dhadhutijñānahāreśṛī laṃjātiyātisma.* Collected Works of His Holiness Dudjom Rinpoche, Thimphu (Bhutan: Kunsang Topgay, 1978), p. 32.

28   *"In that way, the reality of the mind is insightfully perceived"*   Panchen Lozang Chökyi Gyaltsen, "Sems gnas pa'i thabs" section of *dGe ldan bKa' brgyud rin po che'i bka' srol phyag rgya chen po'i rtsa ba rgyas par bshad pa yang gsal sgron me.* Asian Classics Input Project, Source CD, Release A, S5939F.ACT, 1993.

32   *"As long as the conditions"*   Atisha, *Lamp for the Path to Enlightenment.* Geshe Sonam Rinchen (comm.); trans. and ed. Ruth Sonam. (Ithaca, N.Y.: Snow Lion Publications, 1042/1997); vs. 39. My translation differs slightly from that in this translation of Atisha's work.

3 The Awareness of Being Aware

35   *"Quiescence without a sign"*   Padmasambhava, *Natural Liberation: Padmasambhava's Teachings on the Six Bardos.* Gyatrul Rinpoche (comm.); trans. B. Alan Wallace. (Boston: Wisdom Publications, 1998), pp. 105–113.

40   *"The sheer awareness and the sheer clarity"*   Cited in B. Alan Wallace, *The Bridge of Quiescence: Experiencing Tibetan Buddhist Meditation.* (Chicago: Open Court, 1998), p. 173.

41   *"Be unrelenting toward thoughts"*   Panchen Lozang Chökyi Gyaltsen, citation from the "Sems gnas pa'i thabs" section of his *dGe ldan bKa' brgyud rin po che'i bka' srol phyag rgya chen po'i rtsa ba rgyas par bshad pa yang gsal sgron me.* Cf. Geshe Rabten, *Echoes of Voidness*, trans. and ed. Stephen Batchelor. (London: Wisdom Publications, 1986), pp. 113–128.

42   *"Someone with an experience"*   Düdjom Lingpa, *The Vayra Essence*, p. 364.

4 Mindfulness of the Body

54   *"This is the direct path"*   Trans. Bhikkhu Ñānamoli and Bhikkhu Bodhi, *The Middle Length Discourses of the Buddha.* (Boston: Wisdom Publications, 1995); *Satipaṭṭhānasutta*, 2; p. 145.

55   *"In the seen there is only the seen"*   *Udāna*; 1, 10.

63   *"One dwells observing the body"*   *Satipaṭṭhānasutta*; 5.

5 Mindfulness of the Feelings

70   *"This window is crucial"*   Tara Bennett-Goleman, *Emotional Alchemy: How the Mind Can Heal the Heart.* (New York: Harmony Books, 2001), p. 144.

74   *"In this way, one abides"*   *Satipaṭṭhānasutta*; 10, 33.

6 Mindfulness of the Mind

77   *"Monks, this mind is brightly shining"*   Anguttara Nikāya; A.I.9–10.
77   *"When you fall asleep"*   Düdjom Lingpa, *The Vajra Essence;* pp. 46–47.
86   *"Our thinking cannot incorporate"*   Paul Ekman, *Emotions Revealed: Recognizing Faces and Feelings to Improve Communication and Emotional Life.* (New York: Times Books, 2003), pp. 39–40.
89   *"The instant field of the present"*   William James, "Does Consciousness Exist?" in *The Writings of William James,* ed. John J. McDermott (Chicago: University of Chicago Press, 1904/1977), pp. 177–178.
89   *"All phenomena are preceded by the mind"*   The Dhammapada; I: 1.
89   *"All phenomena are preceded by the mind"*   Ratnameghasūtra, cited in Sānntideva (1961). Siksāsamuccaya. ed. P. D. Vaidya, (Darbhanga: Mithila Institute), p. 121.
90   *"The mind, Kashyapa, is like an illusion"*   Ratnacūdasutra, cited in Sāntideva, *Śiksāsamuccaya,* p. 220.

7 Mindfulness of Phenomena

99   *"The aggregates [comprising the body and mind]"*   Lalitavistarasūtra, cited in Sāntideva, *Śiksāsamuccaya;* p. 222.
99   *"Just as when the parts"*   Samyutta-Nikāya; I.135.
100   *"Nameless are all conditions"*   Lokanāthavyākarana, cited in Sānti- deva, *Śiksāsamuccaya,* p. 224.

8 Loving-Kindness

111   *"One who loves himself"*   Udāna; 47.
113   *"When people place a strong emphasis"*   Tim Kasser, *The High Price of Materialism.* (Cambridge, Mass.: MIT Press, 2000), p. 67.
113   *"People who are highly focused"*   Kasser, *The High Price of Materialism;* p. 22.
114   *"Those desiring to escape from suffering"*   Sāntideva, *A Guide to the Bodhisattva Way of Life.* Trans. Vesna A. Wallace and B. Alan Wallace. (Ithaca, N.Y.: Snow Lion Publications, 1997), I: 28.
114   *"The percentage of students"*   Kasser, *The High Price of Materialism,* p. 104.
116   *"Religion is tending to degenerate"*   Alfred North Whitehead, *Science and the Modern World* (New York: Fontana Books, 1925/1975), p. 223.
120   *"Animosity is never quelled with animosity"*   Dhammapada; I: 5.

9 Compassion

126   *"A state of mind that is nonviolent"*   His Holiness the Dalai Lama and Howard C. Cutler. *The Art of Happiness: A Handbook for Living* (New York: Riverhead Books, 1998), p. 114.

127   *"In the same way that physical pain"*   His Holiness the Dalai Lama and Howard C. Cutler. *The Art of Happiness*, p. 211.

127   *"Although it has many divisions"*   Śāntideva, *A Guide to the Bodhisattva Way of Life*, VIII, p. 91.

128   *"I must eliminate the suffering"*   Śāntideva, *A Guide to the Bodhisattva Way of Life*, VIII, pp. 94, 102.

10 Empathetic Joy and Equanimity

139   *"For the moment, what we attend to is reality."*   William James, *The Principles of Psychology* (New York: Dover Publications, 1890/1950), II, p. 322.

150   *"When we feel hatred for someone"*   Geshe Rabten (1988). *Treasury of Dharma: A Tibetan Buddhist Meditation Course* (London: Tharpa Publications, 1988), pp. 143–144.

11 *Bodhichitta:* The Spirit of Awakening

162   *"Those desiring to escape from suffering"*   Śāntideva, *A Guide to the Bodhisattva Way of Life*, I: 28.

163   *"Those who long to overcome"*   Śāntideva, *A Guide to the Bodhisattva Way of Life*, I: 8.

166   *"For as long as space remains"*   Śāntideva, *A Guide to the Bodhisattva Way of Life*, X: 55.

167   *"Holds within it the cause"*   Quoted in Peter Harvey, *The Selfless Mind: Personality, Consciousness and Nirvana in Early Buddhism.* (Surrey, U.K.: Curzon Press, 1995), p. 176.

168   *"If there is something you can do"*   Śāntideva, *A Guide to the Bodhisattva Way of Life*, VI: 10.

169   *"People can handle only a little felicity"*   Gyatrul Rinpoche, *Meditation, Transformation, and Dream Yoga.* Trans. B. Alan Wallace and Sangye Khandro. (Ithaca, N.Y.: Snow Lion Publications, 2002), p. 23.

12 Daytime Dream Yoga

179   *"There is no picture of the object"*   Antonio Damasio, *The Feeling of What Happens: Body and Emotion in the Making of Consciousness* (New York: Harcourt, 1999), p. 321.

13 Nighttime Dream Yoga

186   *"Sometimes false awakenings"* Stephen LaBerge, *Lucid Dreaming: The Power of Being Awake and Aware in Your Dreams* (New York: Ballantine Press, 1985), pp. 129–131.

195   *"In the morning when you wake up"* Padmasambhava, *Natural Liberation: Padmasambhava's Teachings on the Six Bardos.* Gyatrul Rinpoche (comm.); trans. B. Alan Wallace. (Boston: Wisdom Publications, 1998), p. 153.

14 The Great Perfection

198   *"A beginner may be able"* Cited in His Holiness the Dalai Lama, *Dzogchen: The Heart Essence of the Great Perfection.* Trans. Geshe Thupten Jinpa and Richard Barron. (Ithaca, N.Y.: Snow Lion Publications, 2000), p. 66.

199   *"Be at ease, like a brahmin spinning yarn. Be loose,"* Cited in Karma Chagmé, *A Spacious Path to Freedom: Practical Instructions on the Union of Mahāmudrā and Atiyoga.* Gyatrul Rinpoche (comm.); trans. B. Alan Wallace. (Ithaca, N.Y.: Snow Lion Publications, 1998), pp. 141–44.

202   *"While reflecting on the development"* Trans. and ed. B. Alan Wallace. *The Life and Teachings of Geshé Rabten: A Tibetan Lama's Search for Truth* (London: George Allen and Unwin, 1980), p. 116.

205   *"This all-penetrating, unimpeded awareness"* Cited in His Holiness the Dalai Lama, *Dzogchen: The Heart Essence of the Great Perfection,* p. 68.

209   *"To our amazement, Lama Putse remained"* "News from Ka-Nying Shedrub Ling Monastery, Boudhanath, Nepal." *Boudha Sangha News,* April 16, 1998.

211   *"If we can establish as an anthropological fact"* Gail B. Holland, "The Rainbow Body," *IONS: Noetic Sciences Review* (no. 59, March–May, 2002): 33.

211   *"Everyone mentioned his faithfulness"* Gail B. Holland, "The Rainbow Body," p. 34.

212   *"Those having the most superior"* Düdjom Lingpa, *The Vajra Essence,* pp. 464–65.

213   *"In spite of our modern arrogance"* John. R. Searle, *The Rediscovery of the Mind* (Cambridge, Mass.: MIT Press, 1994), p. 247.

Recommended Reading

Introduction

His Holiness the Dalai Lama. *Ethics for the New Millennium*. New York: Riverhead Books, 1999.

Seligman, Martin. *Authentic Happiness: Using the New Positive Psychology to Realize Your Potential for Lasting Fulfillment*. New York: Free Press, 2004.

I Mindfulness of Breathing

Bhikkhu, Buddhadasa. *Mindfulness of Breathing: A Manual for Serious Beginners*. Trans. Santikaro Bhikkhu. Boston: Wisdom Publications, 1996.

Wallace, B. Alan. *The Four Immeasurables: Cultivating a Boundless Heart*. rev. ed. Ithaca, N.Y.: Snow Lion Publications, 2004; chapters 2–3.

2 Settling the Mind in Its Natural State

His Holiness the Dalai Lama and Alex Berzin. *The Gelug/Kagyü Tradition of Mahamudra*. Ithaca, N.Y.: Snow Lion Publications, 1997; part III, chapter 4.

Namgyal, Takpo Tashi. *Mahāmudrā: The Quintessence of Mind and Meditation*. Trans. Lobsang P. Lhalungpa. Boston: Shambhala, 1986; Book One, chapters 1–2; Book Two, part II, chapter 3.

3 The Awareness of Being Aware

Padmasambhava. *Natural Liberation: Padmasambhava's Teachings on the Six Bardos*. Commentator Gyatrul Rinpoche; trans. B. Alan Wallace. Boston: Wisdom Publications, 1998, pp. 105–114.

4 Mindfulness of the Body

Klein, Anne Carolyn. *Knowing, Naming, and Negation: A Sourcebook on Tibetan Sautrantika*. Ithaca, N.Y.: Snow Lion Publications, 1991.

Thera, Nyanaponika. *The Heart of Buddhist Meditation*. New York: Samuel Weiser, 1973.

5 Mindfulness of the Feelings

Bennett-Goleman, Tara. *Emotional Alchemy: How the Mind Can Heal the Heart*. New York: Harmony Books, 2001.

Ekman, Paul. *Emotions Revealed: Recognizing Faces and Feelings to Improve Communication and Emotional Life*. New York: Times Books, 2003.

Segal, Z. V., J. M .G. Williams, and J. D. Teasdale. *Mindfulness-based Cognitive Therapy for Depression: A New Approach to Relapse Prevention*. New York: Guildford Press, 2000.

6 Mindfulness of the Mind

Harvey, Peter. *The Selfless Mind: Personality, Consciousness and Nirvana in Early Buddhism*. Surrey, U.K.: Curzon Press, 1995.

Rabten, Geshe. *The Mind and Its Functions*. 2nd ed. Trans. Stephen Batchelor. Mont Pèlerin: Edition Rabten, 1992.

Varela, Francisco J., and Jonathan Shear, eds. *The View from Within: First-person Approaches to the Study of Consciousness*. Thorverton, U.K.: Imprint Academic, 1999.

7 Mindfulness of Phenomena

Buddhaghosa. *The Path of Purification*. Trans. Bhikkhu Ñanamoli. Kandy, Sri Lanka: Buddhist Publication Society, 1979.

Soma Thera. *The Way of Mindfulness: The Satipatthana Sutta and Commentary*. Kandy, Sri Lanka: Buddhist Publication Society, 1975.

Paravahera Vajirañana Mahathera. *Buddhist Meditation in Theory and Practice*. Kuala Lumpur, Malaysia: Buddhist Missionary Society, 1975.

8 Loving-Kindness

His Holiness the Dalai Lama and Howard C. Cutler. *The Art of Happiness: A Handbook for Living*. New York: Riverhead Books, 1998.

Kasser, Tim. *The High Price of Materialism*. Cambridge, Mass.: MIT Press, 2002.

Post, Stephen G. *Unlimited Love: Altruism, Compassion, and Service*. Philadelphia: Templeton Foundation Press, 2003.

Salzberg, Sharon. *Lovingkindness: The Revolutionary Art of Happiness*. Boston: Shambhala, 2002.

9 Compassion

Davidson, Richard J., and Anne Harrington, eds., *Visions of Compassion: Western Scientists and Tibetan Buddhists Examine Human Nature*. New York: Oxford University Press, 2002.

Ladner, Lorne. *The Lost Art of Compassion: Discovering the Practice of Happiness in the Meeting of Buddhism and Psychology*. San Francisco: Harper San Francisco, 2004.

Śāntideva. *A Guide to the Bodhisattva Way of Life*. Trans. Vesna A. Wallace and B. Alan Wallace. Ithaca, N.Y.: Snow Lion Publications, 1997.

Wallace, B. Alan. *Seven-Point Mind Training*. Ithaca, N.Y.: Snow Lion Publications, 2004.

10 Empathetic Joy and Equanimity

His Holiness the Dalai Lama. *Kindness, Clarity, and Insight*. Ithaca, N.Y.: Snow Lion Publications, 1984.

Wallace, B. Alan. *The Four Immeasurables: Cultivating a Boundless Heart*. Ithaca, N.Y.: Snow Lion Publications. 2004.

11 *Bodhichitta:* The Spirit of Awakening

Khyentse, Dilgo. *Enlightened Courage: An Explanation of Atisha's Seven Point Mind Training*. Trans. Padmakara Translation Group. Ithaca, N.Y.: Snow Lion Publications, 1993.

Rabten, Geshe, and Geshe Dhargyey. *Advice from a Spiritual Friend*. Trans. Brian Beresford. Boston: Wisdom Publications, 1977/1996.

Śāntideva. *A Guide to the Bodhisattva Way of Life*. Trans. Vesna A. Wallace and B. Alan Wallace. Ithaca, N.Y.: Snow Lion Publications, 1997.

Wallace, B. Alan. *Buddhism with an Attitude: The Tibetan Seven-Point Mind-Training*. Ithaca, N.Y.: Snow Lion Publications, 2001.

12 Daytime Dream Yoga

Rinpoche, Gyatrul. *Meditation, Transformation, and Dream Yoga*. B. Trans. Alan Wallace and Sangye Khandro. Ithaca, N.Y.: Snow Lion Publications, 2002.

LaBerge, Stephen, and Howard Rheingold. *Exploring the World of Lucid Dreaming*. New York: Ballantine Books, 1990.

Wallace, B. Alan. *The Taboo of Subjectivity: Toward a New Science of Consciousness.* New York: Oxford University Press, 2000.

Wallace, B. Alan, ed., *Buddhism and Science: Breaking New Ground.* New York: Columbia University Press, 2003.

13 Nighttime Dream Yoga

LaBerge, Stephen. *Lucid Dreaming: The Power of Being Awake and Aware in Your Dreams.* New York: Ballantine Books, 1985.

Norbu, Namkhai. *Dream Yoga and the Practice of the Natural Light.* Ithaca, N.Y.: Snow Lion Publications, 1992.

Padmasambhava. *Natural Liberation: Padmasambhava's Teachings on the Six Bardos.* Gyatrul Rinpoche, commentator; trans. B. Alan Wallace. Boston: Wisdom Publications, 1998.

Rinpoche, Tenzin Wangyal. *Tibetan Yogas of Dream and Sleep.* Ithaca, N.Y.: Snow Lion Publications, 1998.

14 The Great Perfection

His Holiness the Dalai Lama. *Dzogchen: The Heart Essence of the Great Perfection.* Trans. Geshe Thupten Jinpa and Richard Barron. Ithaca, N.Y.: Snow Lion Publications, 2000.

Lingpa, Dudjom. *Buddhahood without Meditation: A Visionary Account Known as Refining Apparent Phenomena (Nang-jang).* Trans. Richard Barron. Junction City, Calif.: Padma Publishing, 1994.

Chagmé, Karma. *A Spacious Path to Freedom: Practical Instructions on the Union of Mahamudra and Atiyoga.* Gyatrul Rinpoche, commentator; trans. B. Alan Wallace. Ithaca, N.Y.: Snow Lion Publications, 1998.

———. *Naked Awareness: Practical Instructions on the Union of Mahamudra and Dzogchen.* Gyatrul Rinpoche (commentator); trans. B. Alan Wallace. Ithaca, N.Y.: Snow Lion Publications, 2000.

Bibliography

Aristotle. *Nicomachean Ethics*. Trans. Terence Irwin. Indianapolis: Hackett Publication Co., 1985.

Atisha. *Lamp for the Path to Enlightenment*. Geshe Sonam Rinchen (commentator); trans. and ed. Ruth Sonam. Ithaca, N.Y.: Snow Lion, 1042/1997.

Augustine. *The Confessions*. Trans. Maria Boulding. Hyde Park, N.Y.: New City Press, 1997.

―――. *Letters 100–155 (Epistolae)*. Trans. Roland Teske. Hyde Park N.Y.: New City Press, 2003.

Bennett-Goleman, Tara. *Emotional Alchemy: How the Mind Can Heal the Heart*. New York: Harmony Books, 2001.

Buddha. *The Dhammapada*. Trans. John Ross Carter and Mahinda Palihawadana. Oxford: Oxford University Press, 2000.

Buddha. *The Middle Length Discourses of the Buddha*. Trans. Bhikkhu Ñāṇamoli and Bhikkhu Bodhi. Boston: Wisdom Publications, 1995.

―――. *Saṃyutta Nikāya* V, 321–2. *The Connected Discourses of the Buddha*, vol. II. Trans. Bhikkhu Bodhi. Boston Wisdom Publications, 2000.

Buddhadasa Bhikkhu. *Mindfulness of Breathing: A Manual for Serious Beginners*. Trans. Santikaro Bhikkhu. Boston: Wisdom Publications, 1996.

Buddhaghosa. *The Path of Purification*. Bhikkhu Ñāṇamoli (trans.) Kandy, Sri Lanka: Buddhist Publication Society, 1979.

Burnaby, John. *Amor Dei: A Study of the Religion of St. Augustine*. Norwich, U.K.: Canterbury Press, 1938/1991.

His Holiness the Dalai Lama. *Dzogchen: The Heart Essence of the Great Perfection*. Trans. Geshe Thupten Jinpa and Richard Barron. Ithaca, N.Y.: Snow Lion Publications, 2000.

―――. *Ethics for the New Millennium*. New York: Riverhead Books, 1999.

―――. *Four Essential Buddhist Commentaries*. Dharamsala, India: Library of Tibetan Works and Archives, 1982.

―――. *Kindness, Clarity, and Insight*. Ithaca, N.Y.: Snow Lion Publications, 1984.

————. *Transcendent Wisdom: A Teaching on the Wisdom Section of Shantideva's Guide to the Bodhisattva Way of Life*. Trans. and ed. B. Alan Wallace. Ithaca, N.Y.: Snow Lion Publications, 1994.

His Holiness the Dalai Lama and Alex Berzin. *The Gelug/Kagyü Tradition of Mahamudra*. Ithaca, N.Y.: Snow Lion Publications, 1997.

His Holiness the Dalai Lama and Howard C. Cutler. *The Art of Happiness: A Handbook for Living*. New York: Riverhead Books, 1998.

Damasio, Antonio. *The Feeling of What Happens: Body and Emotion in the Making of Consciousness*. New York: Harcourt, 1999.

Davidson, Richard J., and A. Harrington, eds. *Visions of Compassion: Western Scientists and Tibetan Buddhists Examine Human Nature*. New York: Oxford University Press, 2001.

Dhammalankara Ittapana, Sthavira. *Venerable Balangoda Ananda Maitreya, the Buddha Aspirant*. Dehiwala: Sridevi Publication, 1996.

Dilgo Khyentse. *Enlightened Courage: An Explanation of Atisha's Seven Point Mind Training*. Trans. Padmakara Translation Group. Ithaca, N.Y.: Snow Lion Publications, 1993.

Düdjom Lingpa (bDud 'joms gling pa). *Buddhahood without Meditation: A Visionary Account Known as Refining Apparent Phenomena (Nang-jang)*. Trans. Richard Barron. Junction City, Calif: Padma Publishing, 1994.

————. *The Vajra Essence, Dag snang ye shes drva pa las gnas lugs rang byung gi rgyud rdo rje'i snying po*. Sanskrit title: *Vajrahṛdayaśuddhadhutijñānahāreśrilamjātiyātisma*. Collected Works of His Holiness Dudjom Rinpoche, Thimphu, Bhutan: Kunsang Topgay, 1978.

Einstein, Albert. *Ideas and Opinions*. Trans. Sonya Bangmann. New York: Crown, 1954.

Ekman, Paul. *Emotions Revealed: Recognizing Faces and Feelings to Improve Communication and Emotional Life*. New York: Times Books, 2003.

Freud, Sigmund. *Civilization and Its Discontents*. Trans. and ed. James Strachey. New York: W. W. Norton and Co., 1961.

Goleman, Daniel, ed. *Healing Emotions: Conversations with the Dalai Lama on Mindfulness, Emotions, and Health*. Boston: Shambhala Publications, 1997.

Gyatrul Rinpoche. *Meditation, Transformation, and Dream Yoga*. Trans. B. Alan Wallace and Sangye Khandro. Ithaca, N.Y.: Snow Lion Publications, 2002.

Harvey, Peter. *The Selfless Mind: Personality, Consciousness and Nirvana in Early Buddhism*. Surrey, U.K.: Curzon Press, 1995.

Hayward, J. W., and F. J. Varela, eds. *Gentle Bridges: Conversations with the Dalai Lama on the Sciences of the Mind*. Boston: Shambhala, 1992.

Heisenberg, Werner. *Physics and Beyond: Encounters and Conversations*. New York: Harper and Row, 1971.

————. *Physics and Philosophy: The Revolution in Modern Science*. New York: Harper and Row, 1962.

Holland, Gail Bernice. "The Rainbow Body." *IONS: Noetic Sciences Review,* March–May 2002 (no. 59): 32–35.

Houshmand, Z., R. B. Livingston, and B. A. Wallace, eds. *Consciousness at the Crossroads: Conversations with the Dalai Lama on Brain Science and Buddhism.* Ithaca, N.Y.: Snow Lion, 1999.

James, William. *The Principles of Psychology.* New York: Dover, 1890/1950.

———. *The Varieties of Religious Experience.* New York: Modern Library, 1902/1929.

———. "Does Consciousness Exist?" In *The Writings of William James,* ed. John J. McDermott. Chicago: University of Chicago Press, 1904/1977, 169–83.

Jamyang Sakya and Julie Emery. *Princess in Land of Snows: The Life of Jamyang Sakya in Tibet.* Boston: Shambhala, 2001.

Karma Chagmé. *Naked Awareness: Practical Teachings on the Union of Mahāmudrā and Dzogchen.* Gyatrul Rinpoche (commentator); trans. B. Alan Wallace. Ithaca, N.Y.: Snow Lion Publications, 2000.

———. *A Spacious Path to Freedom: Practical Instructions on the Union of Mahāmudrā and Atiyoga.* Gyatrul Rinpoche (commentator); trans. B. Alan Wallace. Ithaca, N.Y.: Snow Lion Publications, 1998.

Kasser, Tim. *The High Price of Materialism.* Cambridge, Mass.: MIT Press, 2002.

Klein, Anne Carolyn. *Knowing, Naming, & Negation: A Sourcebook on Tibetan Sautrantika.* Ithaca, N.Y.: Snow Lion Publications, 1991.

LaBerge, Stephen. *Lucid Dreaming: The Power of Being Awake and Aware in Your Dreams.* New York: Ballantine Books, 1985.

LaBerge, Stephen, and Howard Rheingold. *Exploring the World of Lucid Dreaming.* New York: Ballantine, 1990.

Ladner, Lorne. *The Lost Art of Compassion: Discovering the Practice of Happiness in the Meeting of Buddhism and Psychology.* San Francisco: Harper San Francisco, 2004.

Gen Lamrimpa. *Calming the Mind: Tibetan Buddhist Teachings on the Cultivation of Meditative Quiescence.* Trans. B. Alan Wallace. Ithaca, N.Y.: Snow Lion, 1995.

———. *Realizing Emptiness: Madhyamaka Insight Meditation.* Trans. B. Alan Wallace. Ithaca, N.Y.: Snow Lion, 2002.

Lerab Lingpa. (gTer ston las rab gling pa). *rDzogs pa chen po man ngag sde'i bcud phur man ngag thams cad kyi rgyal po klong lnga'i yi ge dum bu gsum pa lce btsun chen po'i vī ma lái zab tig gi bshad khrid chu 'babs su bkod pa snying po'i bcud dril ye shes thig le.* Ven. Taklung Tsetrul Pema Wangyal, ed. Darjeeling: Orgyan Kunsang Chokhor Ling, n.d.

Panchen Lobzang Chökyi Gyaltsen. (Panchen blo bzang chos kyi rgyal mtshan). *dGe ldan bKa' brgyud rin po che'i bka' srol phyag rgya chen po'i rtsa ba rgyas par bshad pa yang gsal sgron me.* Asian Classics Input Project, Source CD, Release A, S5939F.ACT, 1993.

Lobsang Gyatso. *Memoirs of a Tibetan Lama*. Gareth Sparham, ed. Ithaca, N.Y.: Snow Lion, 1998.

Maitreya, Arya, and Acarya Asanga. *The Changeless Nature*. Eskdalemuir, Dumfriesshire, U.K.: Karma Drubgyud Darjay Ling, 1985.

McDermott, John J., ed. *The Writings of William James*. Chicago: University of Chicago Press, 1977.

Nāgārjuna. *The Fundamental Wisdom of the Middle Way*. Trans. Jay Garfield. New York: Oxford University Press, 1995.

Namkhai Norbu. *Dream Yoga and the Practice of the Natural Light*. Ithaca, N.Y.: Snow Lion Publications, 1992.

Bhikkhu Ñāṇamoli. *The Life of the Buddha: According to the Pali Canon*. Kandy, Sri Lanka: Buddhist Publication Society, 1992.

Geshey Ngawang Dhargyey. *Tibetan Tradition of Mental Development: Oral Teachings of Tibetan Lama Geshey Ngawang Dhargyey*. Dharamsala, India: Library of Tibetan Works and Archives, 1974.

Nyanaponika Thera. *The Heart of Buddhist Meditation*. New York: Samuel Weiser, 1973.

Padmasambhava. *Natural Liberation: Padmasambhava's Teachings on the Six Bardos*. Gyatrul Rinpoche (commentator); trans. and ed. B. Alan Wallace. Boston: Wisdom Publications, 1998.

Palden Gyatso. *The Autobiography of a Tibetan Monk*. Trans. Tsering Shakya. New York: Grove Press, 1997.

Plato. *Phaedo*. Trans. Robin Waterfield. Oxford: Oxford University Press, 2002.

Post, Stephen G. *Unlimited Love: Altruism, Compassion, and Service*. Philadelphia: Templeton Foundation Press, 2003.

Geshe Rabten. *Echoes of Voidness*. Trans. and ed. Stephen Batchelor. London: Wisdom Publications, 1986.

———. *The Mind and Its Functions*. 2nd ed. Trans. Stephen Batchelor. Mont Pèlerin: Edition Rabten, 1992.

———. *The Preliminary Practices*. Trans. Gonsar Tulku; ed. Georges Driessens. Dharamsala, India: Library of Tibetan Works and Archives, 1974.

Geshe Rabten and Geshe Dhargyey. *Advice from a Spiritual Friend*. Trans. Brian Beresford. Boston: Wisdom Publications, 1977/1996.

Rao, K. Ramakrishna. *Consciousness Studies: Cross-Cultural Perspectives*. London: McFarland and Co., 2002.

Salzberg, Sharon. *Lovingkindness: The Revolutionary Art of Happiness*. Boston: Shambhala, 2002.

Śāntideva. *A Guide to the Bodhisattva Way of Life*. Trans. Vesna A. Wallace and B. Alan Wallace. Ithaca, N.Y.: Snow Lion, 1997.

———. *Sikṣasamuccaya: A Compendium of Buddhist Doctrine*. Trans. Cecil Bendall and W. H. D. Rouse. Delhi: Motilal Banarsidass, 1971.

Searle, John. R. *The Rediscovery of the Mind*. Cambridge, Mass.: MIT Press, 1994.

Segal, Z. V., J. M.G., Williams, and J. D. Teasdale. *Mindfulness-Based Cognitive Therapy for Depression: A New Approach to Relapse Prevention*. New York: Guildford Press, 2000.

Seligman, Martin. *Authentic Happiness: Using the New Positive Psychology to Realize Your Potential for Lasting Fulfillment*. New York: Free Press, 2004.

Snyder, C. R., and Shane J. Lopez, eds. *Handbook of Positive Psychology*. New York: Oxford University Press, 2002.

Sogyal Rinpoche. *Dzogchen & Padmasambhava*. Berkeley: Rigpa Fellowship, 1989.

———. *The Tibetan Book of Living and Dying*. San Francisco: Harper San Francisco, 1992.

Soma Thera. *The Way of Mindfulness: The Satipaṭṭāna Sutta and Commentary*. Kandy, Sri Lanka: Buddhist Publication Society, 1975.

Stevenson, Ian. *Where Reincarnation and Biology Intersect*. London: Praeger, 1997.

Targ, Russell. *Mind-Reach: Scientists Look at Psychic Ability*. New York: Delacorte Press, 1977.

Takpo Tashi Namgyal. *Mahāmudrā: The Quintessence of Mind and Meditation*. Trans. Lobsang P. Lhalungpa. Boston: Shambhala Publications, 1986.

Teasdale, John. *Mindfulness-Based Cognitive Therapy in the Prevention of Relapse and Recurrence in Major Depression*. In M. Kwee and Y. Haruki, eds. *Meditation as Health Promotion: A Lifestyle Modification Approach*. Delft, Holland: Eburon Publishers, 1999.

Tenzin Wangyal Rinpoche. *Tibetan Yogas of Dream and Sleep*. Ithaca, N.Y.: Snow Lion Publications, 1998.

Tsong-kha-pa. *The Great Treatise on the Stages of the Path to Enlightenment*. Trans. Lamrim Chenmo Translation Committee. Ithaca, N.Y.: Snow Lion Publications, 1402/2000.

U. Sīlānandà. *The Four Foundations of Mindfulness*. Boston: Wisdom Publications, 2002.

Paravahera Vajirañāna. *Buddhist Meditation in Theory and Practice*. Kuala Lumpur, Malaysia: Buddhist Missionary Society, 1975.

Varela, Francisco J., ed. *Sleeping, Dreaming, and Dying: An Exploration of Consciousness with the Dalai Lama*. Trans. Geshe Thubten Jinpa and B. Alan Wallace. Boston: Wisdom Publications, 1997.

Varela, Francisco J., and Jonathan Shear (eds.). *The View from Within: First-person Approaches to the Study of Consciousness*. Thorverton, U.K.: Imprint Academic, 1999.

Wallace, B. Alan. *The Bridge of Quiescence: Experiencing Tibetan Buddhist Meditation*. Chicago: Open Court Press, 1998.

———. *Buddhism with an Attitude: The Tibetan Seven-Point Mind-Training*. Ithaca, N.Y.: Snow Lion Publications, 2001.

———. "The Buddhist Tradition of *Samatha*: Methods for Refining and Examining Consciousness." *Journal of Consciousness Studies* 6 (no. 2–3, 1999): 175–187.

———. *Choosing Reality: A Buddhist View of Physics and the Mind.* Ithaca, N.Y.: Snow Lion Publications, 1996.

———. *The Four Immeasurables: Cultivating a Boundless Heart*, rev. ed. Ithaca, N.Y.: Snow Lion Publications, 2004.

———. "Intersubjectivity in Indo-Tibetan Buddhism." *Journal of Consciousness Studies*, 8, No. 5–7, 2001: 209–230.

Wallace, B. Alan, trans. and ed. *The Life and Teachings of Geshé Rabten: A Tibetan Lama's Search for Truth.* London: George Allen & Unwin, 1980.

———. *A Passage from Solitude: Training the Mind in a Life Embracing the World.* Ithaca, N.Y.: Snow Lion Publications, 1992.

———. *The Taboo of Subjectivity: Toward a New Science of Consciousness.* New York: Oxford University Press, 2000.

Wallace, B. Alan (ed.). *Buddhism & Science: Breaking New Ground.* New York: Columbia University Press, 2003.

Whitehead, Alfred North. *Science and the Modern World*, New York: Fontana Books, 1925/1975.

Index